Created by Aimee Major Steinberger (6'-0")
Layout Assistant – Sandra Powers (5'-7")
Editorial Assistant– Mallory Reaves (5'-5")
Translation Notes – Christine Schilling (5'-9")
Senior Editor – Brynne Chandler (5'-2")
Designer – James Dashiell (6'-0")
Creative Director – Audry Taylor (5'-1")
Publisher – David Wise (5'-11½")

Published by Go! Media Entertainment, LLC

Japan Ai: A tall girl's adventures in Japan
© Aimee Major Steinberger 2007

Visit us online at www.gocomi.com
e-mail: info@gocomi.com

ISBN 978-1-933617-83-1

First printed in December 2007

1 2 3 4 5 6 7 8 9

Manufactured in the United States of America

日本愛 Japan Ai

A tall girl's adventures in Japan

By

Aimee Major Steinberger

go!comi

TABLE OF CONTENTS

CHAPTER ONE:
Dreams of Japan

This is me, Aimee.

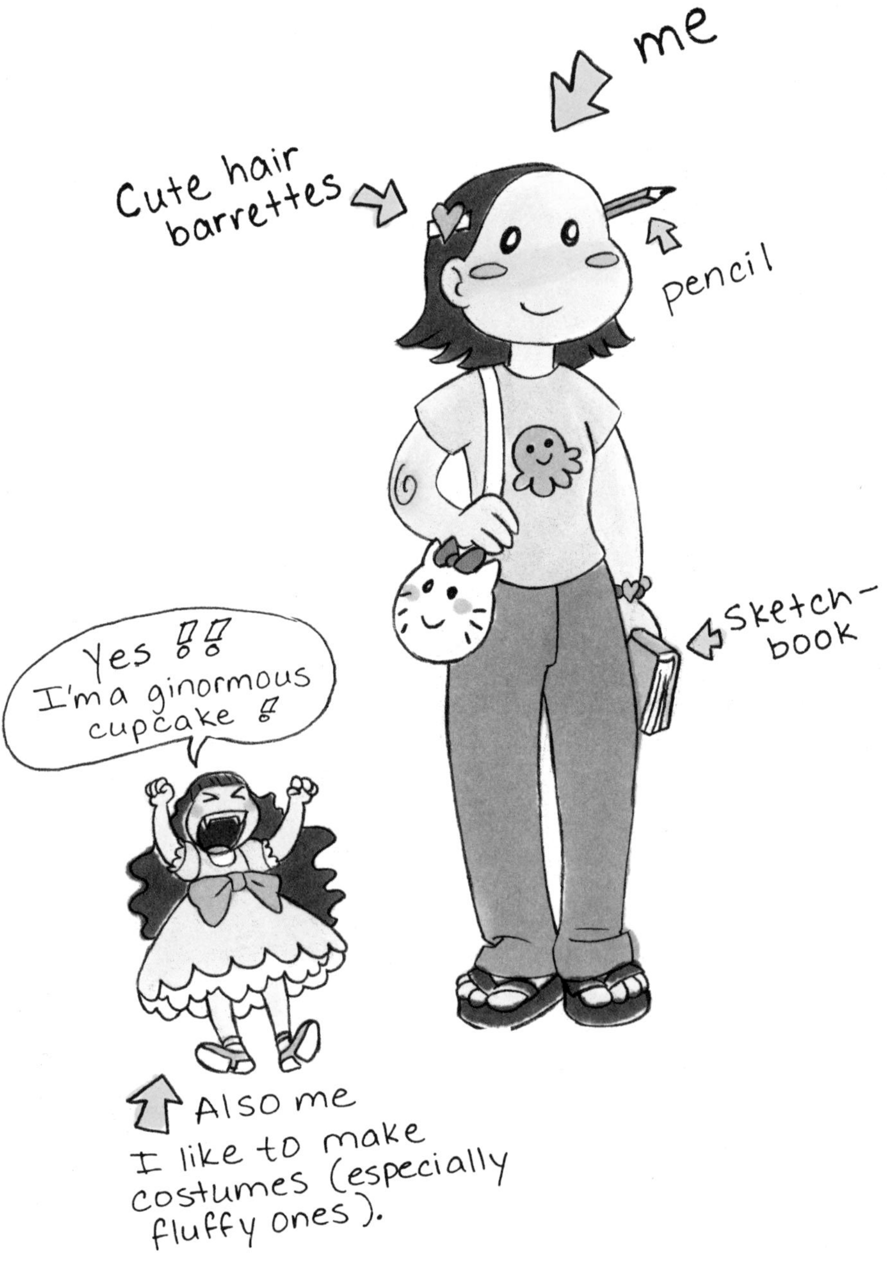
me
Cute hair barrettes
pencil
Sketch-book
Yes !! I'm a ginormous cupcake !
Also me
I like to make costumes (especially fluffy ones).

I'm a girl but I like video games and comic books.

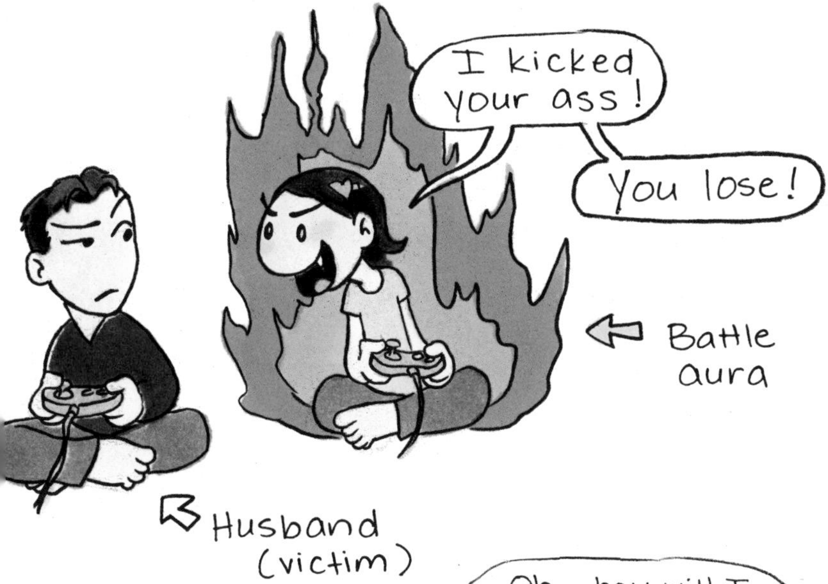
I kicked your ass!
You lose!
Battle aura
Husband (victim)

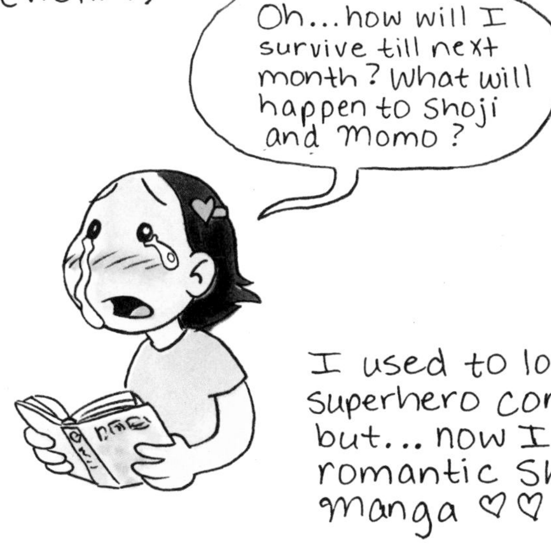
Oh... how will I survive till next month? What will happen to Shoji and Momo?

I used to love superhero comics but... now I love romantic Shojo manga ♡♡

I really am 6 feet tall.

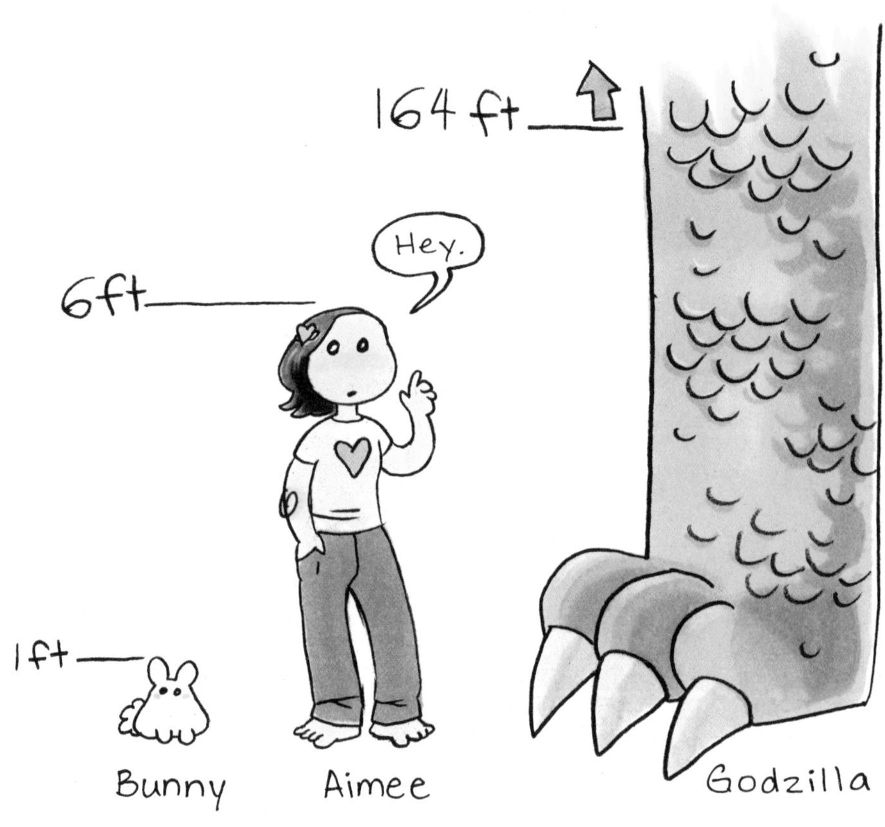

164 ft
6ft
Hey.
1ft
Bunny
Aimee
Godzilla

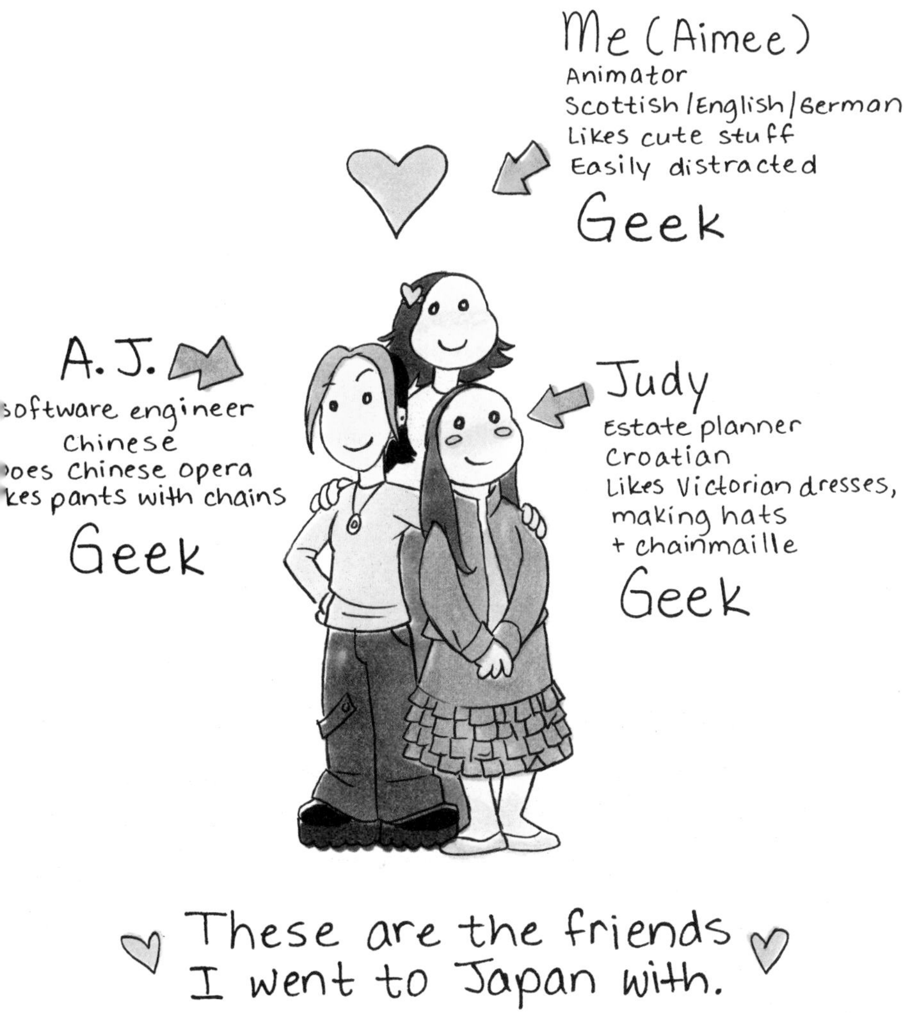
Me (Aimee)
Animator
Scottish/English/German
Likes cute stuff
Easily distracted
Geek
A. J.
software engineer
Chinese
oes Chinese opera
kes pants with chains
Geek
Judy
Estate planner
Croatian
Likes Victorian dresses, making hats + chainmaille
Geek
These are the friends I went to Japan with.

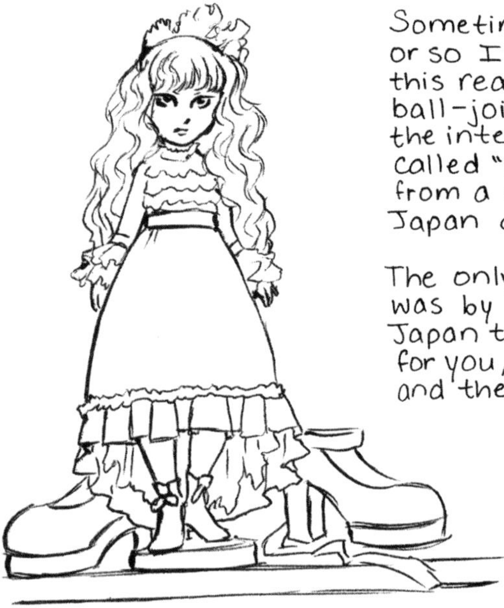

Sometime around 2002 or so I discovered this really beautiful ball-jointed doll on the internet. It was called "Super Dollfie" from a company in Japan called VOLKS.

The only way to get one was by paying someone in Japan to visit a VOLKS store for you, purchase the doll and then mail it to you.

After buying a few dolls that way, I fantasized about visiting the dream-like, flower-filled stores in Japan. I never thought that I would be able to go.

Meanwhile, I helped start one of the first English websites about these dolls. That led to a staff writing position at Haute Doll Magazine.

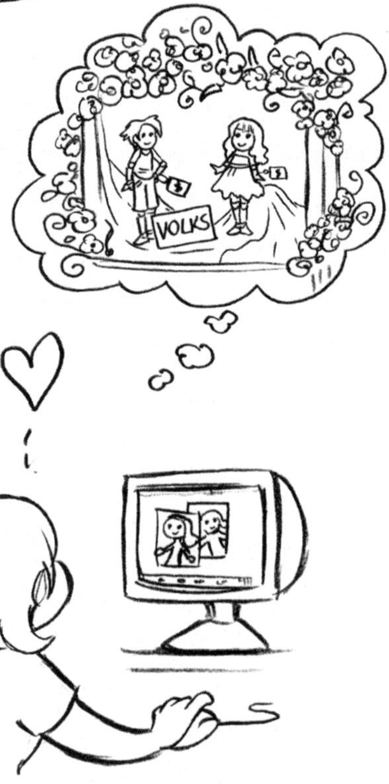
VOLKS

The more involved I got in the hobby, the more I wanted to visit VOLKS in Japan.

Finally, I couldn't take it anymore. I decided to go to Japan and to visit VOLKS and asked if they would allow me to ask them some questions.

Imagine my surprise when they told me they knew who I was! They had been reading my articles in Haute Doll Magazine and had been visiting my website! Not only were they willing to answer my questions, but they wanted me to visit their offices as a guest and have dinner with the president of the company!

At that very moment, one of my friends' (and my) favorite musicals was playing in Japan. I shot a pleading email to my buddies playing up all the great things we could do if we went to Japan.

We bought our plane tickets the next day.

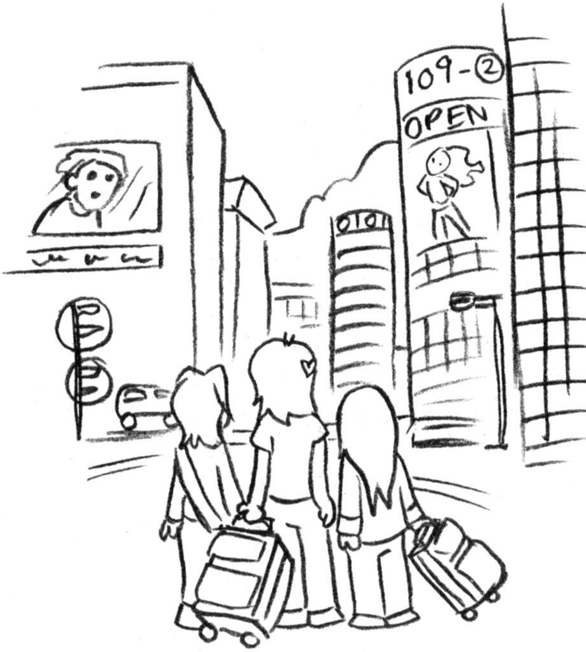
109-②
OPEN
0101

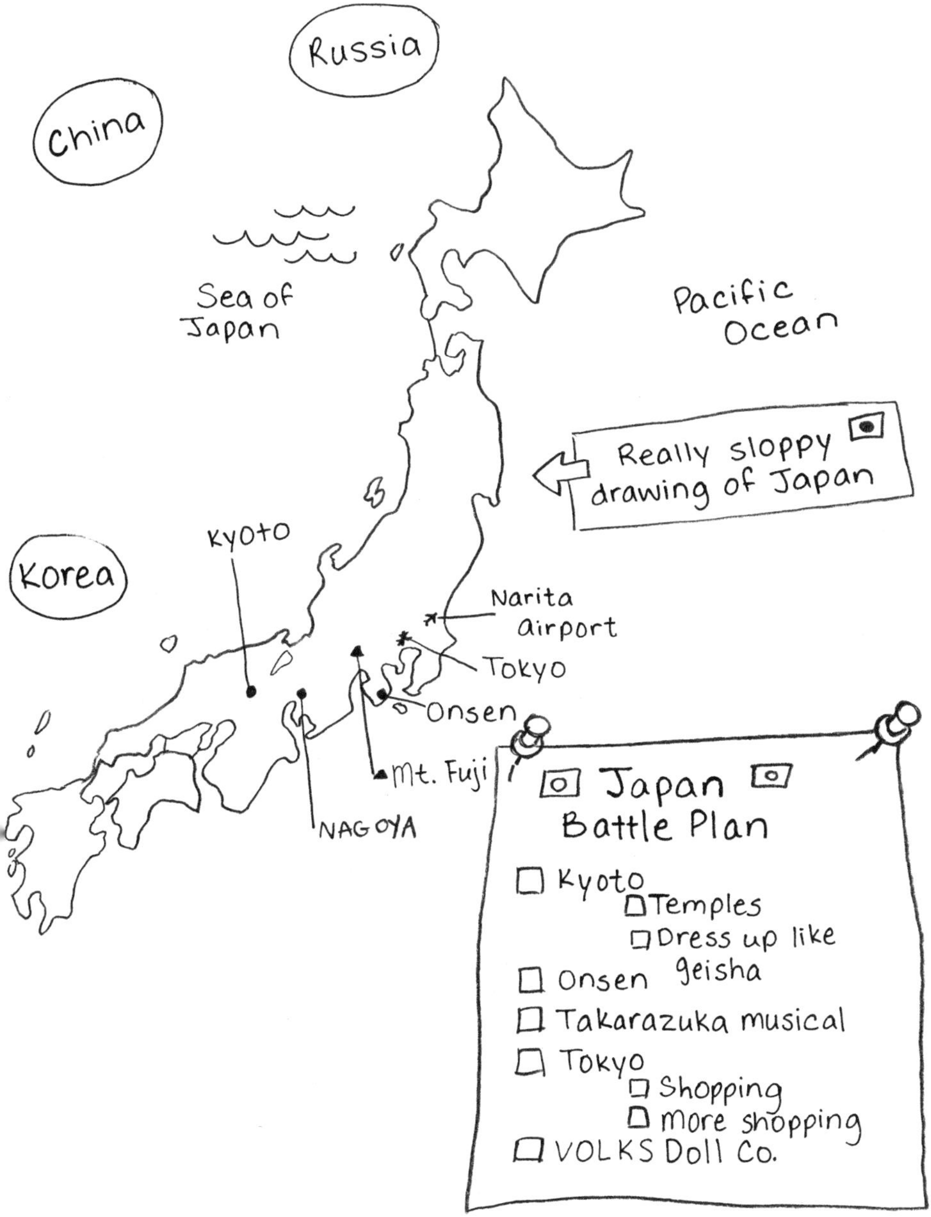
Russia
China
Sea of Japan
Pacific Ocean
Really sloppy drawing of Japan
KYOTO
Korea
Narita airport
Tokyo
Onsen
Mt. Fuji
NAGOYA
Japan Battle Plan
Kyoto
Temples
Dress up like geisha
Onsen
Takarazuka musical
Tokyo
Shopping
more shopping
VOLKS Doll Co.

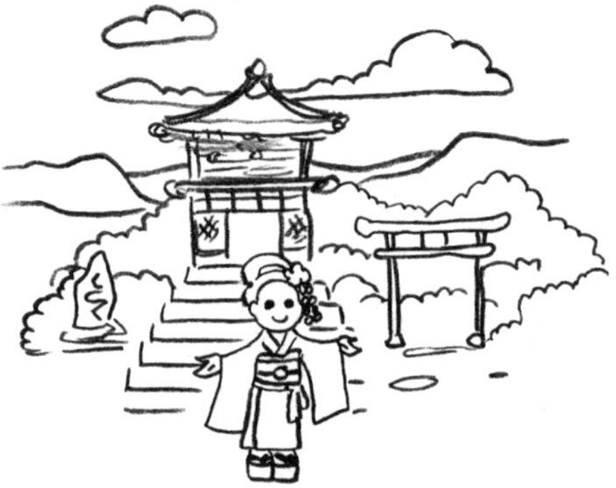

Kyoto

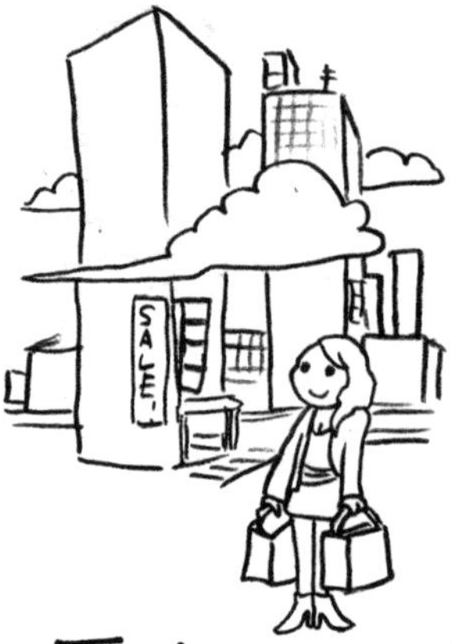
SALE!

Tokyo

We would mostly be
seeing two cities...
Kyoto, home of Japanese
traditional culture...
and Tokyo, city of the future.

The plane ride was perfect....

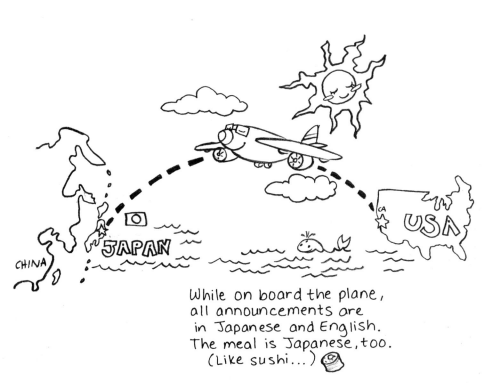

While on board the plane,
all announcements are
in Japanese and English.
The meal is Japanese, too.
(Like sushi...)

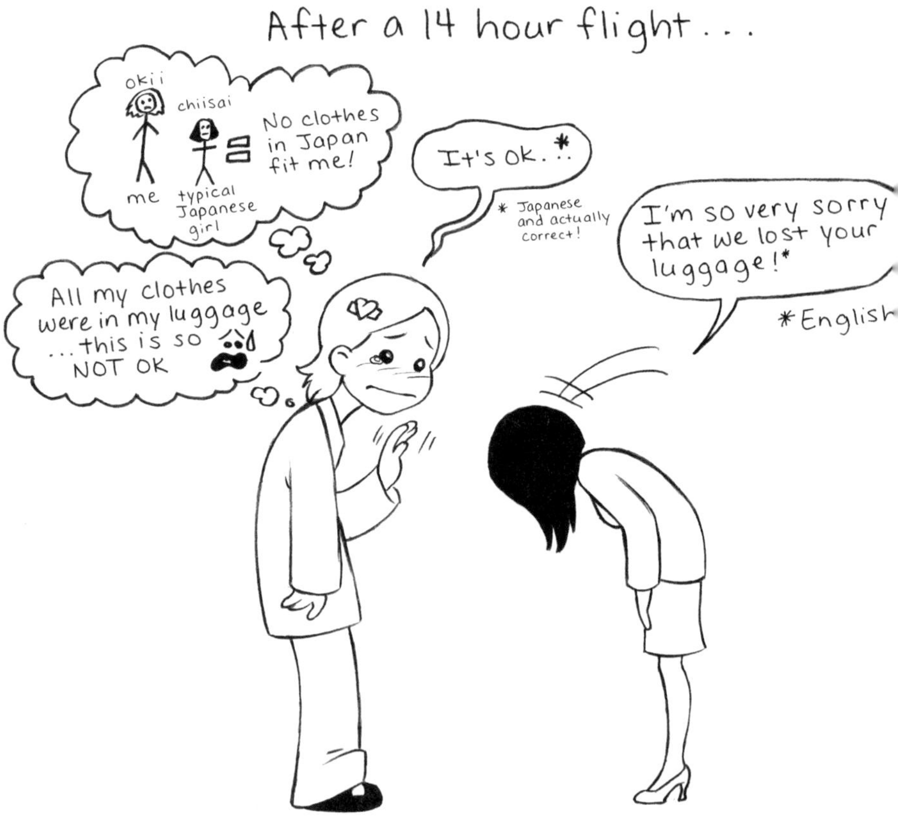
After a 14 hour flight . . .
I'm so very sorry that we lost your luggage!*
*English
It's ok. . .*
* Japanese and actually correct!
All my clothes were in my luggage . . . this is so NOT OK
okii
chiisai
me
typical Japanese girl
No clothes in Japan fit me!

When VOLKS contacted me to schedule the big visit, it turned out that they wanted me to have dinner with them on the same day I was planning to go to the Takarazuka Revue* performance of Aida!

*All-female theatrical troupe

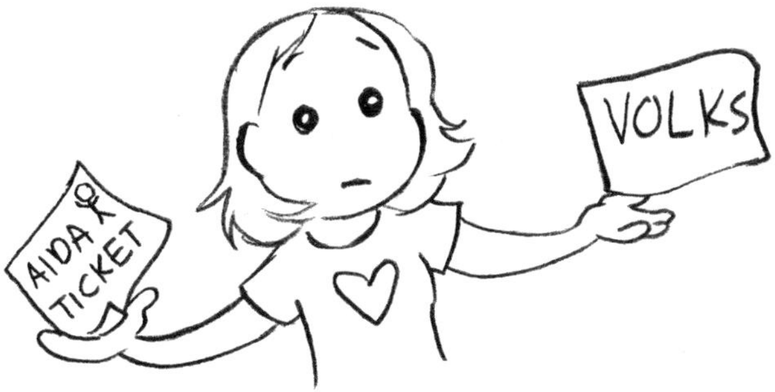
AIDA TICKET
VOLKS

Super Spectacular Musical
OR
the sacred birthplace of my dolls?

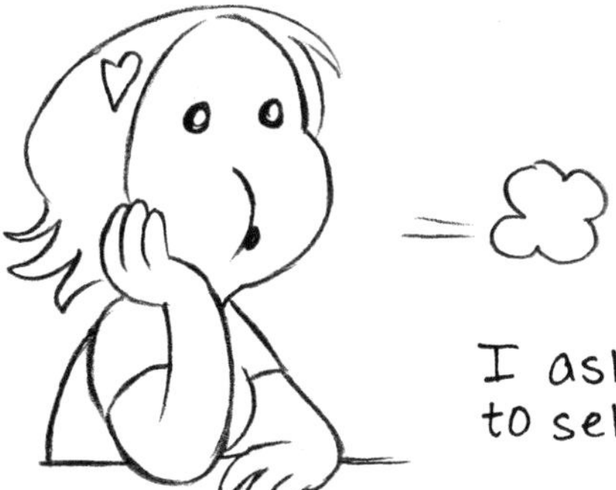

I asked a friend living in Japan to sell my Aida ticket for me.

It was hard for me to stay upset about the Aida ticket, though. I had so much to look forward to

♡ Tomorrow morning we would see our first temples!

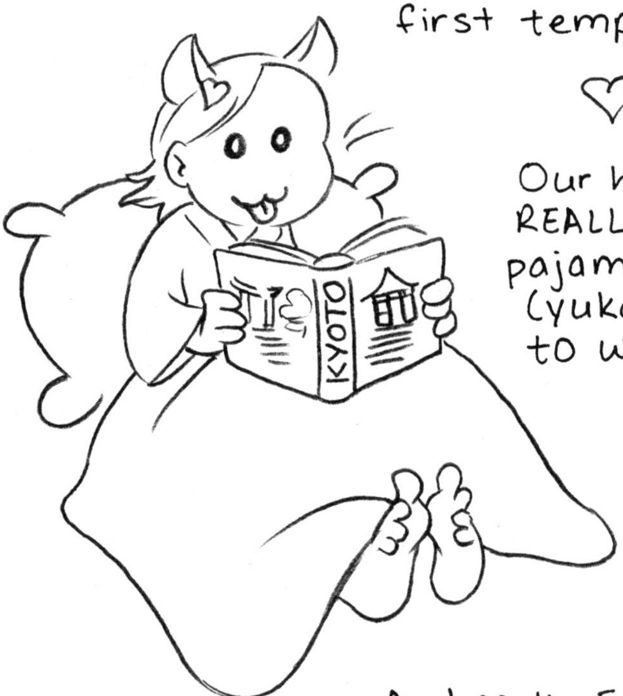
KYOTO

♡

Our hotel* was REALLY comfy, ha pajama kimonos (yukata) for us to wear...

♡

Had tea...

♡

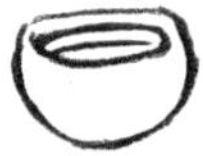

And spoke English. ♡

* Rihga Royal Hotel in Kyoto:
http://www.rihga.com/kyoto/index.html

Chapter Two:

Kyoto Shrines

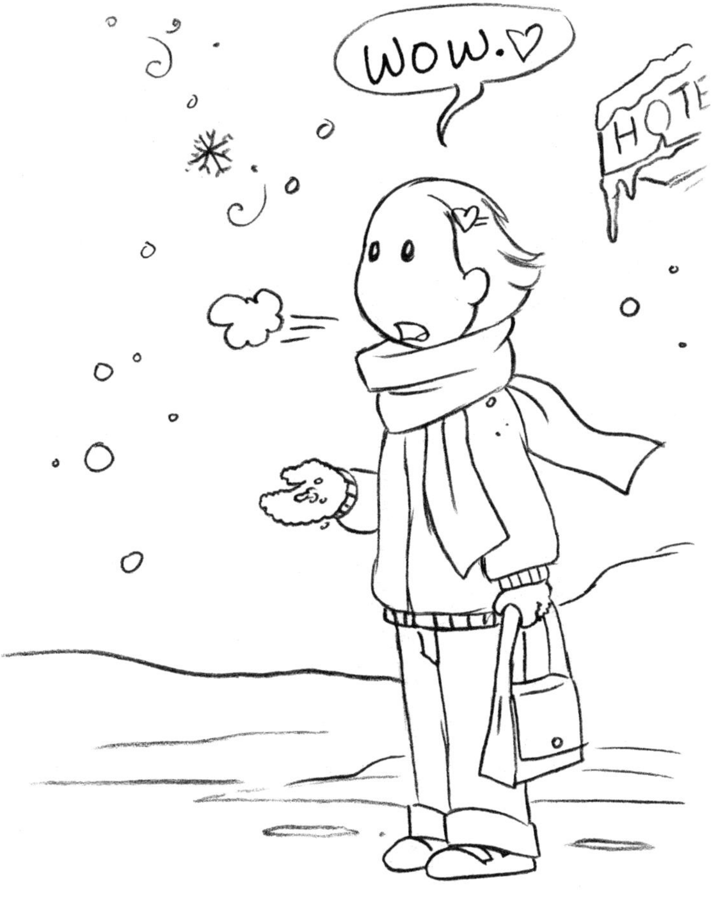
WOW.♡
HOTE

Kyoto

Previous capitol of Japan, over 1,000 years old... one of the best preserved cities in Japan.

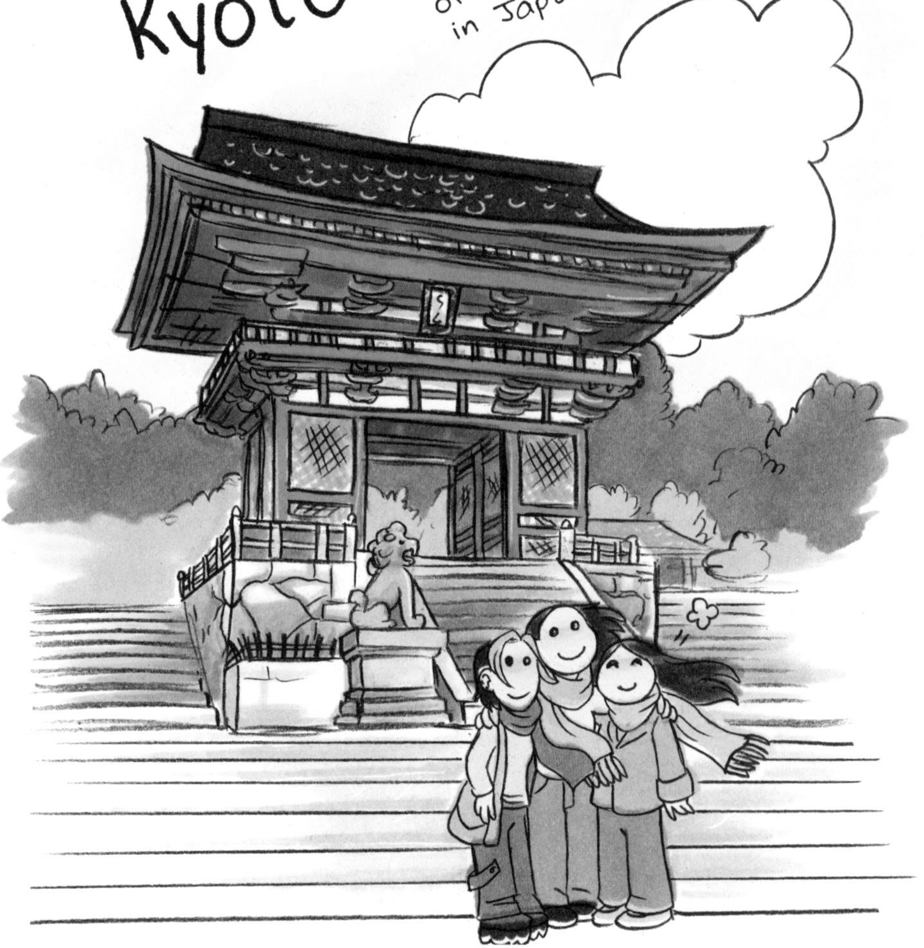

Kyoto is an old town surrounded by forest-covered hills. Everywhere you look there's a temple. we decided to visit the famous temple, Kiyomizu (established 798).

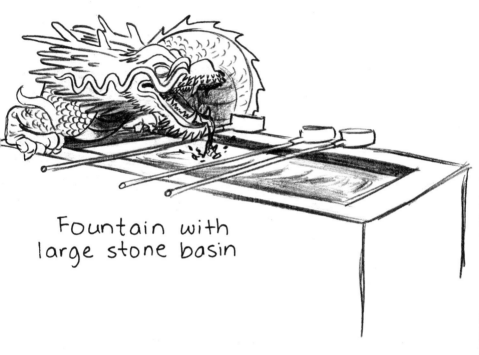

Fountain with
large stone basin

Fountains like this are outside
most temples. You're supposed
to wash your hands and mouth
here before entering (to cleanse
yourself spiritually).

Kiyomizu means "Pure Water".
If you drink from this fountain, "Otowa-No-Taki
you will supposedly get health, long-life
and success in studies.

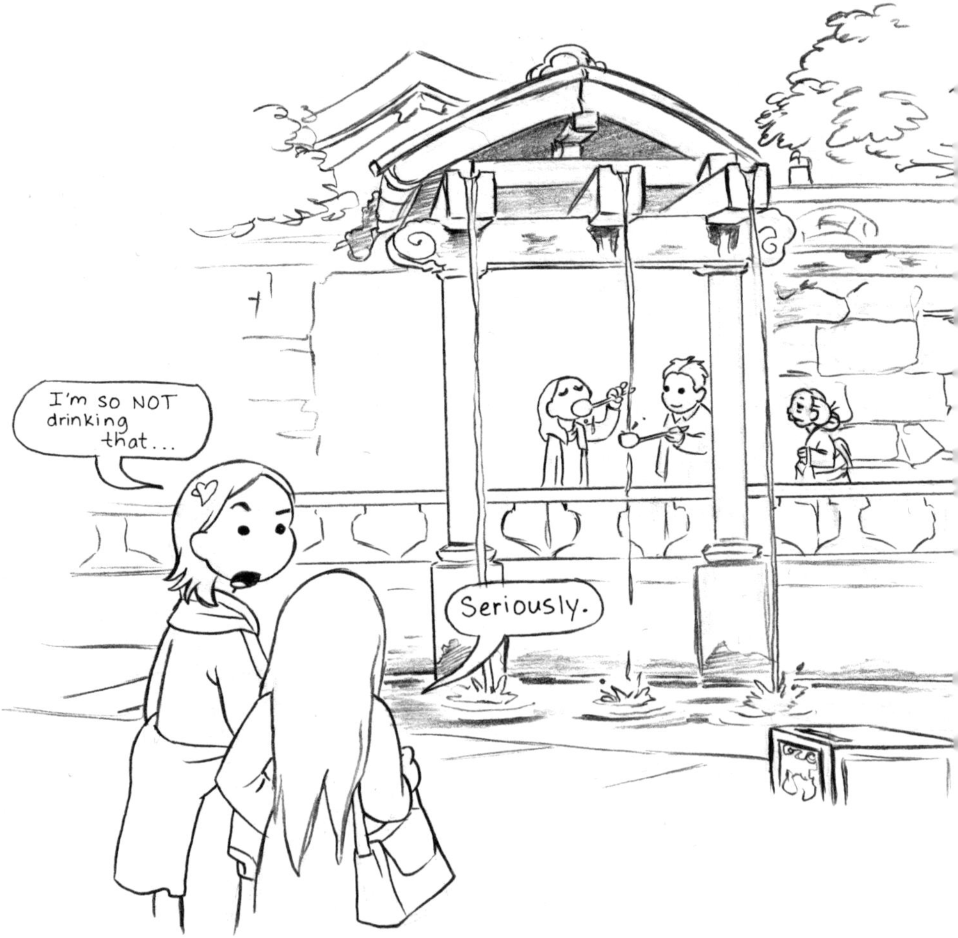
Seriously.
I'm so NOT drinking that...

MIKO
(shinto shrine maidens)

No makeup

white
kimono
top

Red pleated
Hakama

They help keep up shrines
and sell goodluck charms, etc.
at temple events.

Anime fans will remember
Rei from Sailor Moon and
Kikyo from Inuyasha were miko.

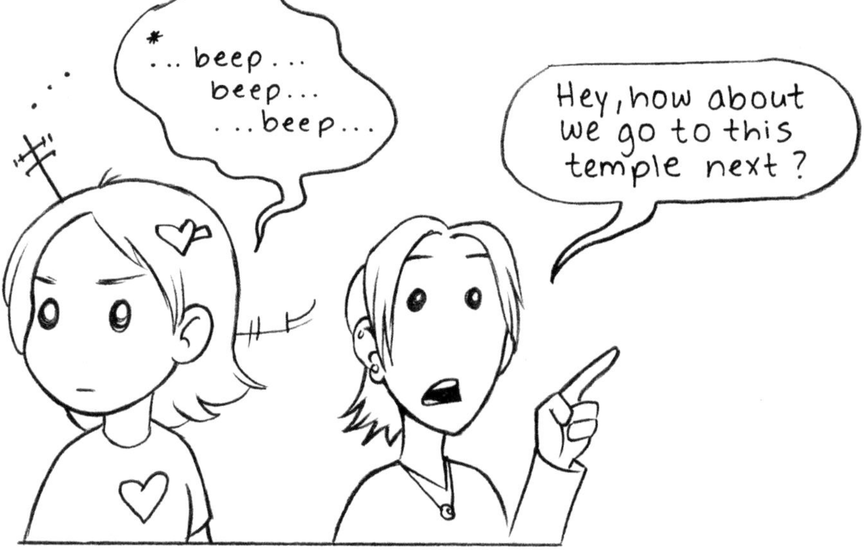
. . .
*. . . beep . . . beep . . . . . . beep . . .
Hey, how about we go to this temple next?

*cute stuff homing device

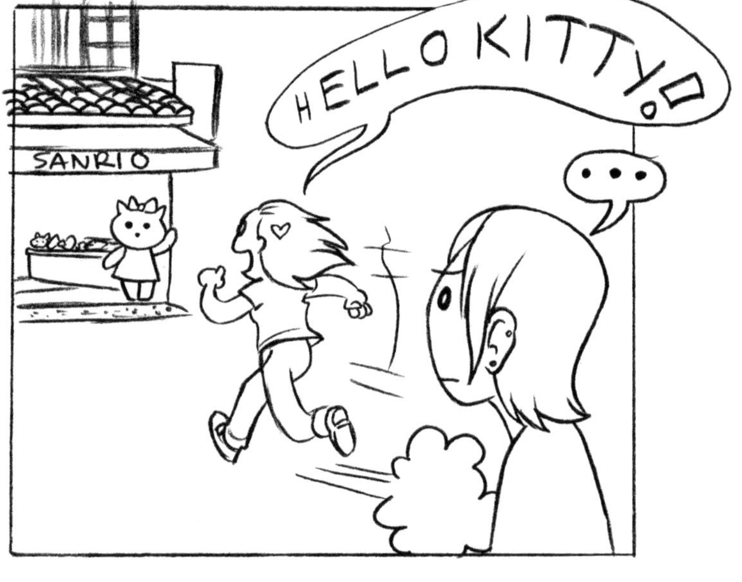
SANRIO
HELLO KITTY!
• • •

We didn't make it to any other temples that day . . .

When we got back to the hotel, my luggage was waiting for me. The airport had delivered it straight to my hotel room!

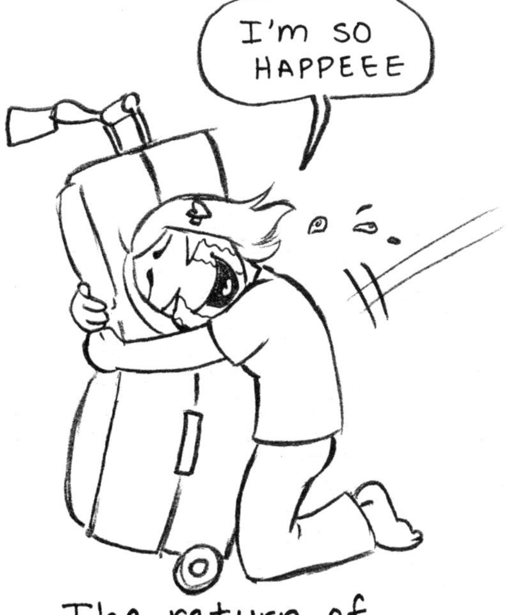
I'm SO HAPPEEE

The return of the LUGGAGE!

Even better,
VOLKS had faxed me!

It turned out that they could meet
me on another day, so I could see
Aida after all!

But that meant...

Have you sold
the ticket yet?

(Luckily she hadn't sold it yet!)

The next day,
we saw a shrine
from the bus and
decided to stop.
Little did we know
we'd come at
exactly the right
time to see a
celebration.

It was "Yasaka Shrine"(est. 656)
patron shrine of the
the Gion Entertainment District.

Today was "Setsubun".

On a covered
platform in the snow,
two geisha perform
a traditional dance.

"Out with the old, in with the new!"

Good Luck Beans

We almost bought some $8 goodluck beans.

Almost.

Setsubun used to be on New Year's before they switched calendars. They still celebrate it on the OLD LUNAR NEW YEAR, which is the beginning of Spring.

It's basically a celebration of the end of the year and the end of winter. In the evening, people dress up in silly costumes, like Carnival.

Ake-mashite-omedetou-gozaimasu!
(Happy New year!)

Clean slate!

young women + girls get dressed up in furisode for New year's. Hair ornament (Kanzashi), fur stole and matching clutch purse are the norm.

The kimono is called "furisode" for the long swinging sleeves...
The pattern is for New year's... "Shou-chiku-bai" (plum, bamboo + pine) The octagonal box is a New year's lunchbox for special dishes called Osechi Ryouri. Other patterns are fine, but you'll often see New year's themes.

In Japan, New year's is a huge holiday. Families come together and visit shrines to make wishes for the New Year. The whole country closes down for the first week of the year. Also, everyone cleans out their house.

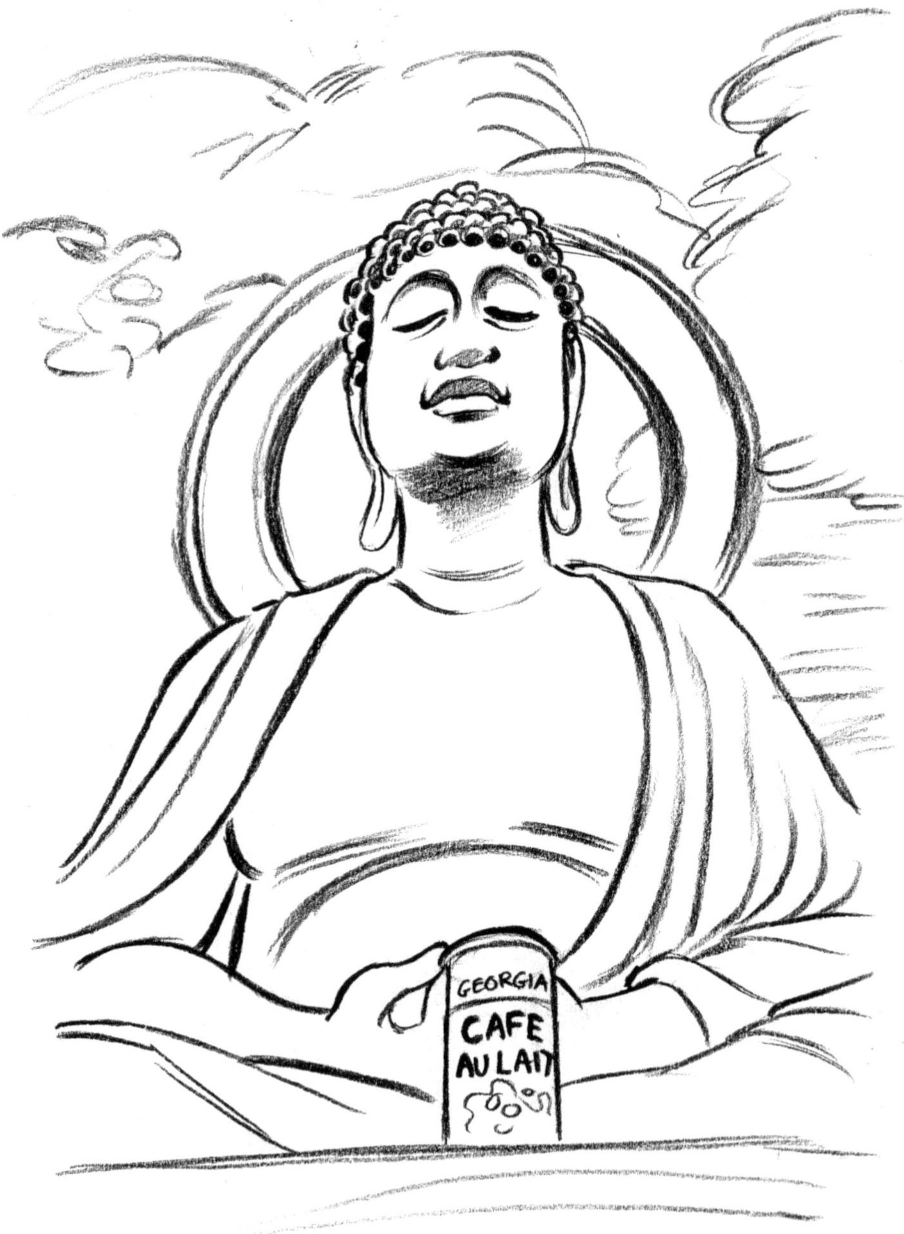
GEORGIA
CAFE
AU LAIT

Buddha likes coffee?
(Statue with can in Kyoto ...)

(The drink is an offering...
it's not litter)

There are drink machines on almost every corner.
They have like 5 kinds of tea, some coffee, hot chocolate... and rarely soda.

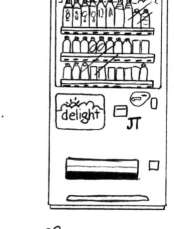

♡ Ocha ♡

I love Japanese tea

Judy doesn't like the bitter taste...

Judy kept buying different teas trying to find a non-bitter one...
She didn't have much success. So I helped her out ♡ ♡

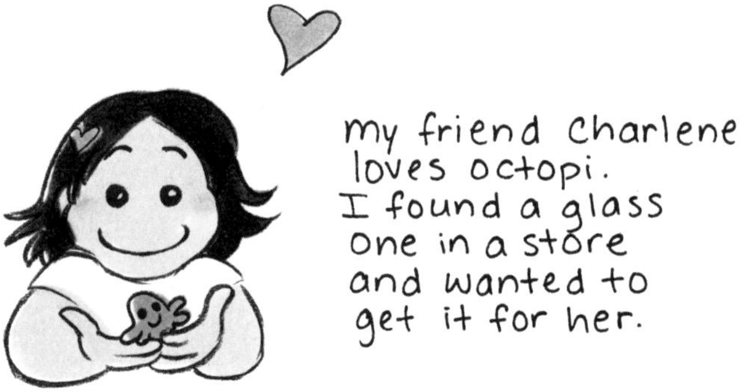
my friend Charlene loves octopi. I found a glass one in a store and wanted to get it for her.

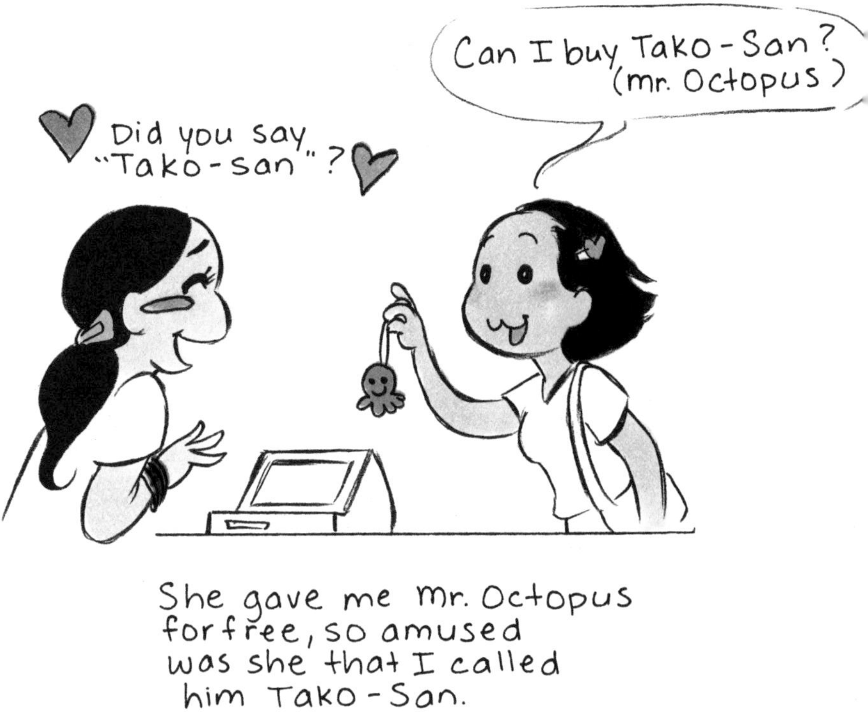
Can I buy Tako-San? (mr. Octopus)
Did you say "Tako-san"?
She gave me mr. Octopus for free, so amused was she that I called him Tako-San.

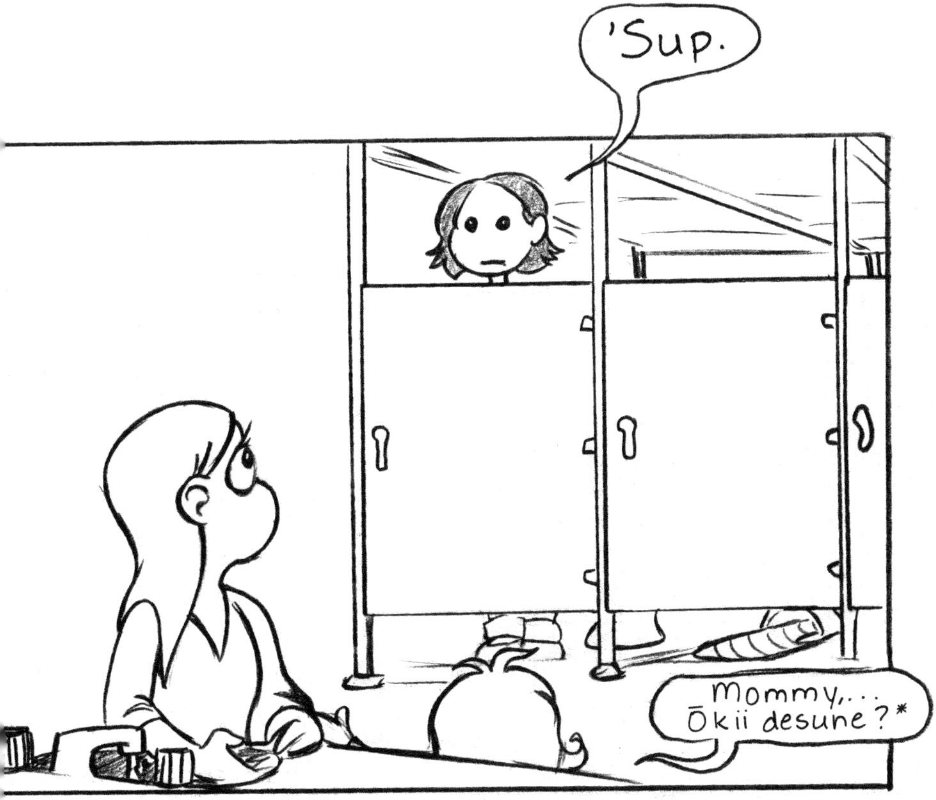
'Sup.
Mommy,...
Ōkii desune?*

I was too tall
for certain bathrooms...

✱ "Big, isn't she?"

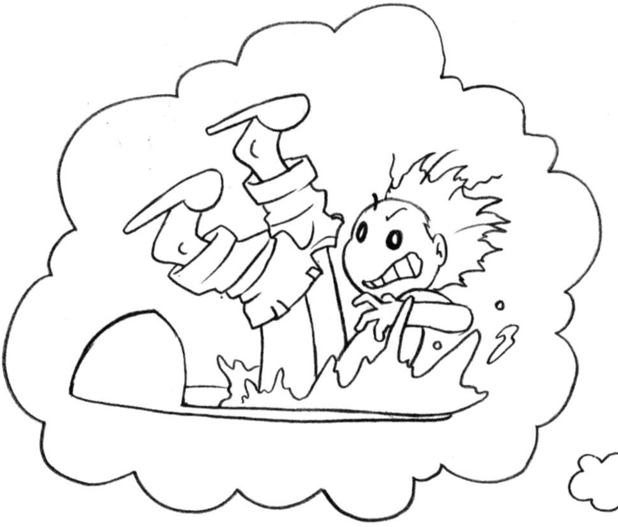

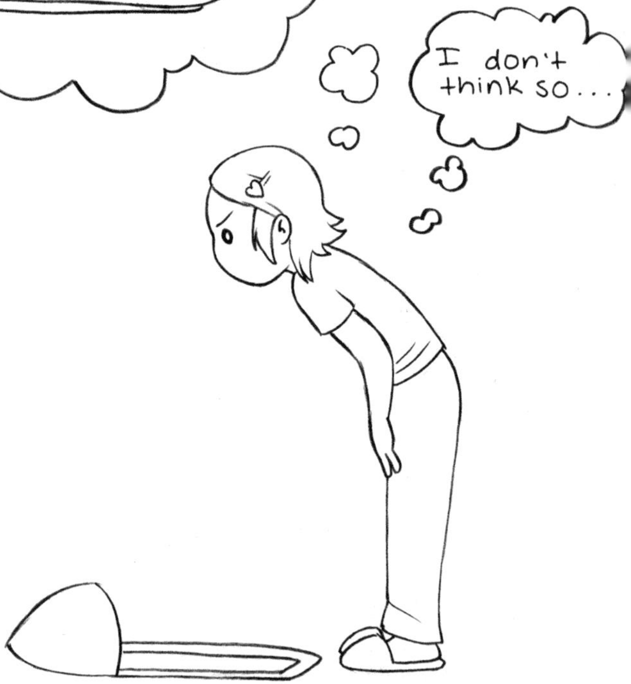
I don't think so...

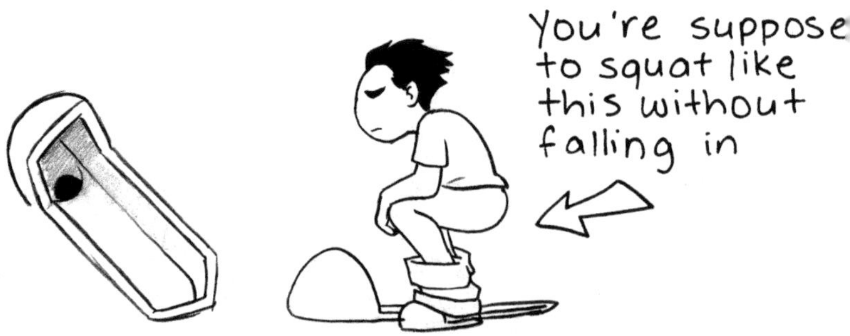
You're suppose to squat like this without falling in

Near Kiyomizu,
here are many cute stores ...
n a fan store ... there
as an adorable cat with
big head, but no visible
store owner.

We joked that the cat was the owner.

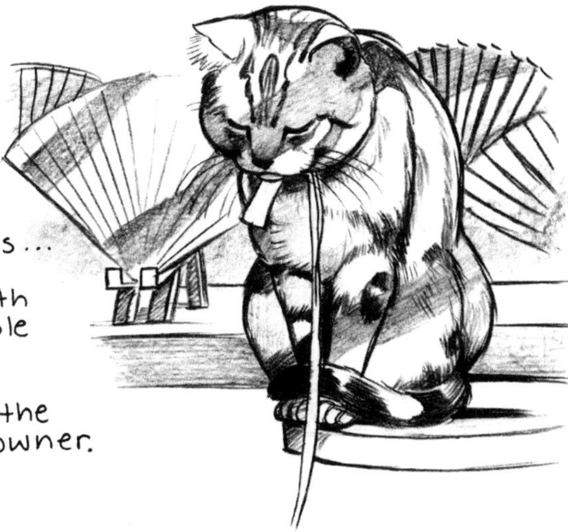

Apparently during rush hour (when the trains are like sardine cans ...), sometimes perverts grab women's butts ... (Never happened to me)

So ... At certain times of day, at least one train car is for women only.

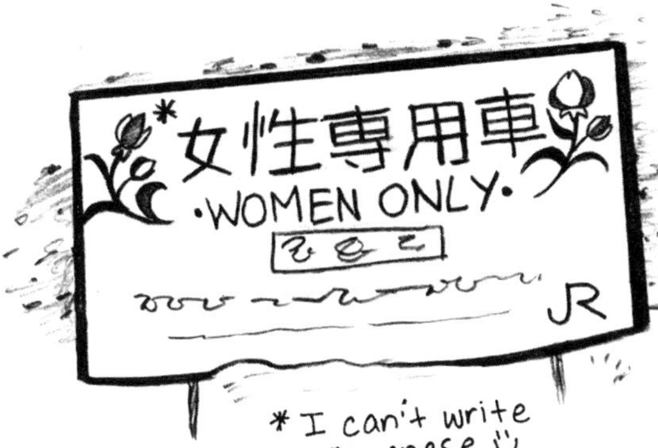
*女性専用車
·WOMEN ONLY·
JR

This sign is on the ground at the station.

* I can't write Japanese ☺

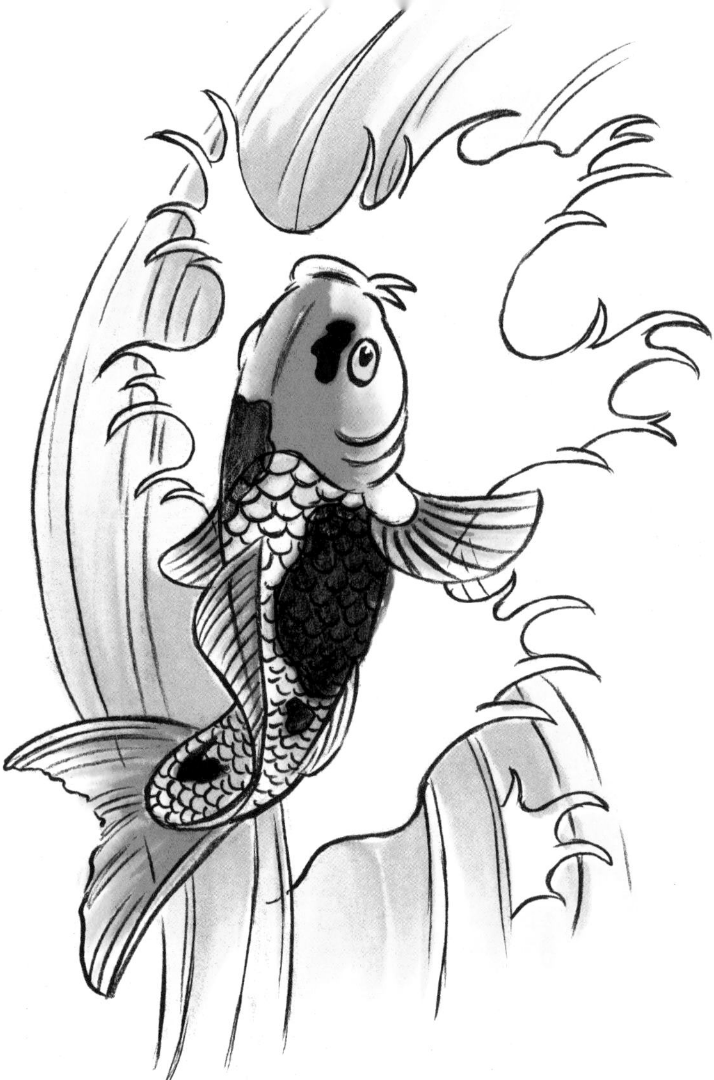

Koi (which look like giant goldfish) swim upstream, like salmon, to spawn.

So you'll often see the image of a Koi swimming upstream as a symbol of not giving up. I think it is beautiful. If I got a tattoo, I would get a Koi. Keep fighting!

Good luck!!

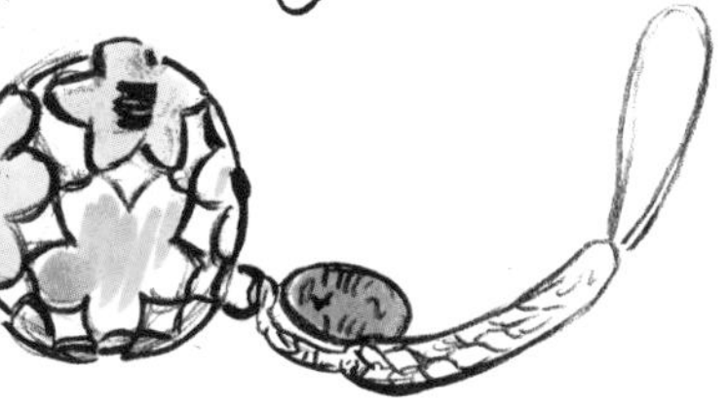

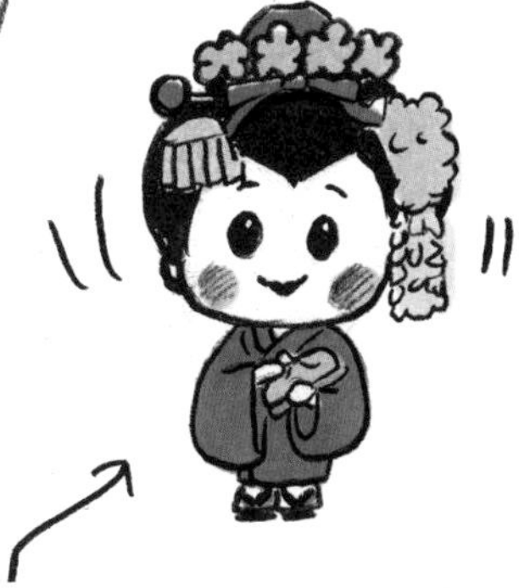

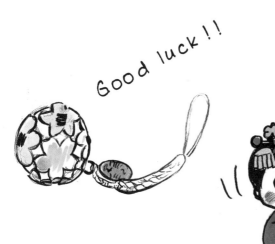

This little bobble-head geisha was on everything from pencil toppers to towels and home products.

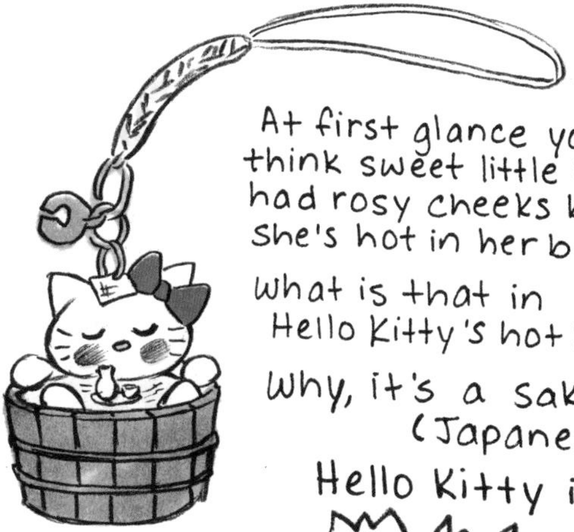

At first glance you'd think sweet little Hello Kitty had rosy cheeks because she's hot in her bath ... but ...

What is that in Hello Kitty's hot bath ... ?

Why, it's a sake bottle! (Japanese rice wine)

Hello Kitty is DRUNK!

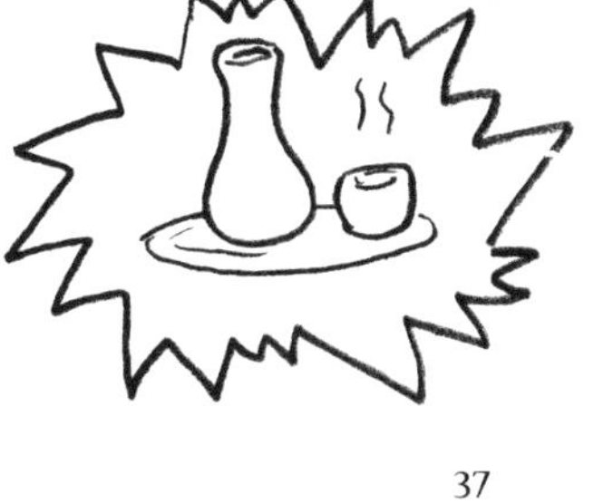

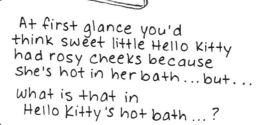

THE REQUIRED TOURIST
PHOTO AT KIYOMIZU

Chapter Three:

Geisha

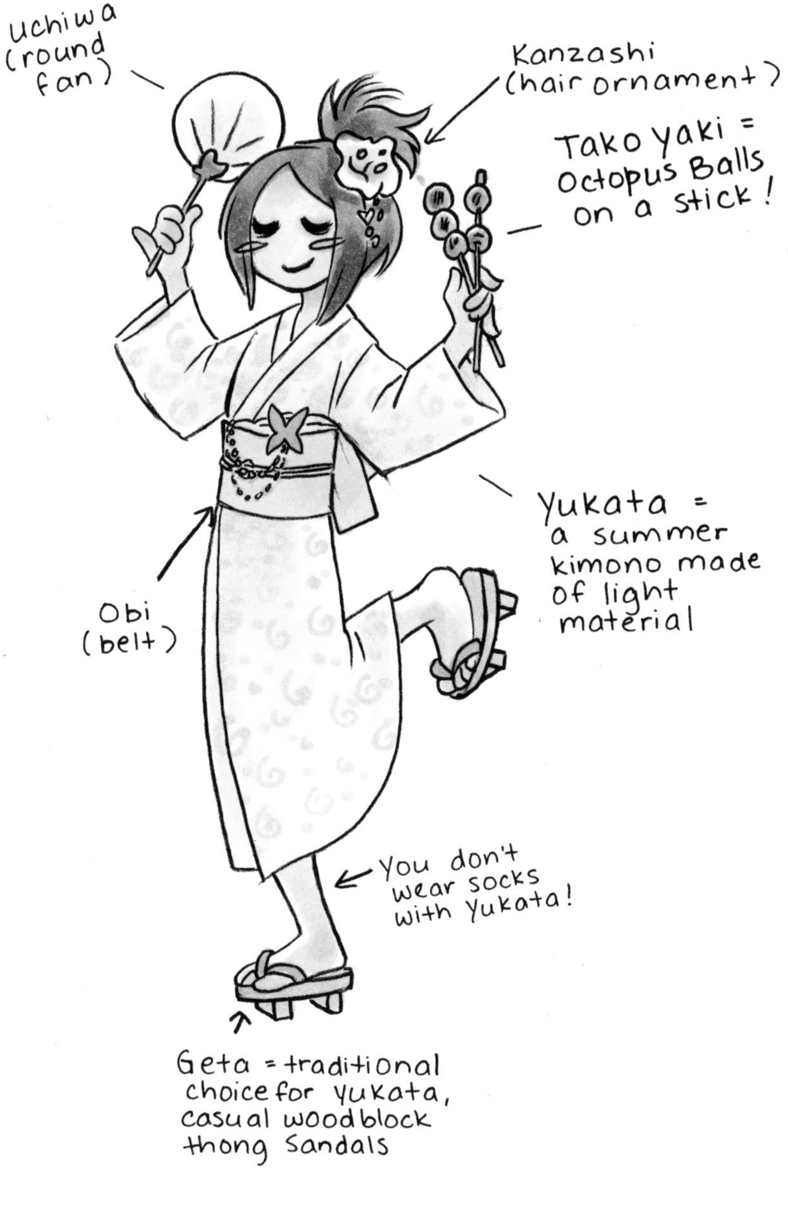

uchiwa (round fan)
Kanzashi (hair ornament)
Tako yaki = Octopus Balls on a stick!
Yukata = a summer kimono made of light material
Obi (belt)
You don't wear socks with Yukata!
Geta = traditional choice for yukata, casual woodblock thong sandals

One of the most well-
known images of Japan
is the Geisha. When I
heard from my friend that
there were photo studios
in Japan that would
dress you up like a
geisha, I knew I had to go!

First... What is a Geisha?

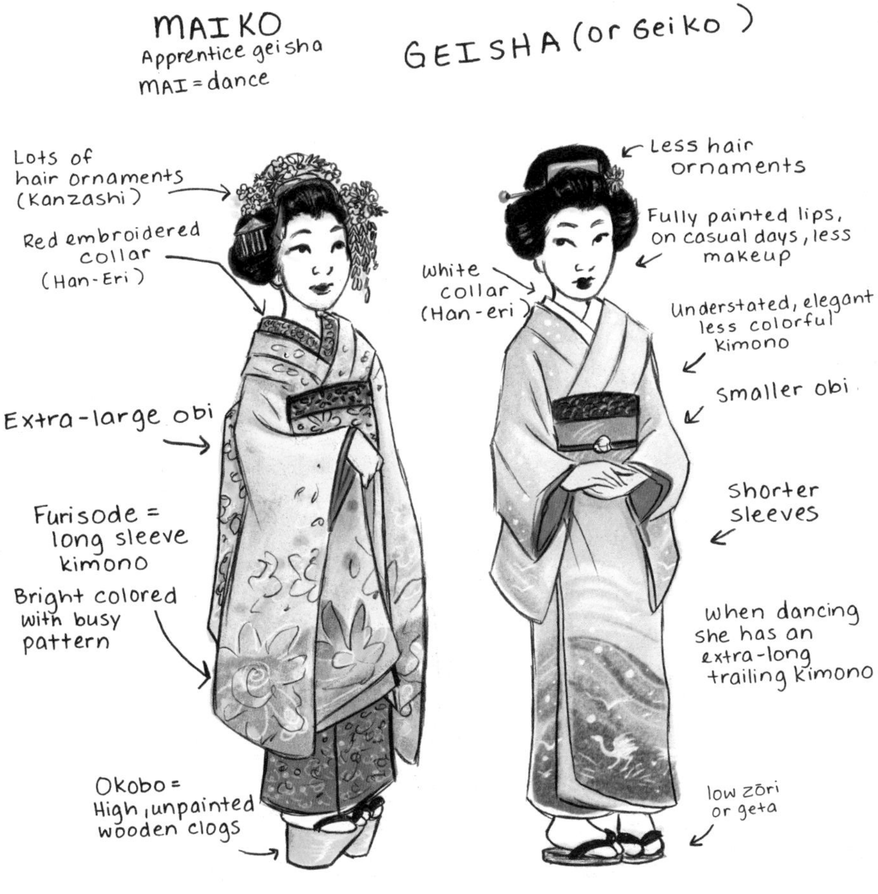
MAIKO
Apprentice geisha
MAI = dance
GEISHA (or Geiko)
Lots of hair ornaments (Kanzashi)
Red embroidered collar (Han-Eri)
Extra-large obi
Furisode = long sleeve kimono
Bright colored with busy pattern
Okobo = High, unpainted wooden clogs
Less hair ornaments
Fully painted lips, on casual days, less makeup
White collar (Han-eri)
Understated, elegant less colorful kimono
Smaller obi
Shorter sleeves
When dancing she has an extra-long trailing kimono
low zōri or geta

Geisha are artisans trained in dance, tea ceremony, musical instruments and conversation. They are keepers of Japanese traditional culture. In Kyoto, Geisha are called "Geiko". Geisha are rare today. Your average Japanese girl doesn't know how to put on a kimono.

OIRAN OR TAYŪ

Unlike Geisha . . . they were prostitutes.

Their overall look compared to a Geisha is flamboyant and flashy.

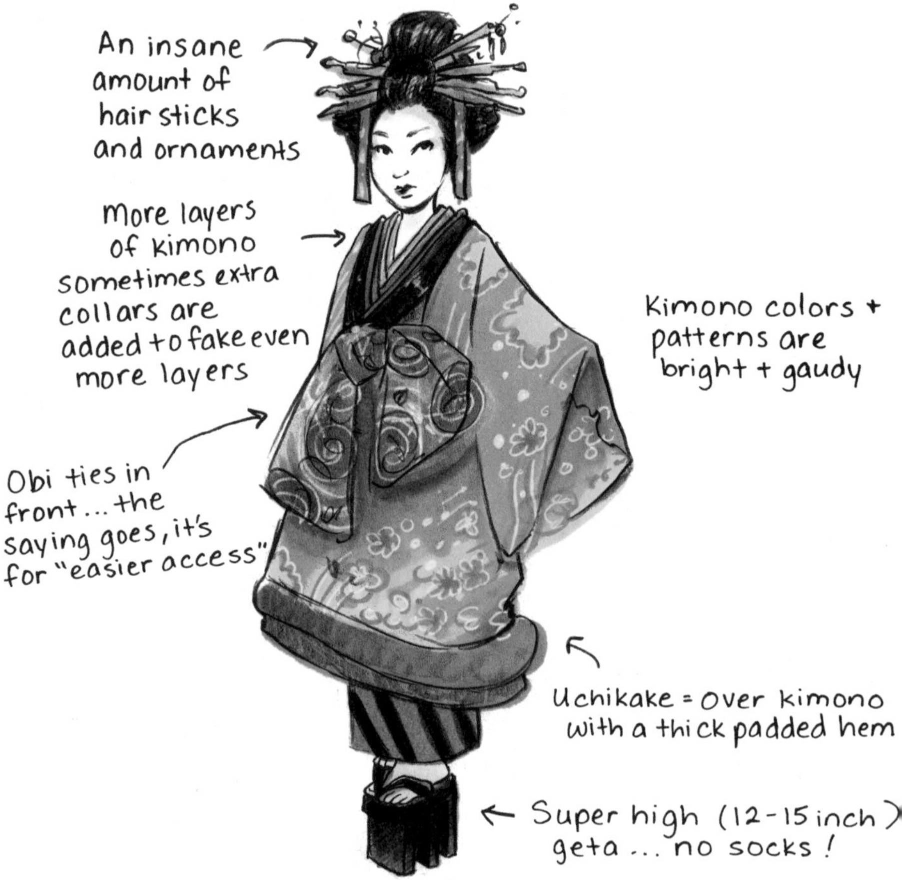
An insane amount of hair sticks and ornaments
More layers of kimono sometimes extra collars are added to fake even more layers
Obi ties in front . . . the saying goes, it's for "easier access"
Kimono colors + patterns are bright + gaudy
Uchikake = Over kimono with a thick padded hem
Super high (12-15 inch) geta . . . no socks !

The sudden snow in Kyoto caused train
+car delays. We got to the maiko-make-up
studio on time, but the photographer
and most of the staff were late.

So we made snow kitties!
It doesn't snow much in
California, after all.

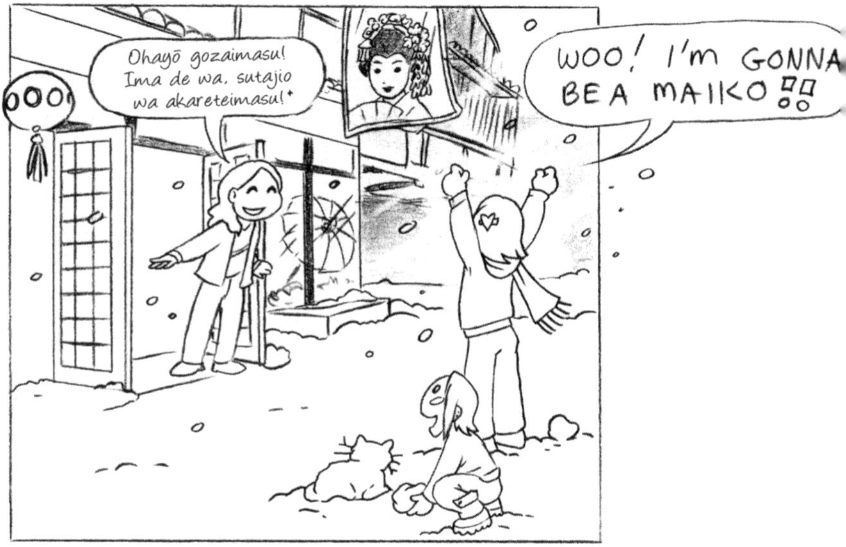
Ohayō gozaimasu! Ima de wa, sutajio wa akareteimasu!*
WOO! I'M GONNA BE A MAIKO!!

* Good morning!
The studio is now open!

I sat down and chose whether to be a maiko or a Geisha.

I picked "Maiko" because they had the prettiest hair ornaments.

The studio was gorgeous with tatami mats and orchids... and stunning photos of previous customers. ♡

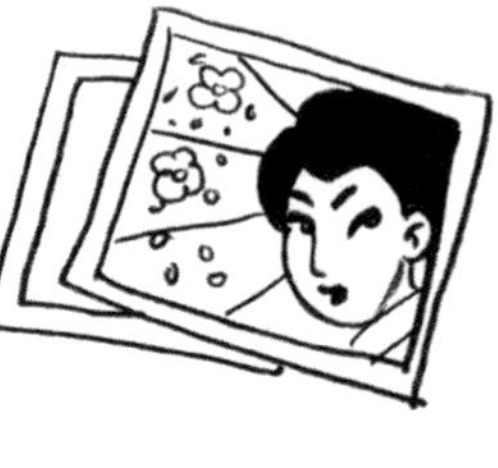

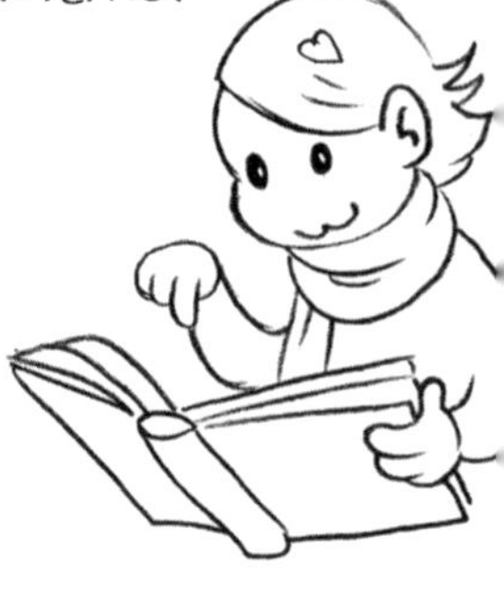

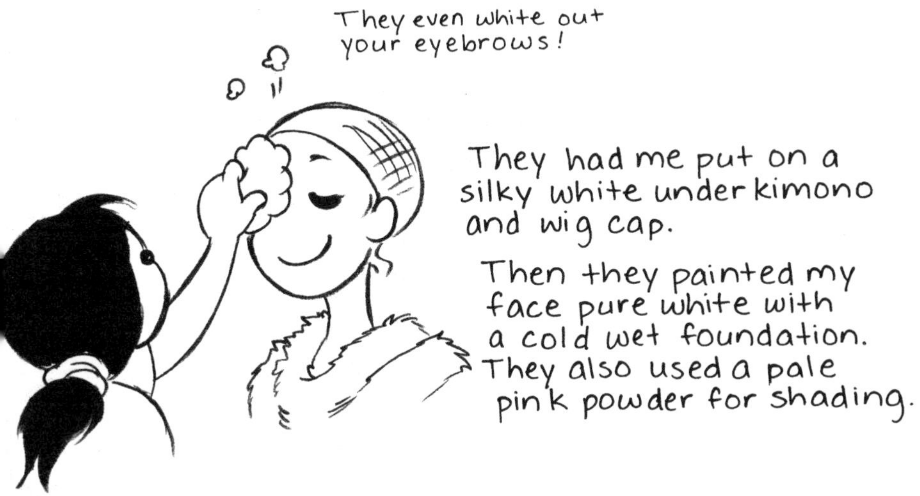
They even white out your eyebrows!
They had me put on a silky white underkimono and wig cap.
Then they painted my face pure white with a cold wet foundation. They also used a pale pink powder for shading.

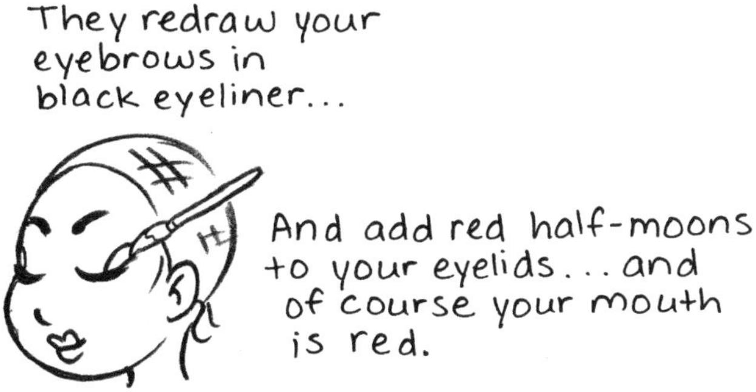
They redraw your eyebrows in black eyeliner...
And add red half-moons to your eyelids... and of course your mouth is red.

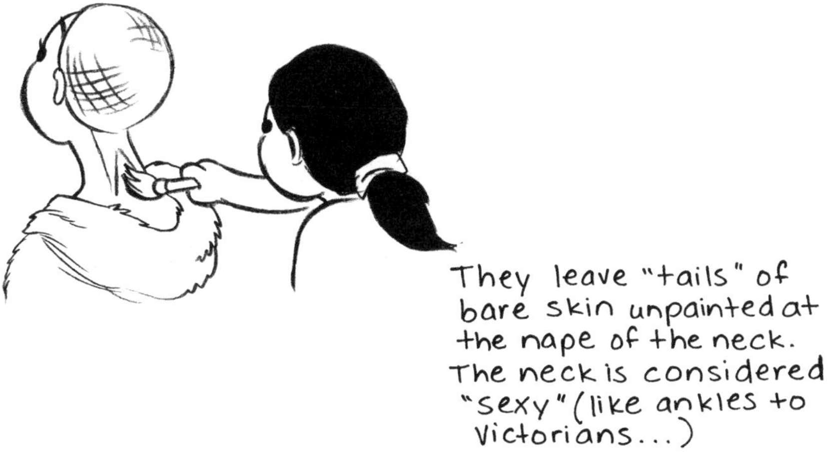
They leave "tails" of bare skin unpainted at the nape of the neck. The neck is considered "sexy" (like ankles to Victorians...)

Then I got to choose a kimono!

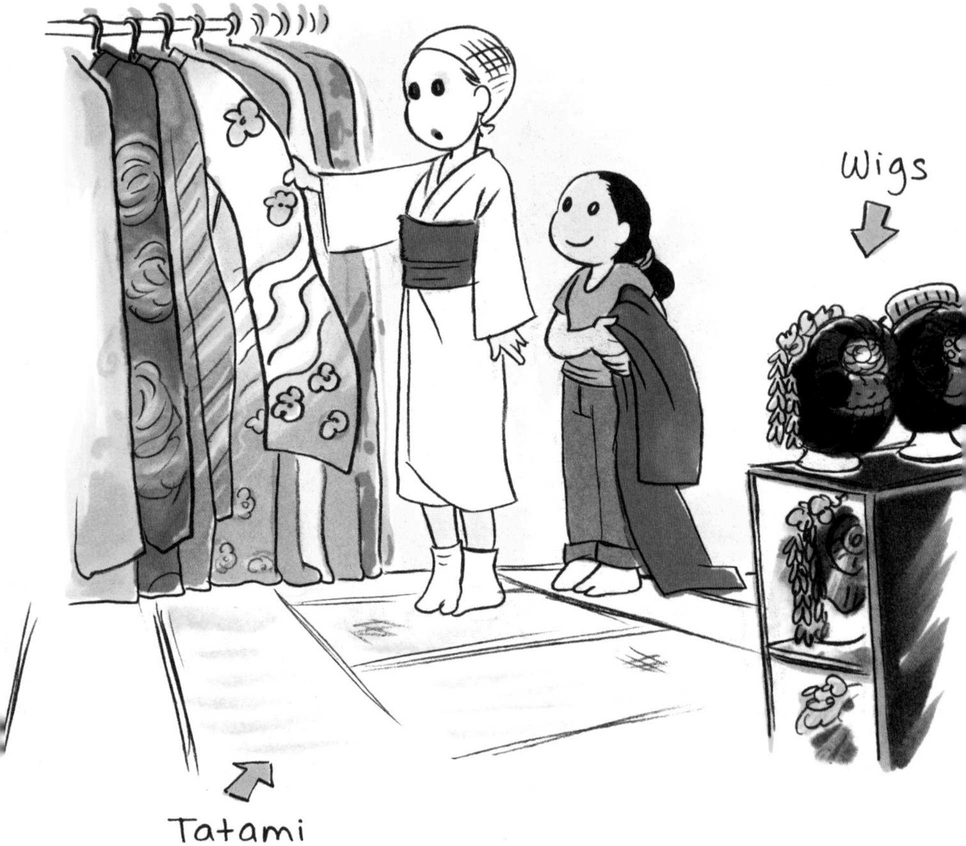
Wigs
Tatami Mats

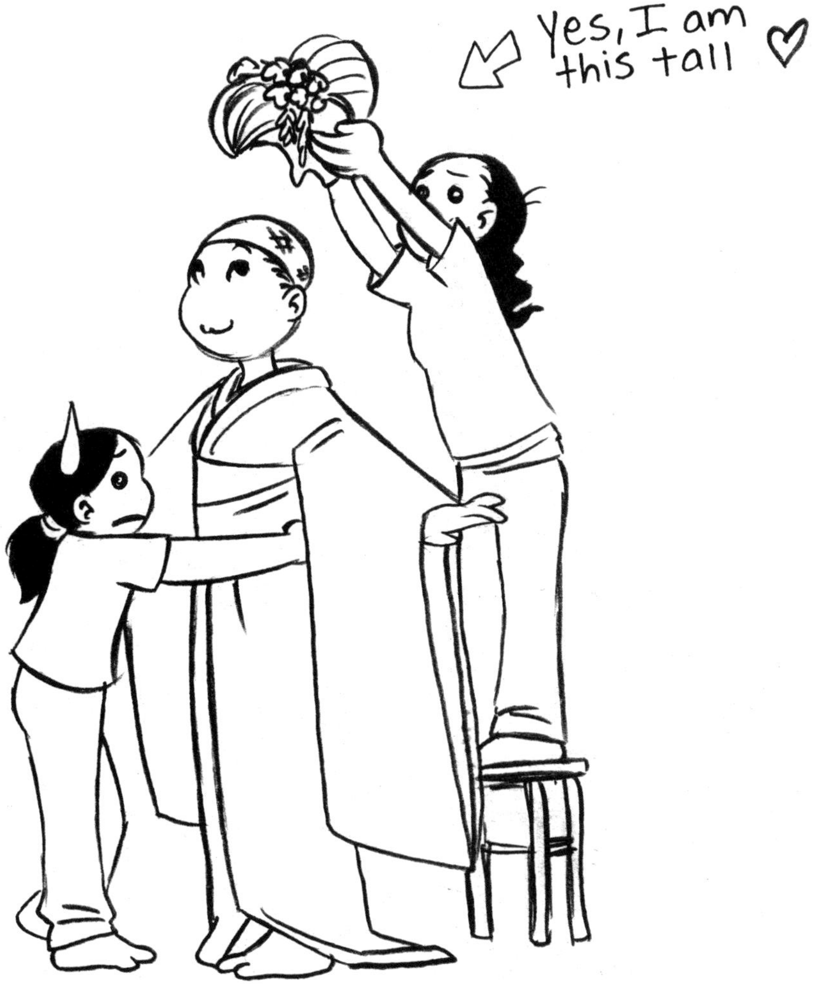
Yes, I am this tall ♡

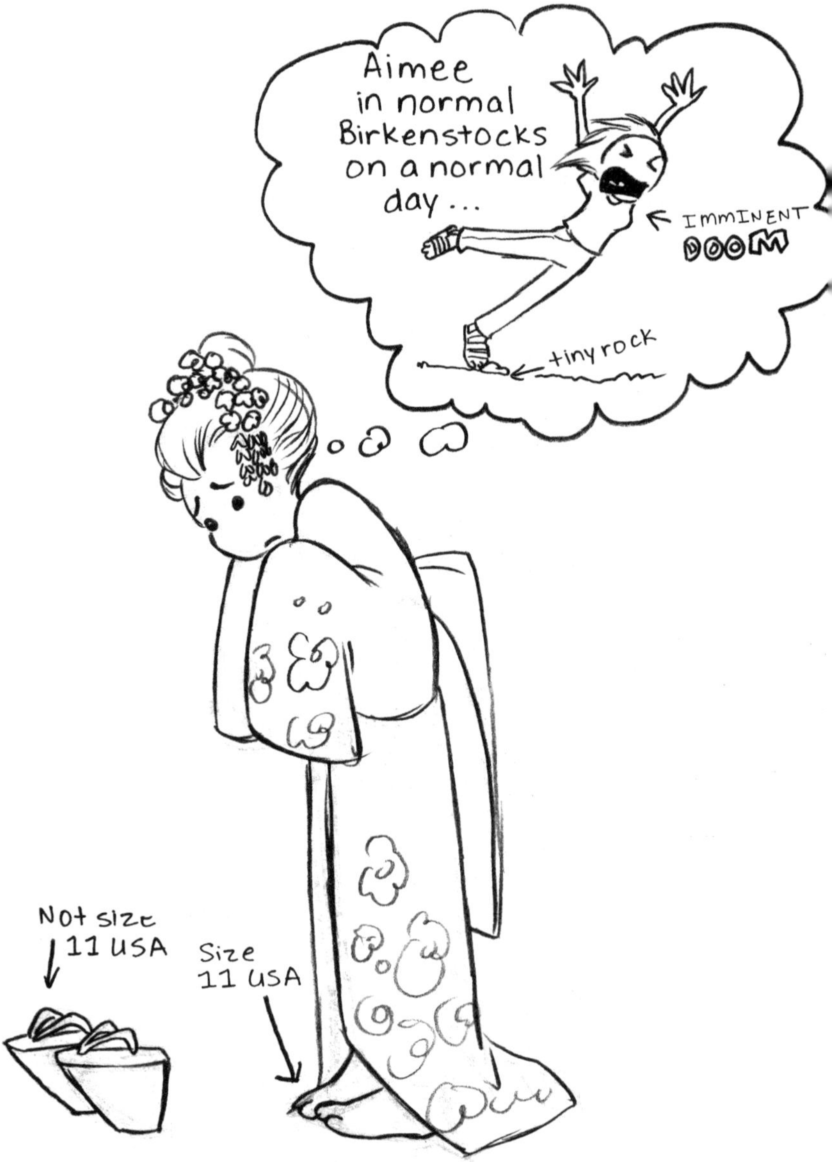
Aimee in normal Birkenstocks on a normal day...
IMMINENT DOOM
tiny rock
Not size 11 USA
Size 11 USA

Aimee trying on maiko gear...

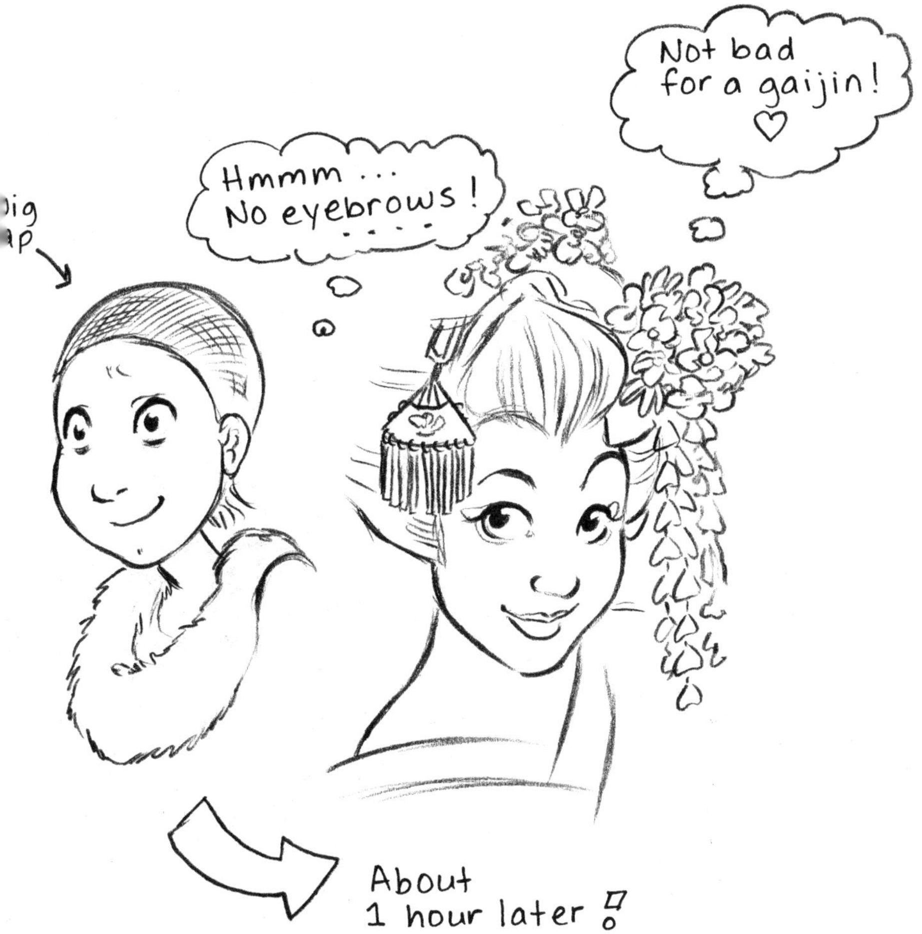
Hmmm ... No eyebrows! ....
Not bad for a gaijin! ♡
About 1 hour later!

I got a CD of my fancy maiko photos... and a few weeks after I got home, I got my printed glossies in the mail!

(And stickers of me as a maiko, too!)

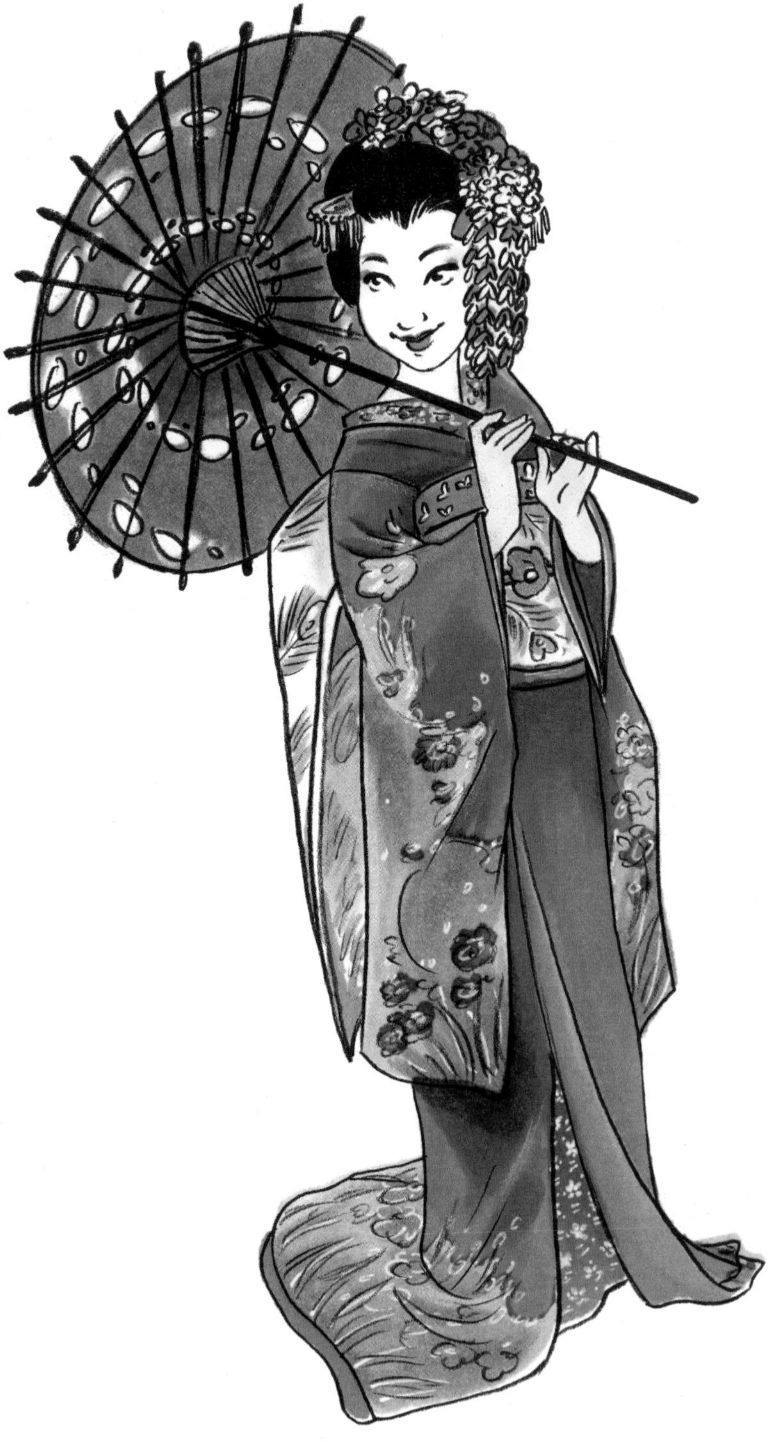

Chapter Four:
Onsen

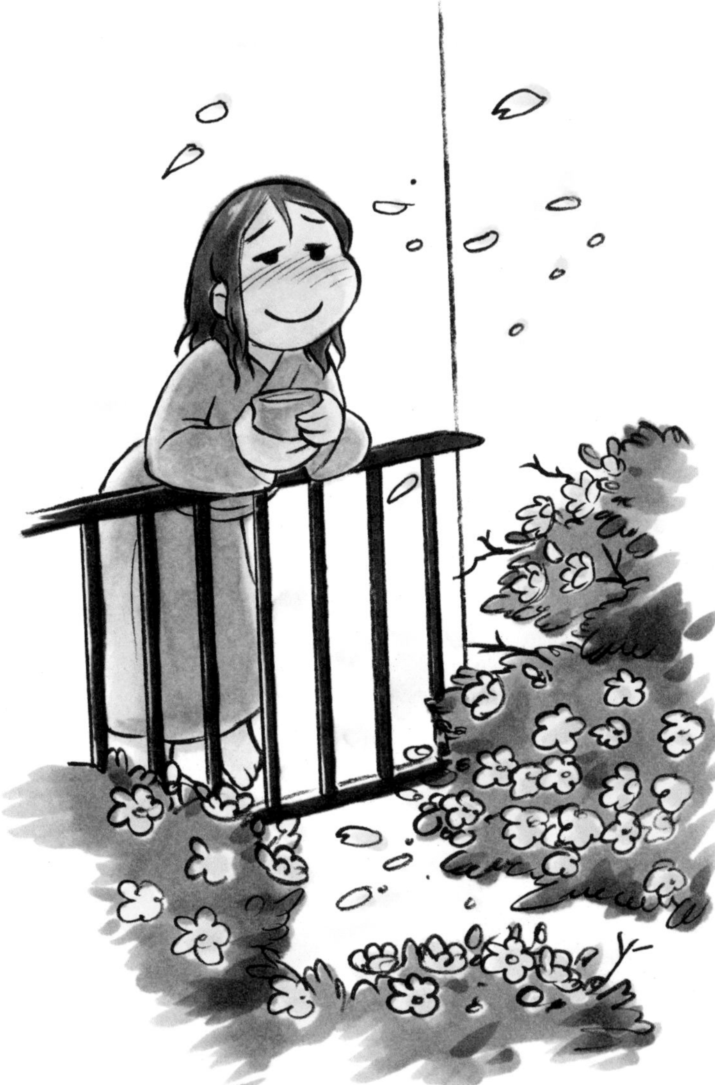

Boarding the Shinkansen

Trains are the main method of transportation, even when traveling from city to city.

⇧
We really saw two maiko waiting to ride the train!

⇘
This yellow bumpy line warns you not to get too clos to the track. (for the blind)

There is a painted area for each door of the train. The train ALWAYS stops at exactly the right spot to line up with the paint.

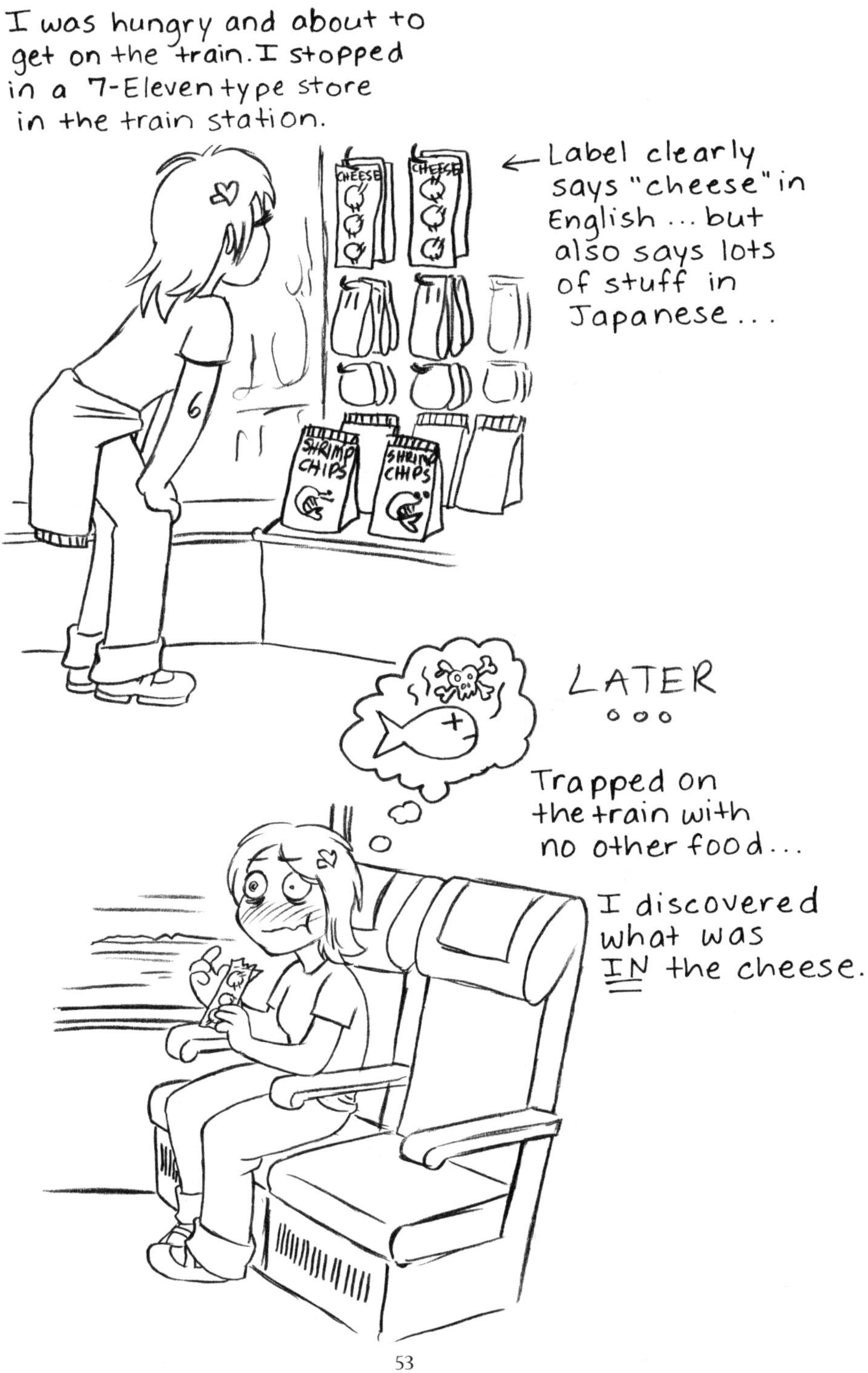
I was hungry and about to get on the train. I stopped in a 7-Eleven type store in the train station.
CHEESE
CHEESE
Label clearly says "cheese" in English ... but also says lots of stuff in Japanese...
SHRIMP CHIPS
SHRIMP CHIPS
LATER ...
Trapped on the train with no other food...
I discovered what was IN the cheese.

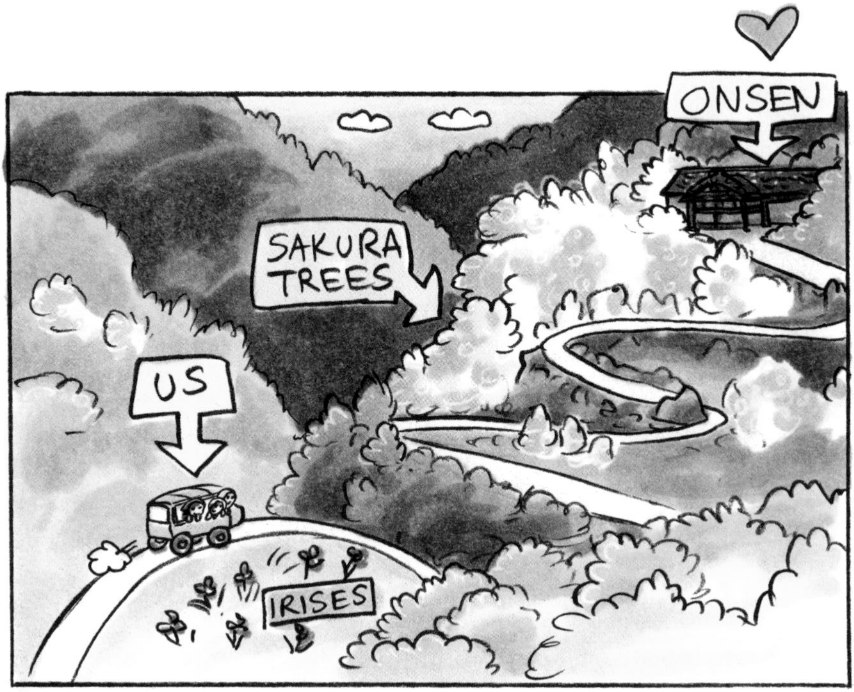
ONSEN
SAKURA TREES
US
IRISES

The next thing on our to-do list was staying at an onsen. Onsen are hot springs. Ours was part of a traditional Japanese inn in a forest on top of flower-filled hills.

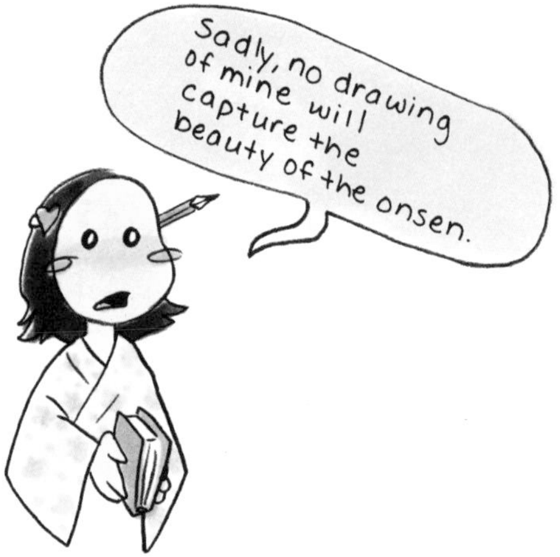
Sadly, no drawing of mine will capture the beauty of the onsen.

We were greeted at the onsen with a hot cup of tea... with sakura petals in it. It tasted mildly salty. I felt like I was drinking something precious. I bought some of the tea before leaving and rationed it over a few months.

Jochū-San (personal hostess)

(You can't see it, but she had a cellphone tucked in the front of her obi!)

Our personal hostess at the onsen. She would bow like this at the door before leaving.

Our room at the onsen.

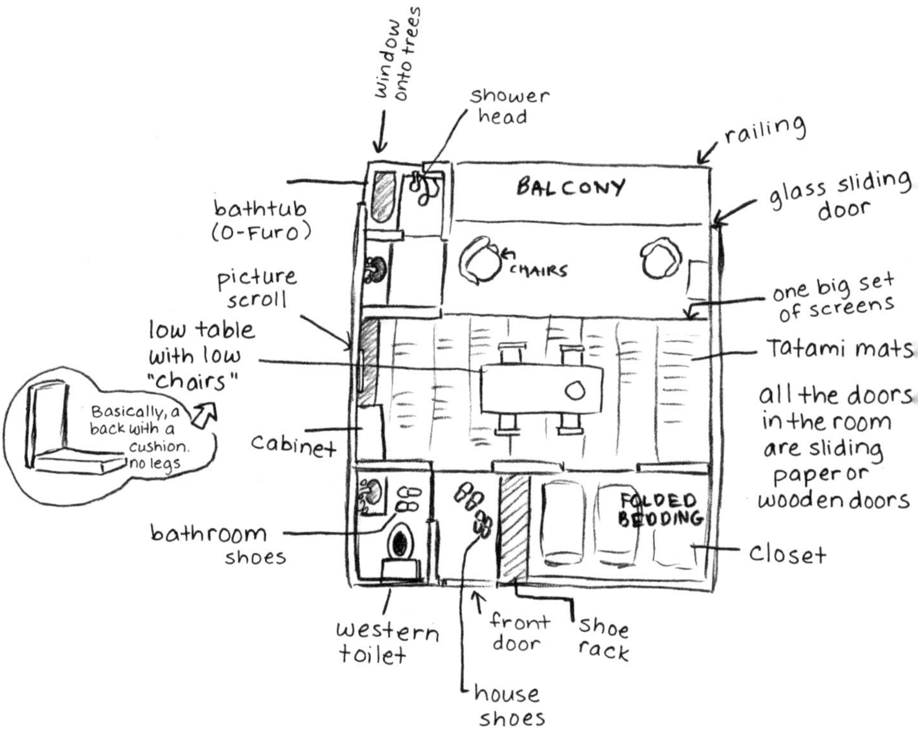

window onto trees
shower head
railing
BALCONY
glass sliding door
bathtub (O-Furo)
CHAIRS
picture scroll
one big set of screens
low table with low "chairs"
Tatami mats
all the doors in the room are sliding paper or wooden doors
Basically, a back with a cushion. no legs
cabinet
FOLDED BEDDING
bathroom shoes
closet
western toilet
front door
shoe rack
house shoes

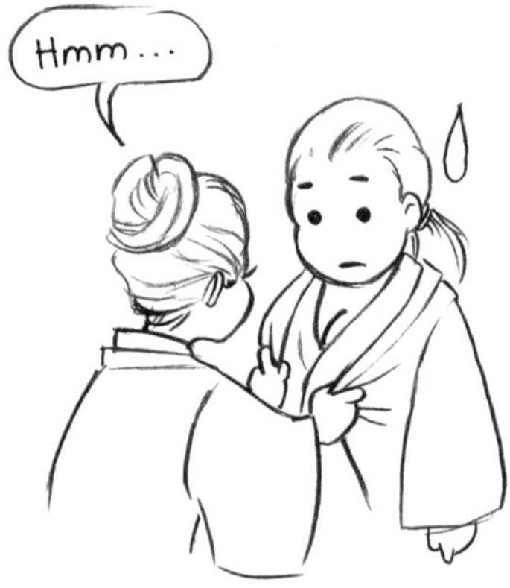

Hmm...

Judy's boobs proved to be too mighty for some kimono... (which is not to say our hostess didn't try!)

Onsen are hot springs in Japan. They are communal baths... most requiring that you bathe naked with complete strangers!

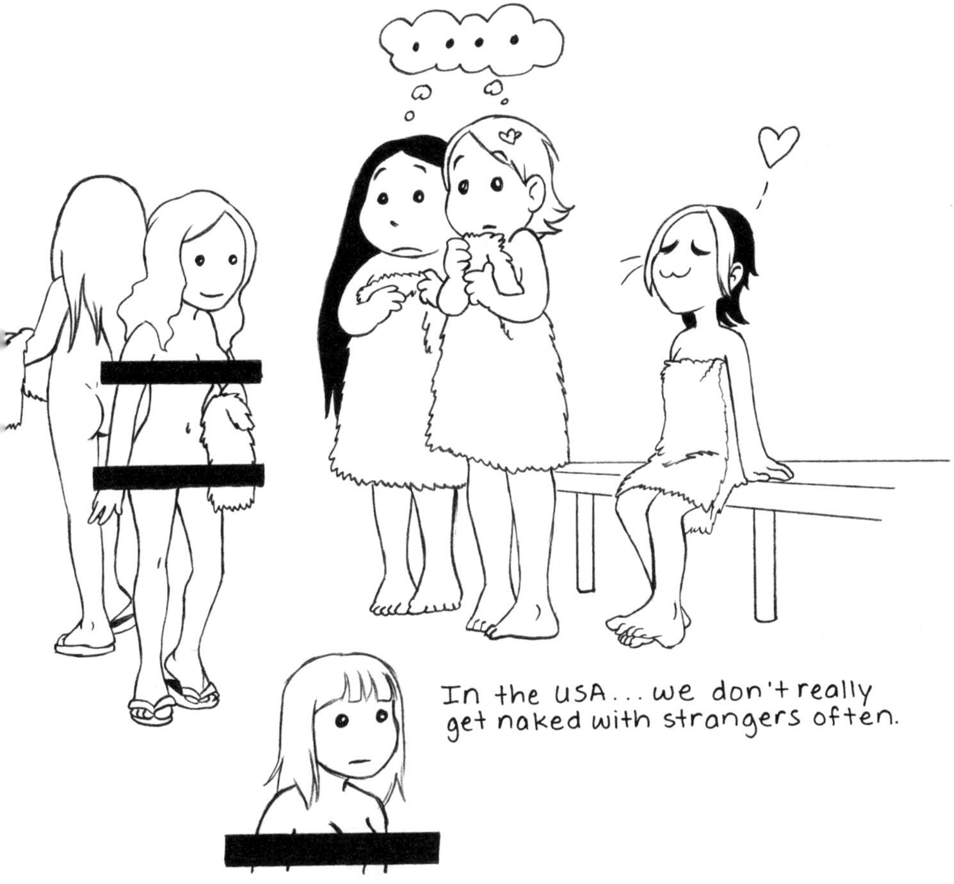
In the USA... we don't really get naked with strangers often.

At the onsen, you rinse off before you bathe in the hot springs... assuming you can FIND them!

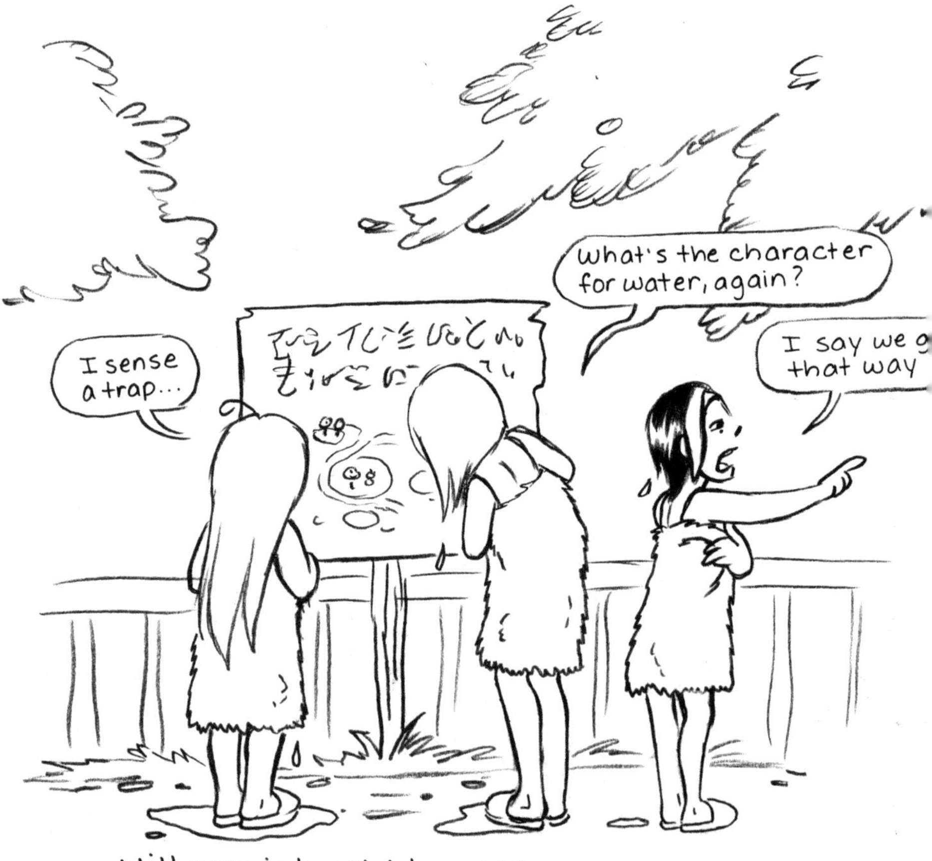
I say we g
that way
What's the character for water, again?
I sense a trap...

Will our intrepid heroes ever find the mythical hot spring?

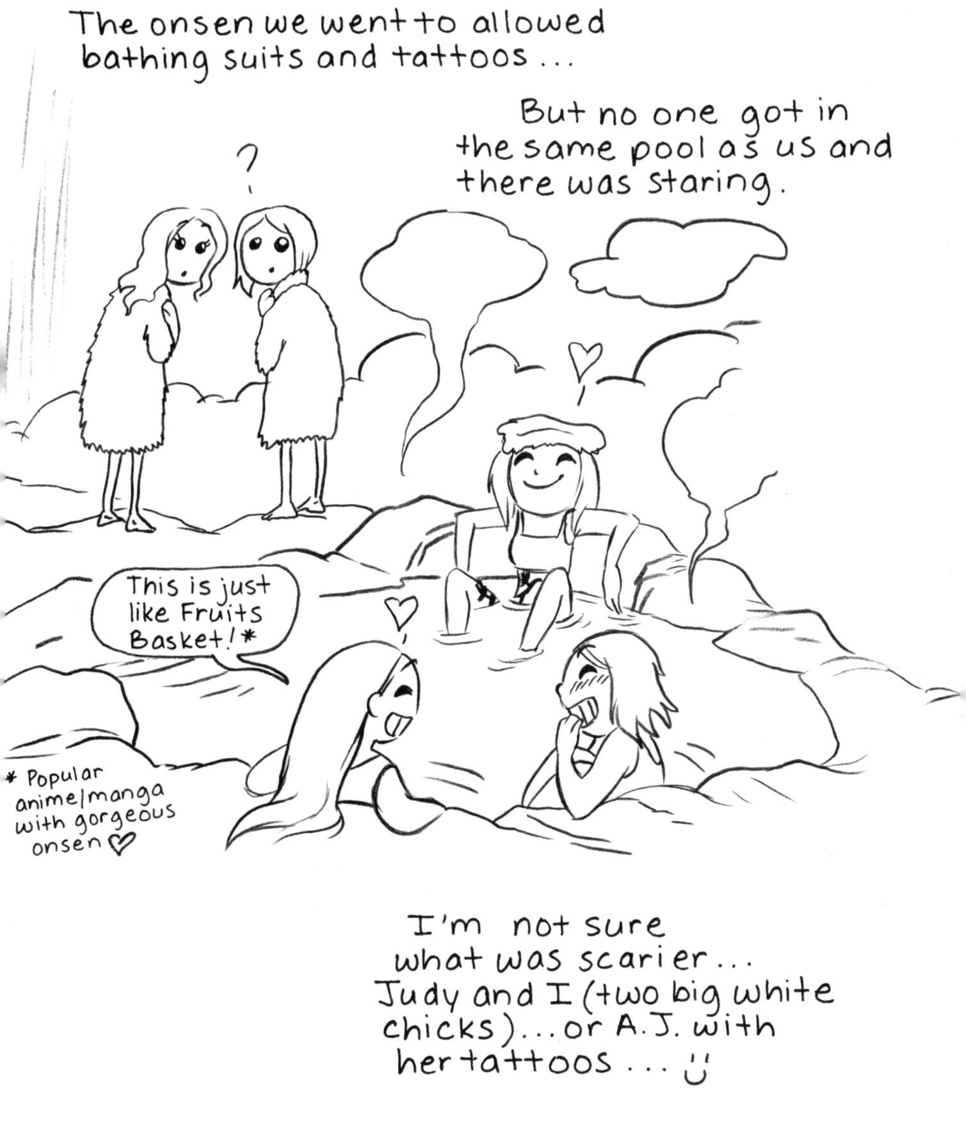
The onsen we went to allowed bathing suits and tattoos...
But no one got in the same pool as us and there was staring.
?
This is just like Fruits Basket! *
* Popular anime/manga with gorgeous onsen
I'm not sure what was scarier... Judy and I (two big white chicks)... or A.J. with her tattoos...

A. J. The Narcoleptic* Ninja

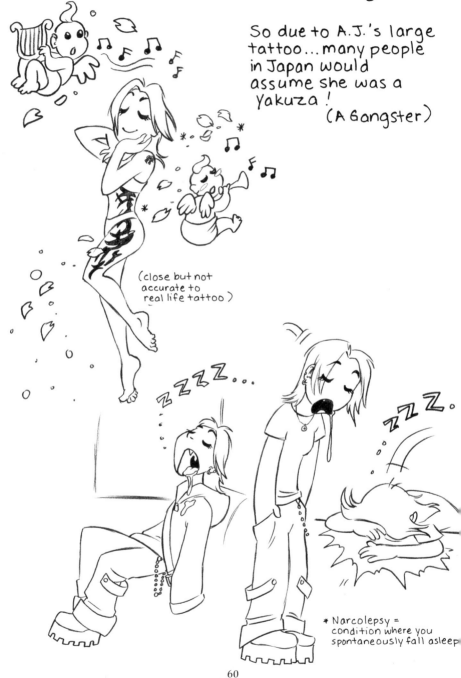

So due to A.J.'s large tattoo... many people in Japan would assume she was a Yakuza!
(A Gangster)

(close but not accurate to real life tattoo)

ZZZZ...

ZZZ.

* Narcolepsy = condition where you spontaneously fall asleep

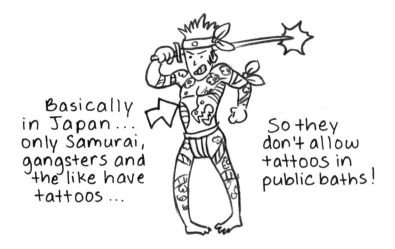

Basically in Japan... only Samurai, gangsters and the like have tattoos...

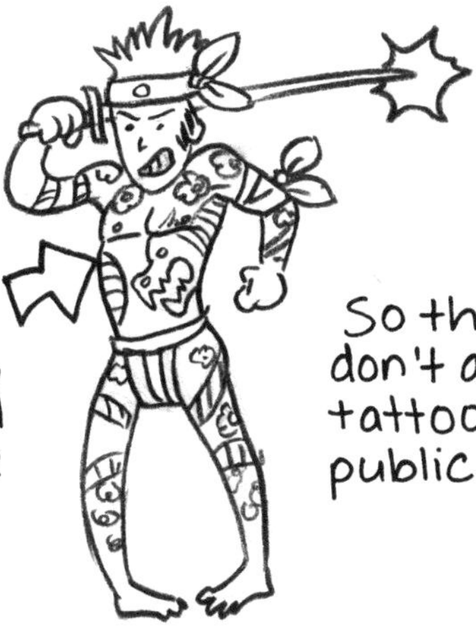

So they don't allow tattoos in public baths!

But in reality, due to her narcoleptic tendencies... she would not make a very good yakuza.

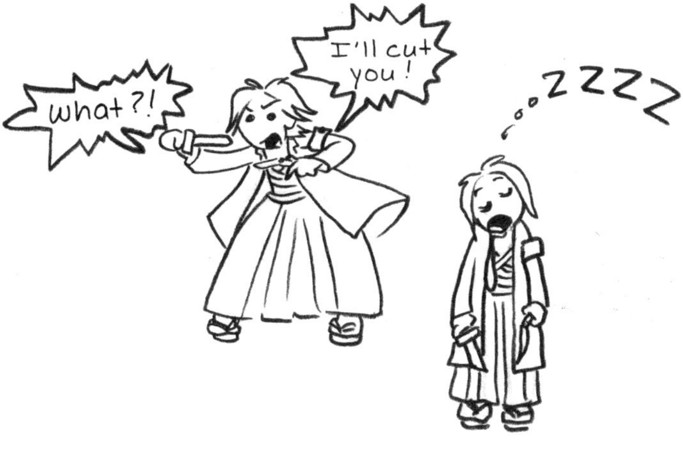
what?!
I'll cut you!
...ZZZZ

(she's not really narcoleptic... she just works too hard...)

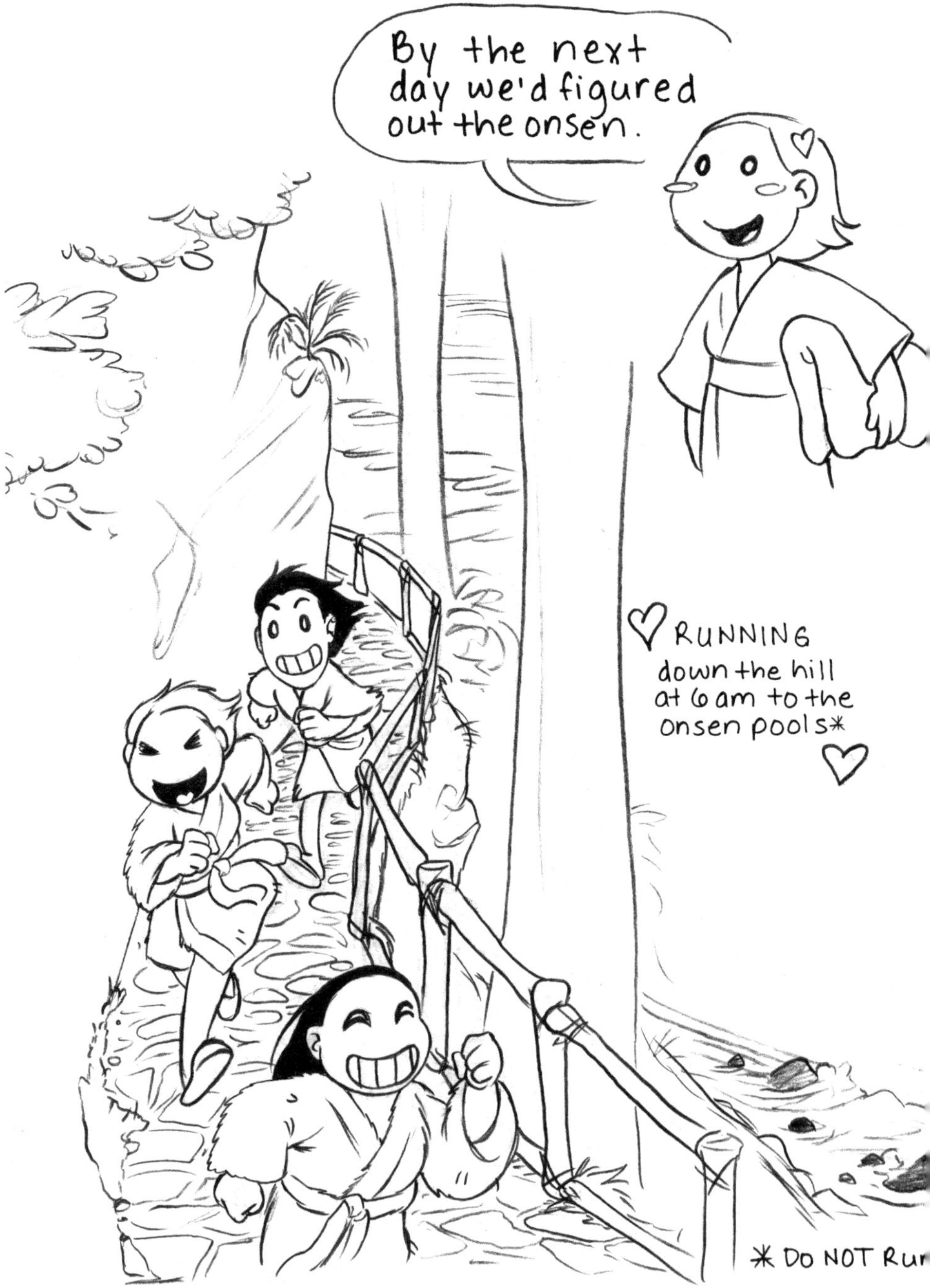
By the next day we'd figured out the onsen.
♡ RUNNING down the hill at 6 am to the onsen pools* ♡
* DO NOT Ru

As we went to sleep that night, I could see sakura blossoms outside the window ... and I could hear the waterfall.

I can't remember a time I have been so relaxed and at peace.

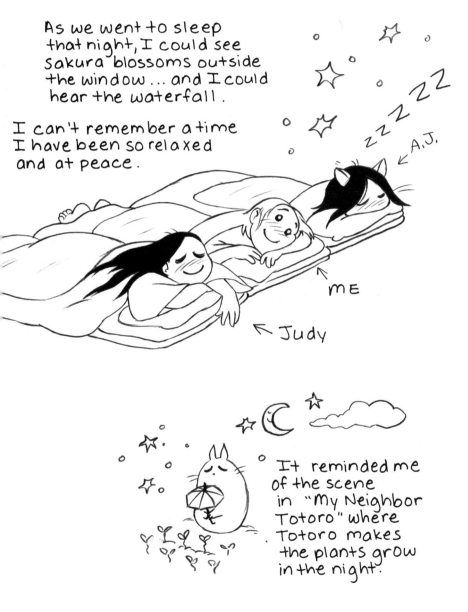

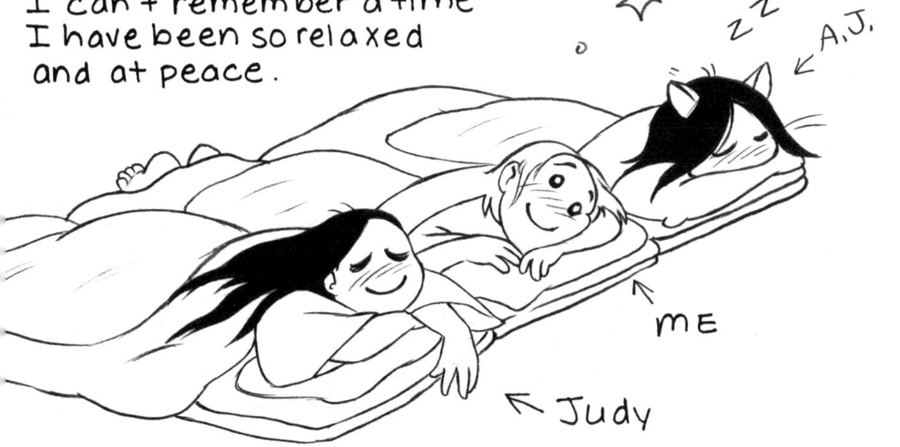
zzzzZZ
A.J.
ME
Judy

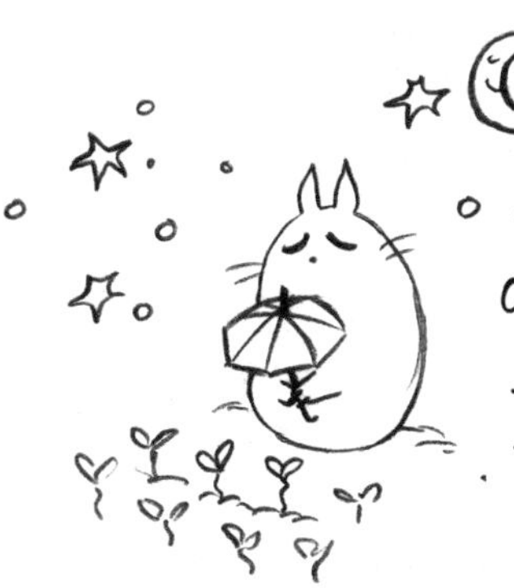

It reminded me of the scene in "My Neighbor Totoro" where Totoro makes the plants grow in the night.

✿ THE TRAIN FROM THE ONSEN ✿

⇦ We decided this
was the train to
Ohtori Academy
(Utena)

Chapter Five:
Takarazuka

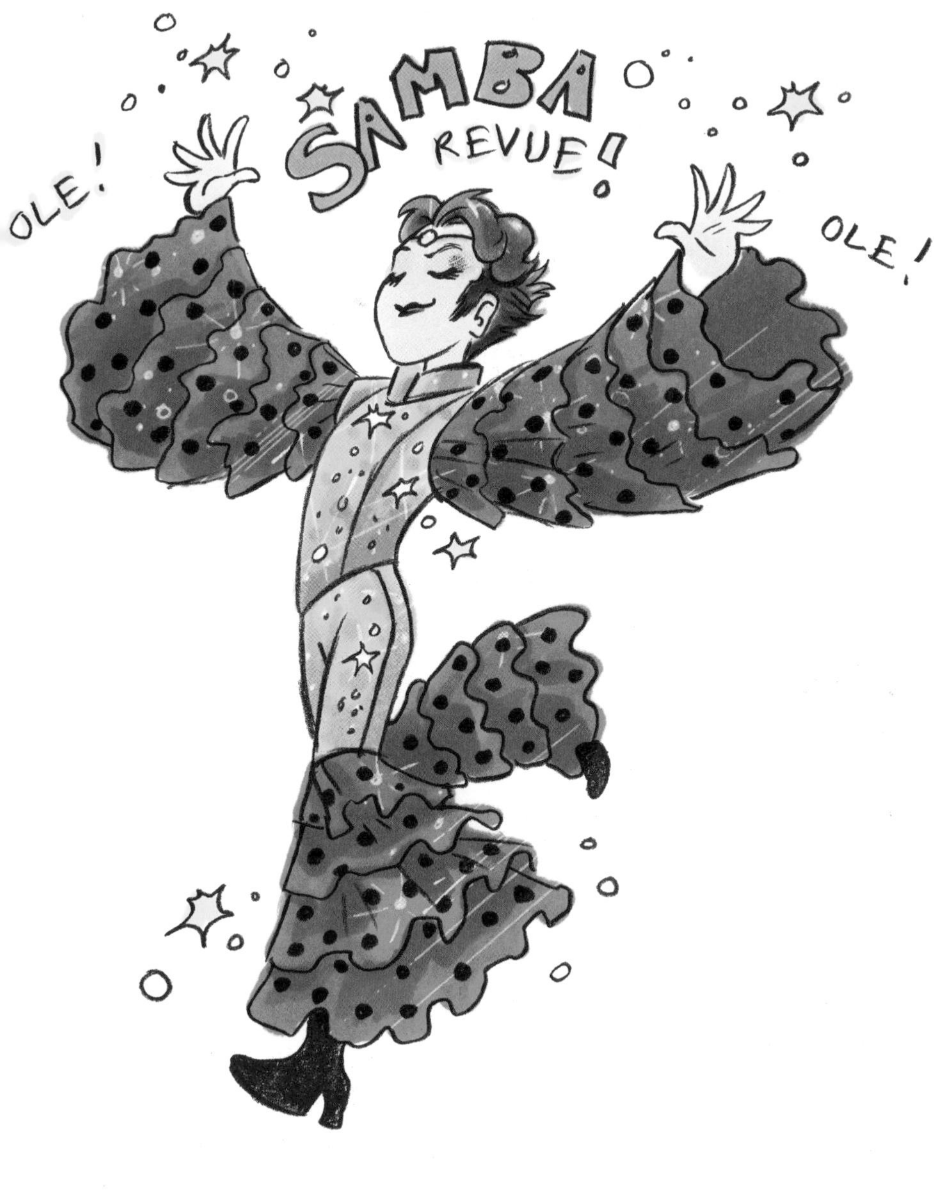
SAMBA
REVUE!
OLE!
OLE!

The Takarazuka Revue was founded in 1913 by the pres. of Hankyu Railways to boost business for the hot spring town, Takarazuka (a stop on the Hankyu line).

At the time western musicals were gaining popularity in Japan and it was thought that an all-girl theater group performing family shows would be well-received.

EE-YA-YA-YA

At the end of each play is an all-out Vegas-style revue complete with huge feathers, sequins and a kick-line.

One performance's revue contained "Egyptian" Samba outfits. So tacky, it's AWESOME.

The Takarazuka Revue does do
traditional Japanese plays, but
they also do western musicals
like "West Side Story" and
"Gone with the Wind." (Seeing Rhett
Butler played by a woman is
endlessly amusing ü)

Kisses are faked with
a turn of the head,
the strategic placement
of a hand or a
just-in-time cut
of the scene.

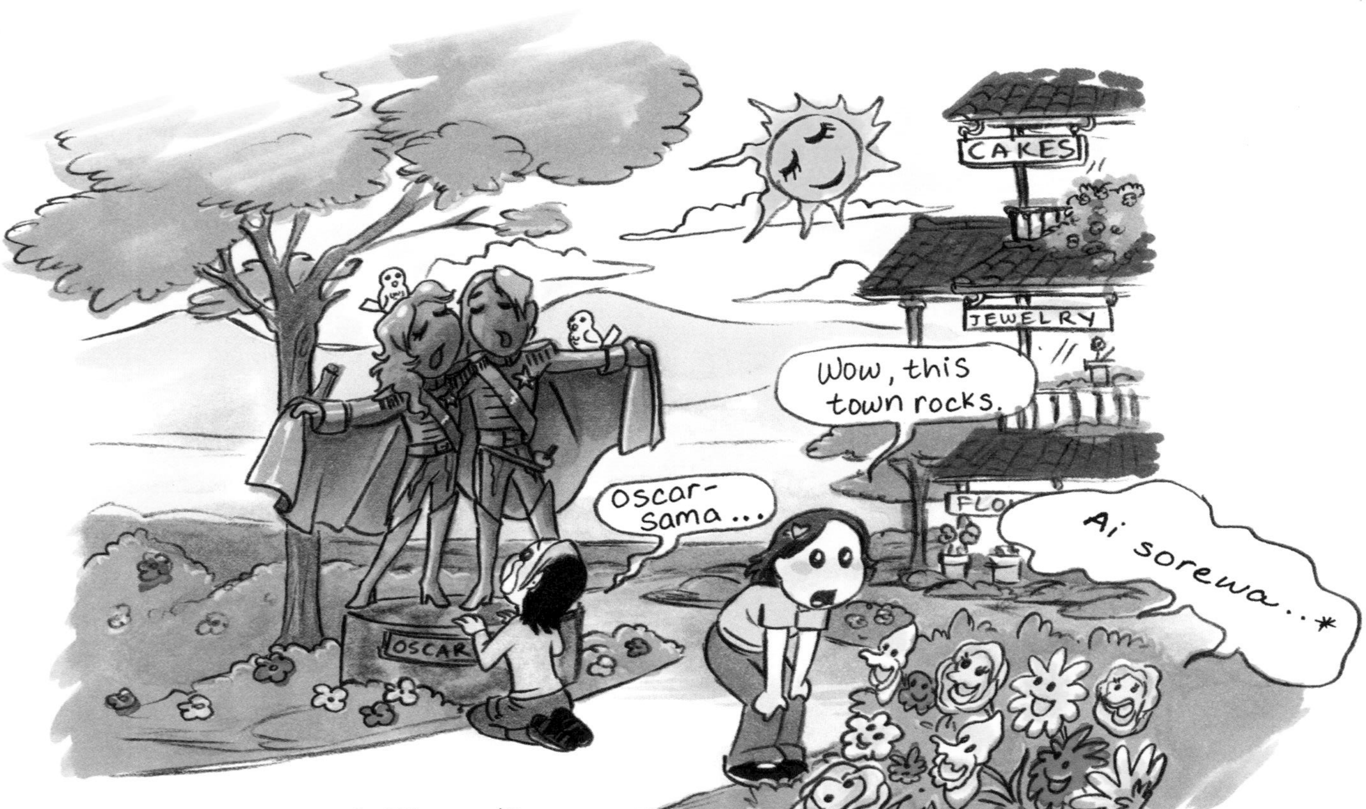
CAKES
JEWELRY
FLO
Wow, this town rocks.
Ai sorewa...*
Oscar-sama...
OSCAR

* The flowers in Takarazuka-town do not sing.

The theater seats are too small for my legs

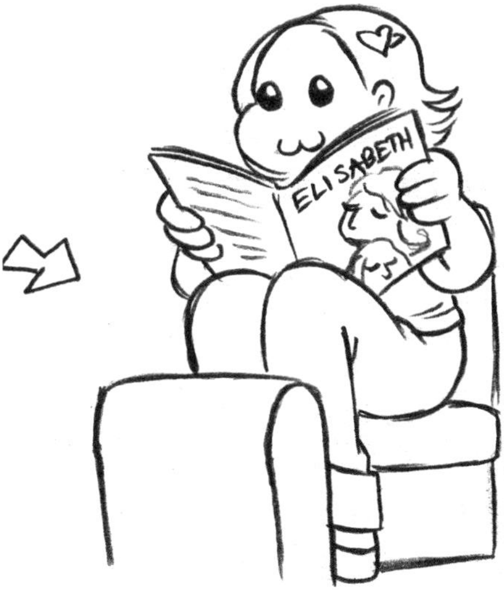
ELISABETH

I knew the basic story by researching the play online, and they also had program books with an English summary, like when you go to the Italian opera.

We saw my two favorite plays... Rose of Versailles (which is based on a famous manga) and Elisabeth (about the Empress Sissi).

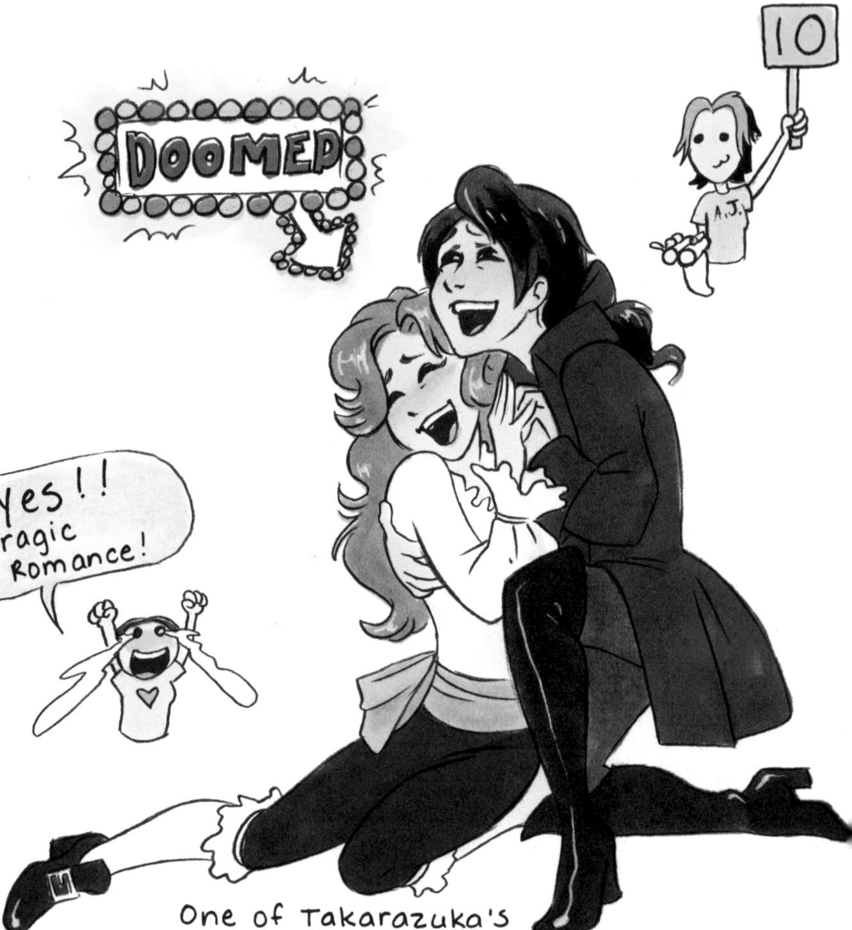
10
DOOMED
A.J.
Yes!!
Tragic Romance!

One of Takarazuka's best-loved couples... "Oscar and Andre" from Rose of Versailles.

Takarazuka likes to take impossible romances and set them to music. All parts are played by women. The "men" are basically taller women in platform boots with deep voices trained to saunter like men.

The first Takarazuka show I saw was "Rose of Versailles," a story about Marie Antoinette and French revolutionary soldiers.

The story basically goes like this... Andre loves Oscar (a girl) his whole life. Oscar doesn't love him back.

Then Oscar finally falls in love with Andre.

The <u>next</u> day Andre dies.

Then they find each other in the afterlife. It's very over dramatic (and awesome). ♥

Oh yeah and Marie A. is in there somewhere.

HEAVEN

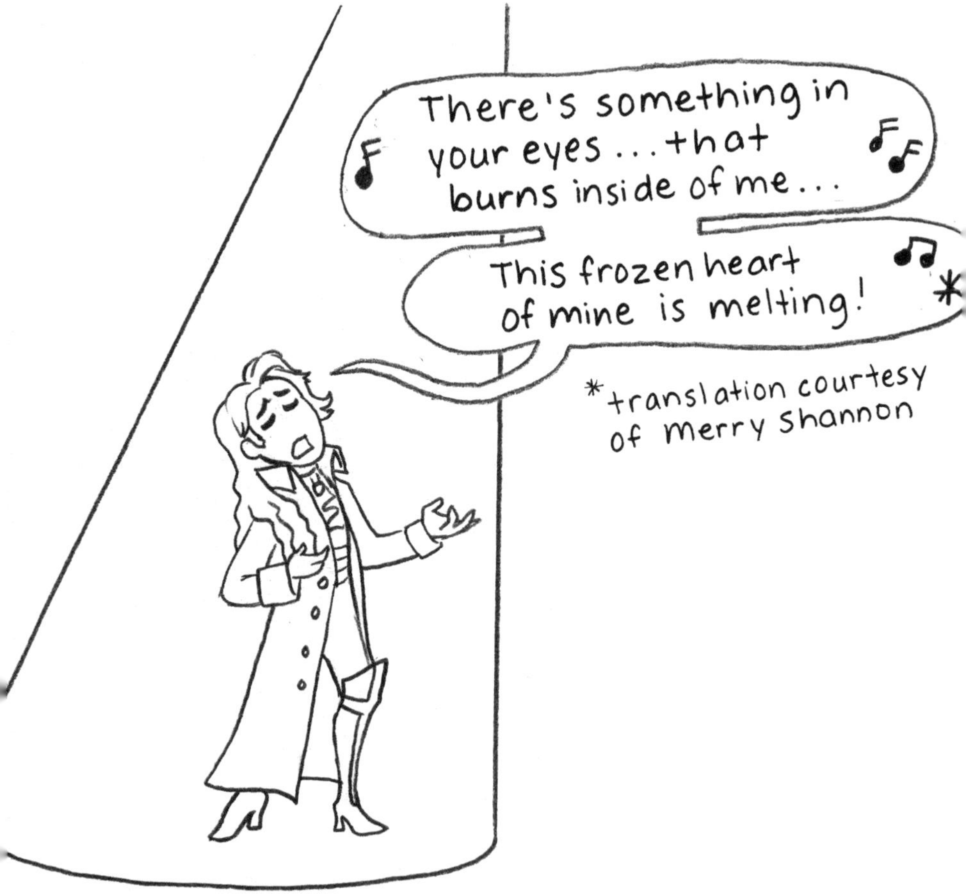
There's something in your eyes ... that burns inside of me...
This frozen heart of mine is melting! *
* translation courtesy of Merry Shannon

Along with their romantic, chick-flick plots, Takarazuka features idealized heroes played by women. These "otokoyaku" (men played by women) are more passionate and sensitive than a real man. At least, that's the idea.

My other favorite play is "Elisabeth," which is about Empress Sissi of Austria + Death personified. (Well she did have a rough life.)

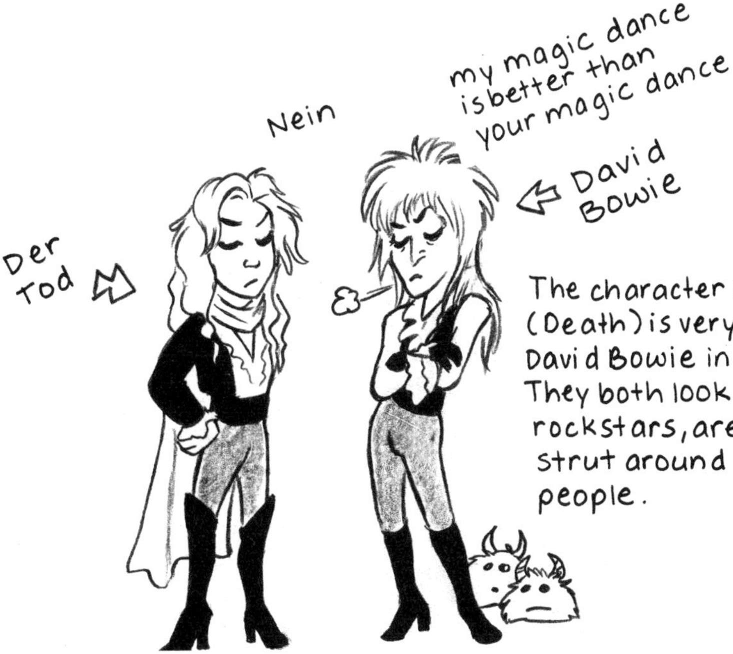
Nein
my magic dance is better than your magic dance
David Bowie
Der Tod

The character of Der Tod (Death) is very much like David Bowie in Labyrinth. They both look like gothy rockstars, are evil and strut around seducing people.

Only, when Der Tod seduces you, his kiss takes you to the netherworld. (Otherwise known as that really foggy part of the stage.)

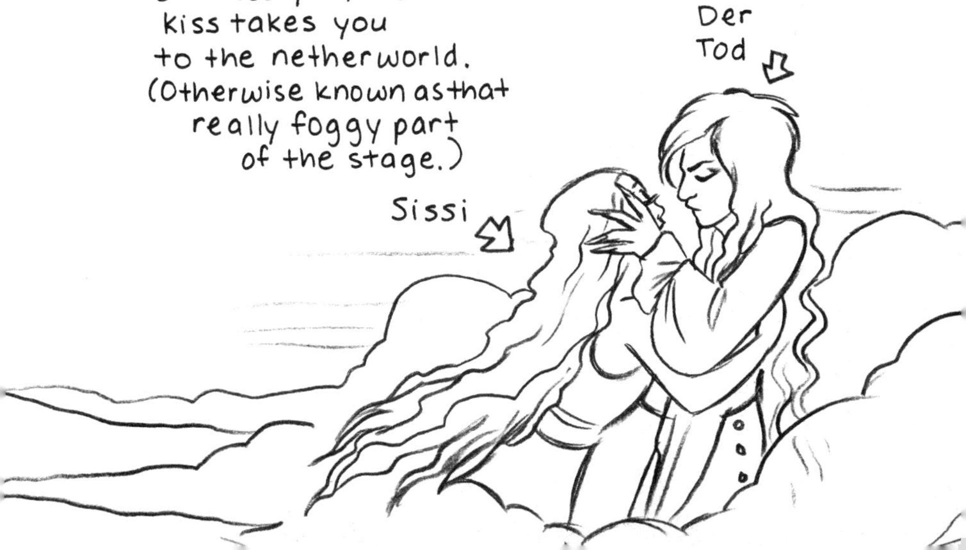
Der Tod
Sissi

Despite not knowing
Japanese, the acting
and songs were so
moving that I cried.

It was the lead (the Top Star's)
retirement performance and
she got a standing ovation.

↑
Yes her Vegas-style
back feathers were
this big. ☺

The fans of Takarazuka stars have created very strict and regimented fanclubs. They sit in neat formations waiting for their favorite star to emerge after the show.

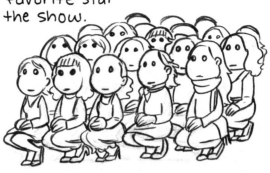

RIGHT!
Fanclub! Synch secret fan watches!

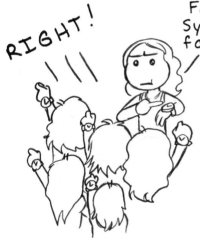

They all sit and stand at the same time, like robots. We didn't hear or see any cue to stand or sit, but somehow they did it synchronized.

Fans give HUGE orchids as gifts after the show. They are left outside the back door.

Not an exaggeration. Really this many flowers and this large.

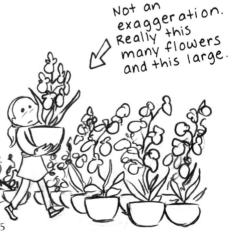

In Takarazuka stores they have a ton of themed merchandise (mostly posters from the plays and glamour shots of the top stars . . .) but they also sell kinda lame run-of-the-mill bags + folders with no real value other than having a TOP STAR's name on them.

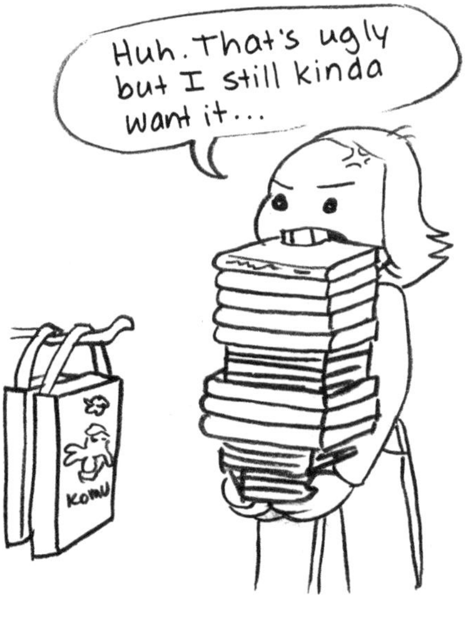
Huh. That's ugly but I still kinda want it...
KOMU

Which is good for me cause I already had my hands full with DVDs I don't understand (but are pretty) and at least 30 postcards of my favorite top stars.

*I can't write Japanese

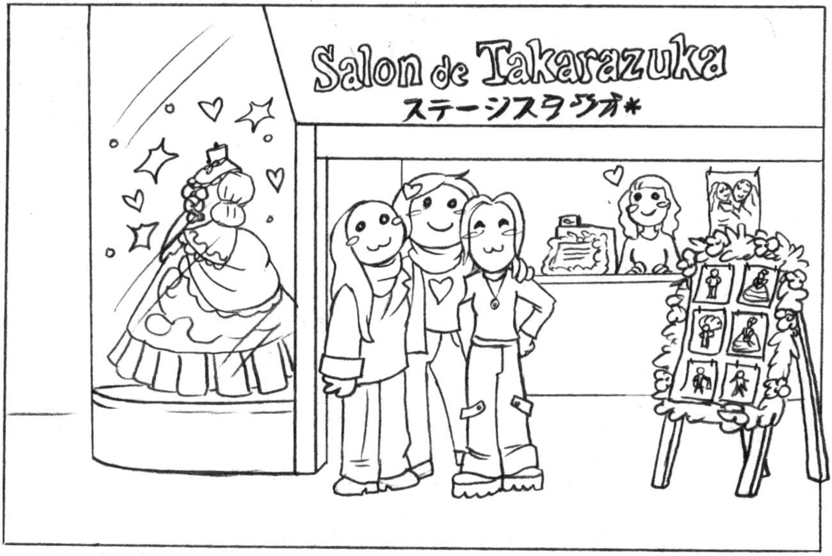
Salon de Takarazuka
ステージスタジオ*

In Takarazuka town there is a salon where you can get dressed up like your favorite Takarazuka stars. Some examples are ...

Scarlett O' Hara, Der Tod, Oscar and Andre, Elisabeth (of Austria), Marie Antoinette, Etc.

For about $80 or so, you get to dress up and get a glamour-shot ☺

First I tried dressing up as Andre from "Rose of Versailles".

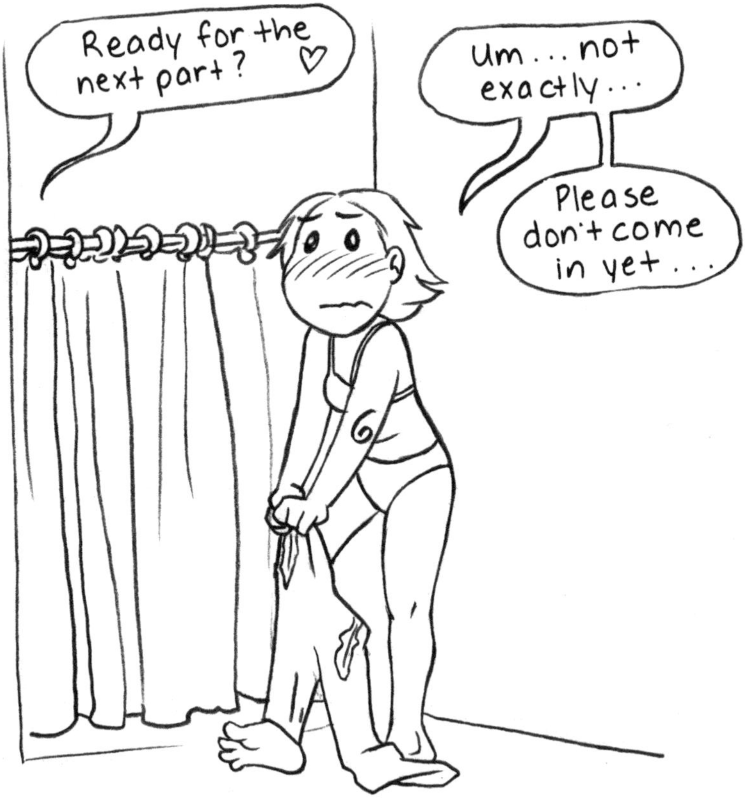
Ready for the next part? ♡
Um... not exactly...
Please don't come in yet...

I figured that the pants wouldn't fit me, but the salon attendants insisted. (Of course, I couldn't get the pants past my knee ü)

That's ok... I made my own Andre costume a month after I got back from Japan (with big pants ü). A.J. was Oscar with me.

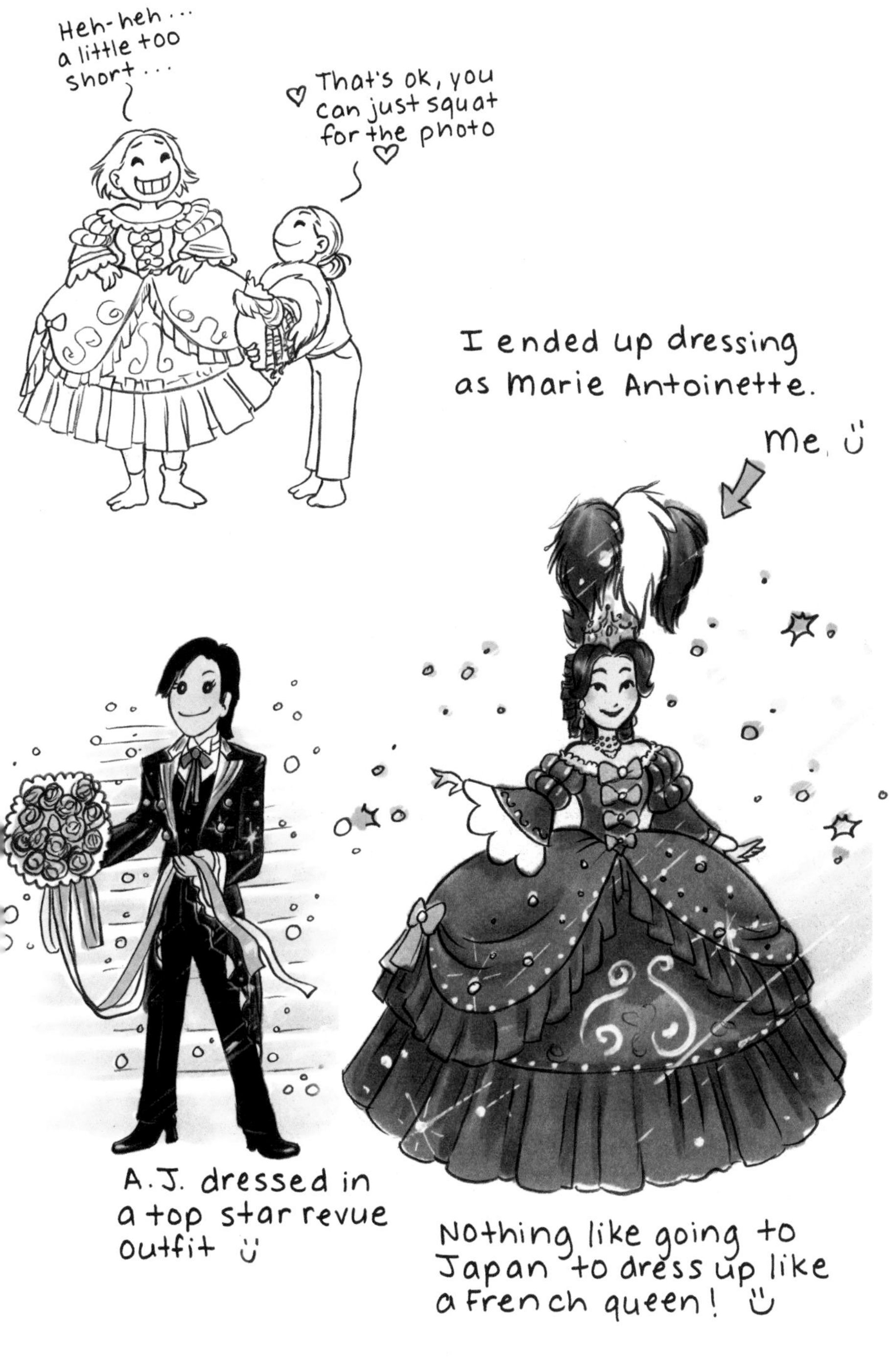
Heh-heh... a little too short...
That's ok, you can just squat for the photo
I ended up dressing as Marie Antoinette.
Me.
A.J. dressed in a top star revue outfit
Nothing like going to Japan to dress up like a French queen!

ROSE OF VERSAILLES

A.J. as Oscar

me as André

We performed on stage
at an anime convention
in the USA and got
"Best in Show". Probably
90% of the audience
didn't know who we were
dressed as, but we
didn't care ... we felt like
real Takarazuka stars. ☺

CHAPTER SIX:

The Big Event!

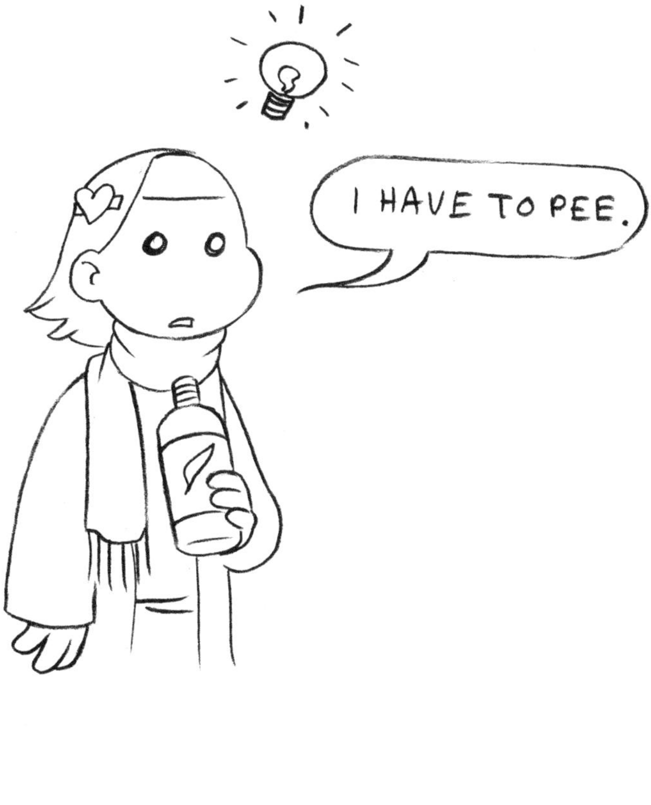
I HAVE TO PEE.

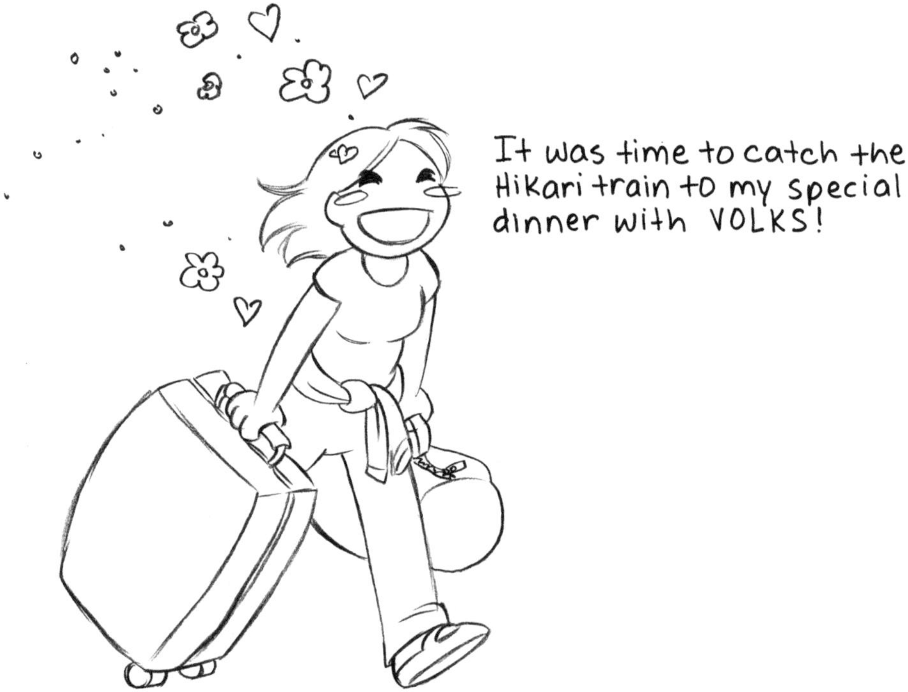
It was time to catch the Hikari train to my special dinner with VOLKS!

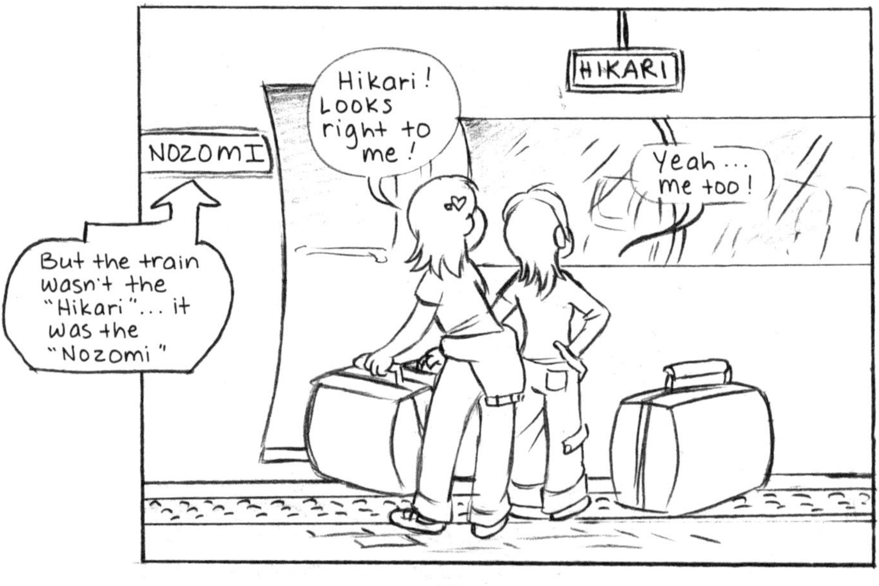
HIKARI
Hikari! Looks right to me!
Yeah... me too!
NOZOMI
But the train wasn't the "Hikari"... it was the "Nozomi"

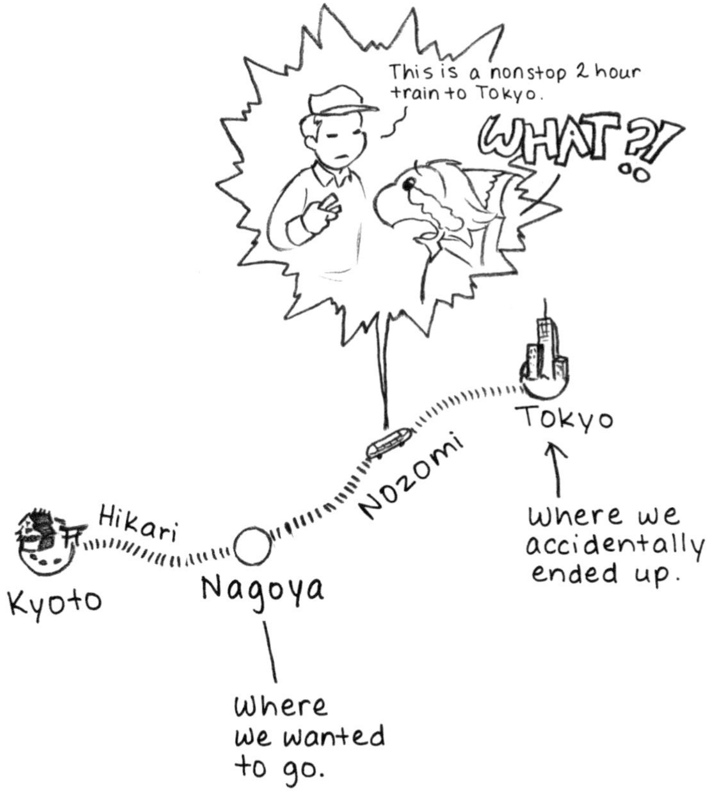
This is a nonstop 2 hour train to Tokyo.
WHAT?!
Tokyo
Nozomi
Hikari
Kyoto
Nagoya
Where we accidentally ended up.
Where we wanted to go.

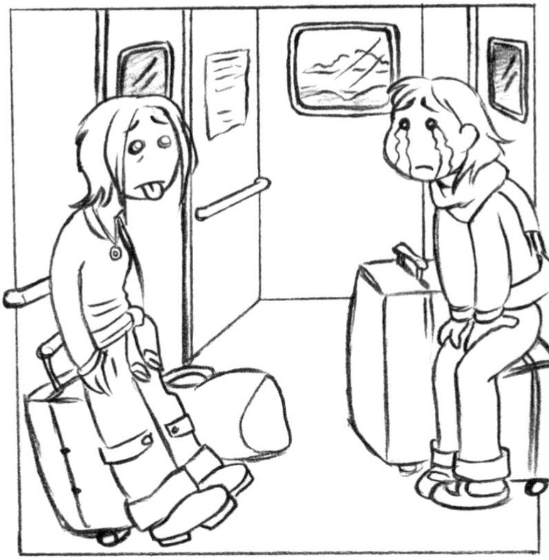

Since we got on the wrong train, we had no tickets. So the conductor made us stand inbetween the train cars for the whole two hour trip.

This was a super fast train, so our trip back would take four hours since we couldn't afford the fast train.

No one seemed to speak English...

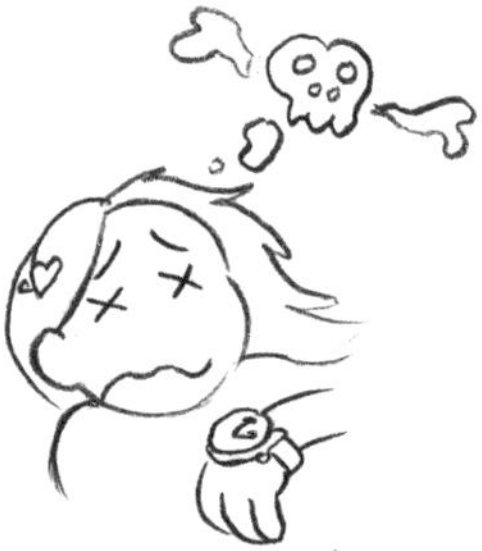

There would be no way we could make it back in time for me to make my dinner.

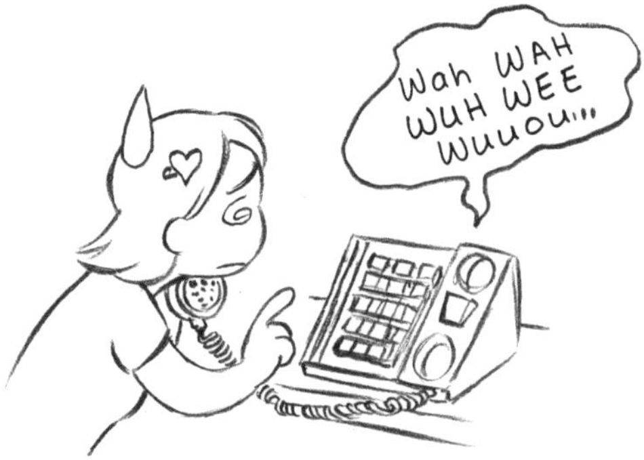
Wah WAH WUH WEE Wuuou...

So I tried to use the train phone... but it was all in Japanese! How would I call VOLKS to cancel dinner?

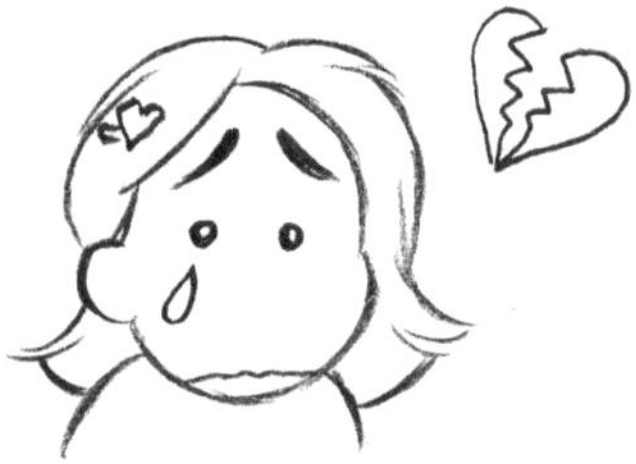

The thought of Volks waiting for me was crushing.

wibble

Then this nice Japanese man noticed my trouble. He not only dialed the # for me, but also let me use his phone card. With his help, I was able to reach VOLKS.

VOLKS was very kind and understanding.

But... I was so crushed by disappointment.

When I finally got back to the hotel, all I could do was put on my yukata and have some green tea in bed.

CHAPTER SEVEN:
Tokyo

To get to our apartment in Tokyo, we had to use the trains during rush hour.

Normally people in Japan are extremely polite... but not at rush hour on the train!

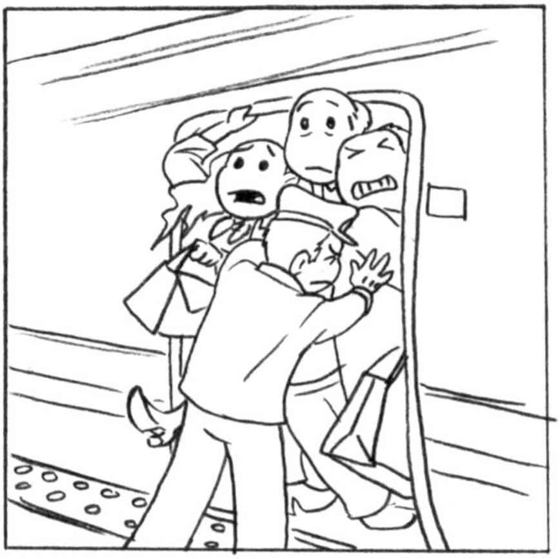

Sometimes the subways are really crowded and the train employees "help" you into the car.

(I only saw it this bad once or twice...)

At least the "helpers" wear white gloves.

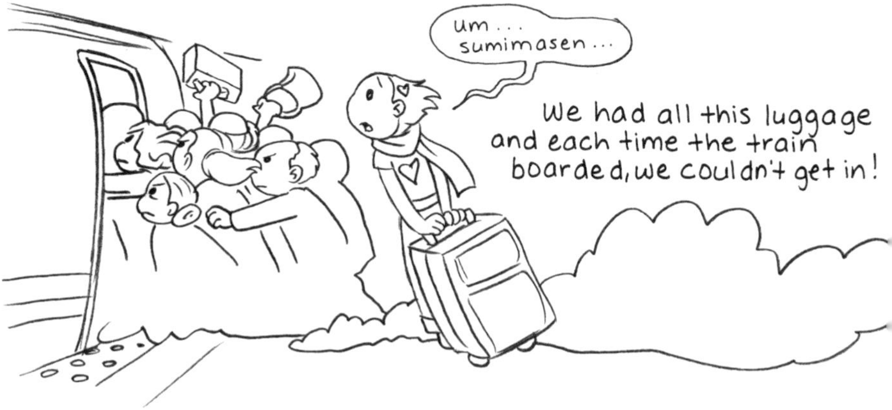
um... sumimasen...

We had all this luggage and each time the train boarded, we couldn't get in!

Eventually we got fed up...

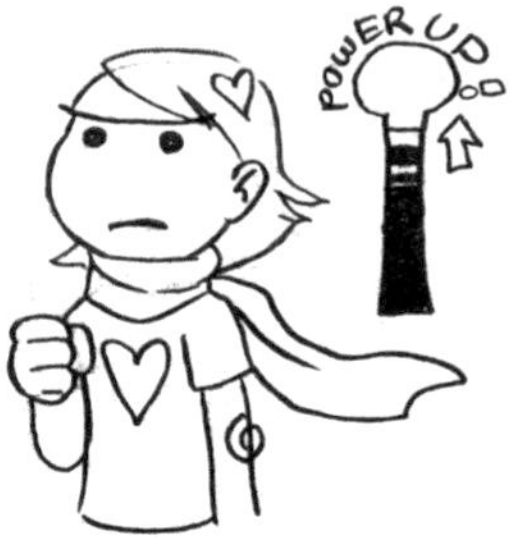
POWER UP!!

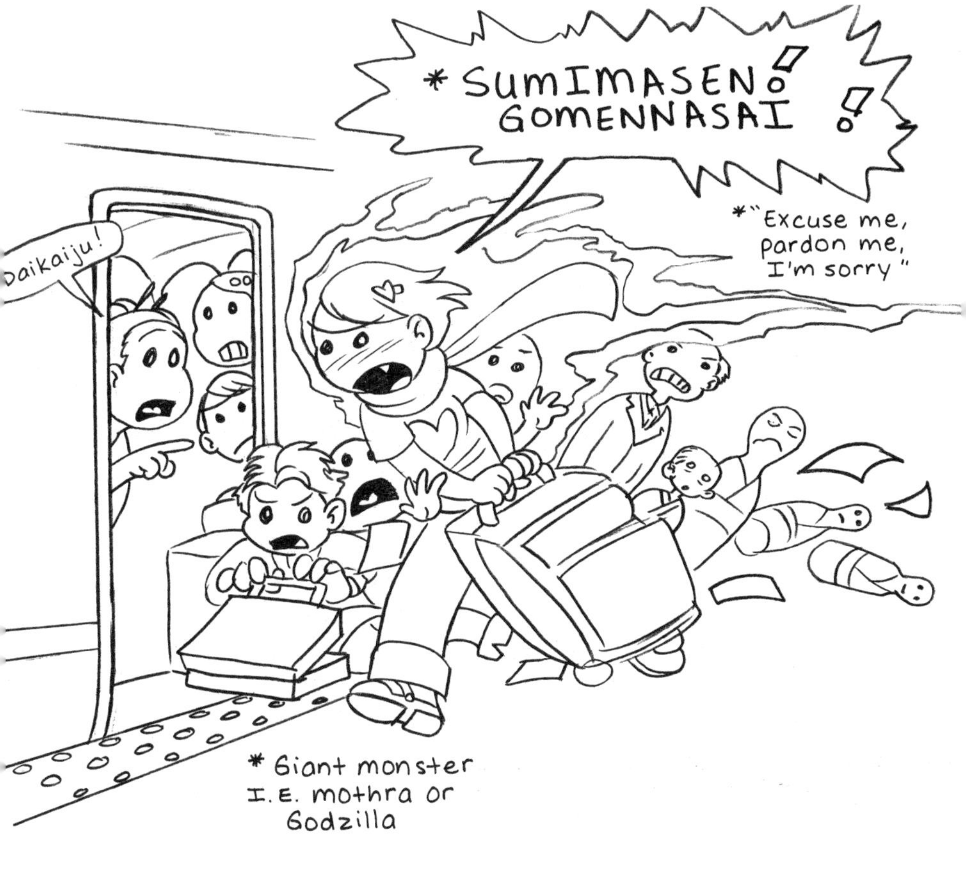
Daikaiju!
*SUMIMASEN!
GOMENNASAI!
*"Excuse me, pardon me, I'm sorry"
* Giant monster I.E. mothra or Godzilla

This is the cute + convenient apt. we rented in Tokyo.

The title of the complex was "Lion's Mansion."
The apt. was nice... but it definitely was not a mansion. ☺

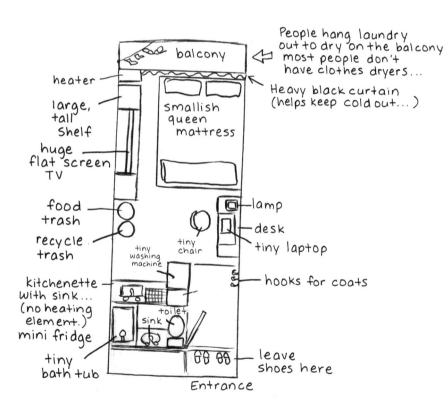

balcony
People hang laundry out to dry on the balcony most people don't have clothes dryers...
heater
Heavy black curtain (helps keep cold out...)
large, tall shelf
smallish queen mattress
huge flat screen TV
food trash
lamp
desk
recycle trash
tiny chair
tiny laptop
tiny washing machine
hooks for coats
kitchenette with sink... (no heating element.)
toilet
sink
mini fridge
tiny bath tub
leave shoes here
Entrance

You turn this lever to switch the water from the sink to the shower

The entire bathroom is about 3 toilets wide...

It feels like it's one connected piece.

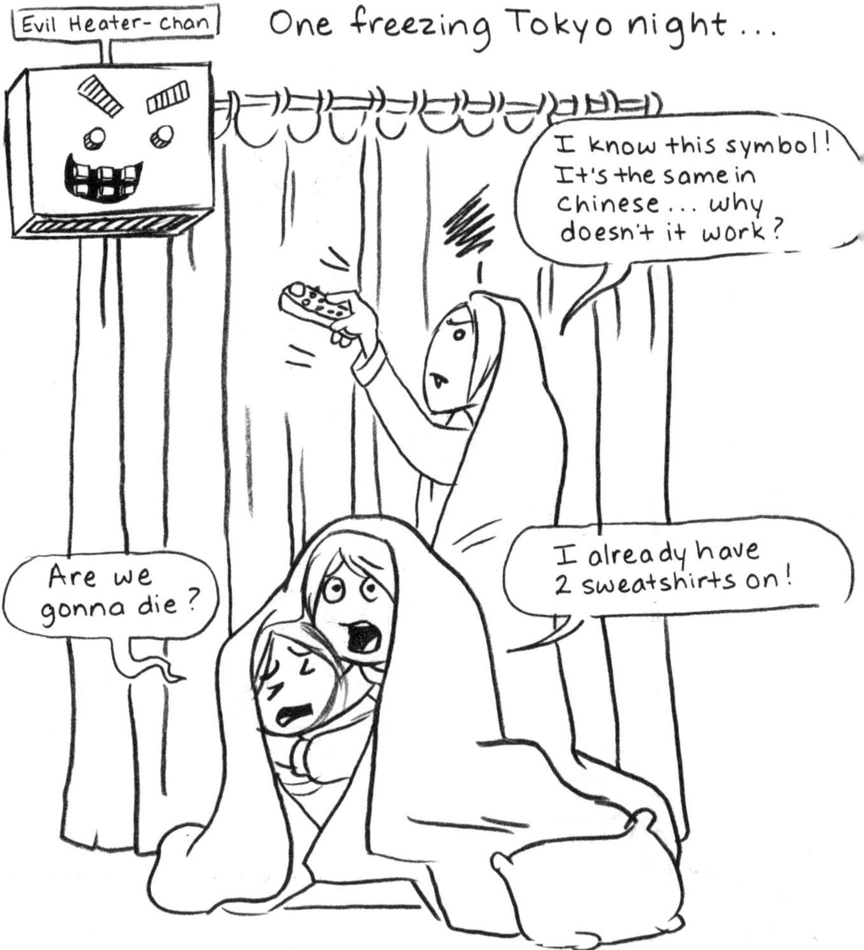
Evil Heater-chan
One freezing Tokyo night...
I know this symbol! It's the same in chinese... why doesn't it work?
Are we gonna die?
I already have 2 sweatshirts on!

Hours later...
We ended up begging the landlord for help. He spoke no English but explained the heater buttons.

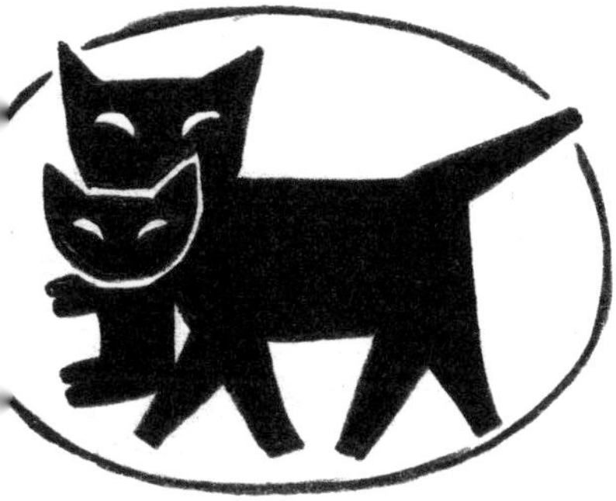

We saw a ton of vans with this logo on it... our first thought was that it was a vet or pet service. Turns out it's a door to door delivery service called "Yamato Transport".

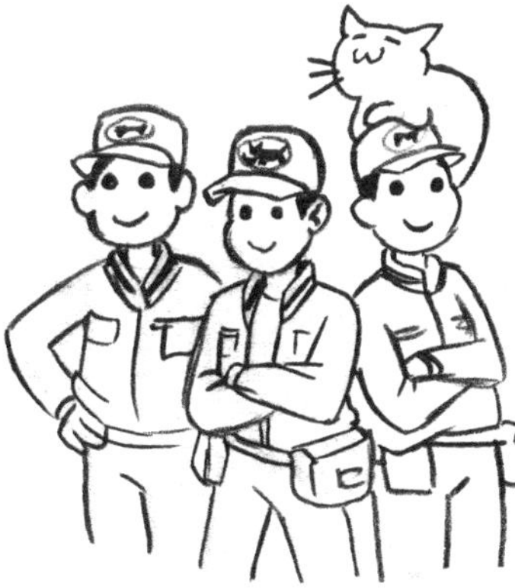

The motto is that they will take care of your package as well as a mother cat carries her kitten.

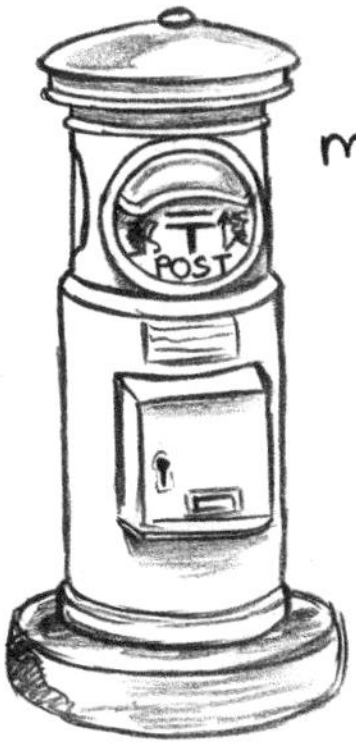
POST

mailbox

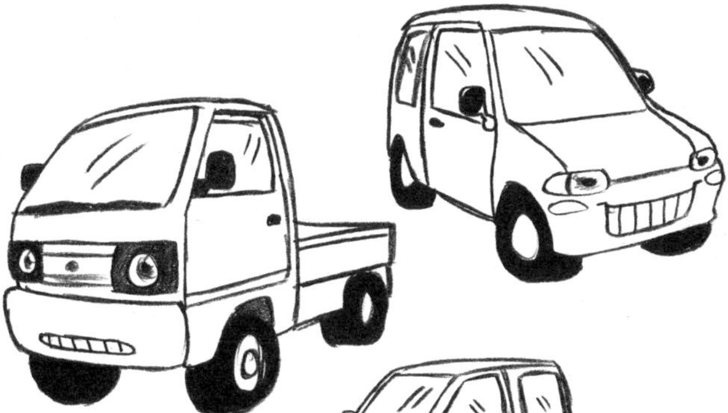

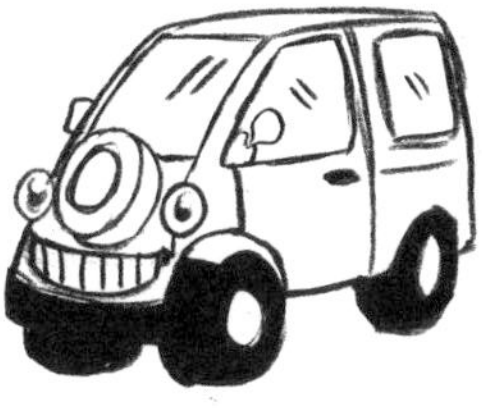

Cars and trucks in Japan are very cute and compact.

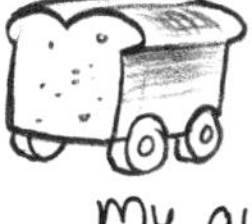

They are shoped like loaves of bread.

My guess is that it's so you can fit the most stuff into the smallest parking space.

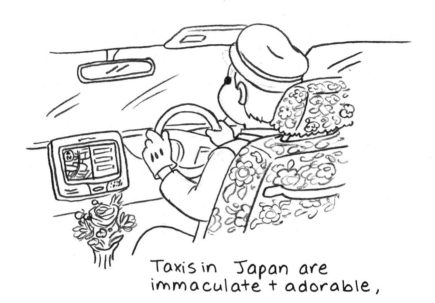

Taxis in Japan are immaculate + adorable,

- Driver has a suit + white gloves
- Seats have white doilies covering them
- Some have flower vases!
- They have really advanced GPS/Navigation systems

One of the adorable taxi signs . . .

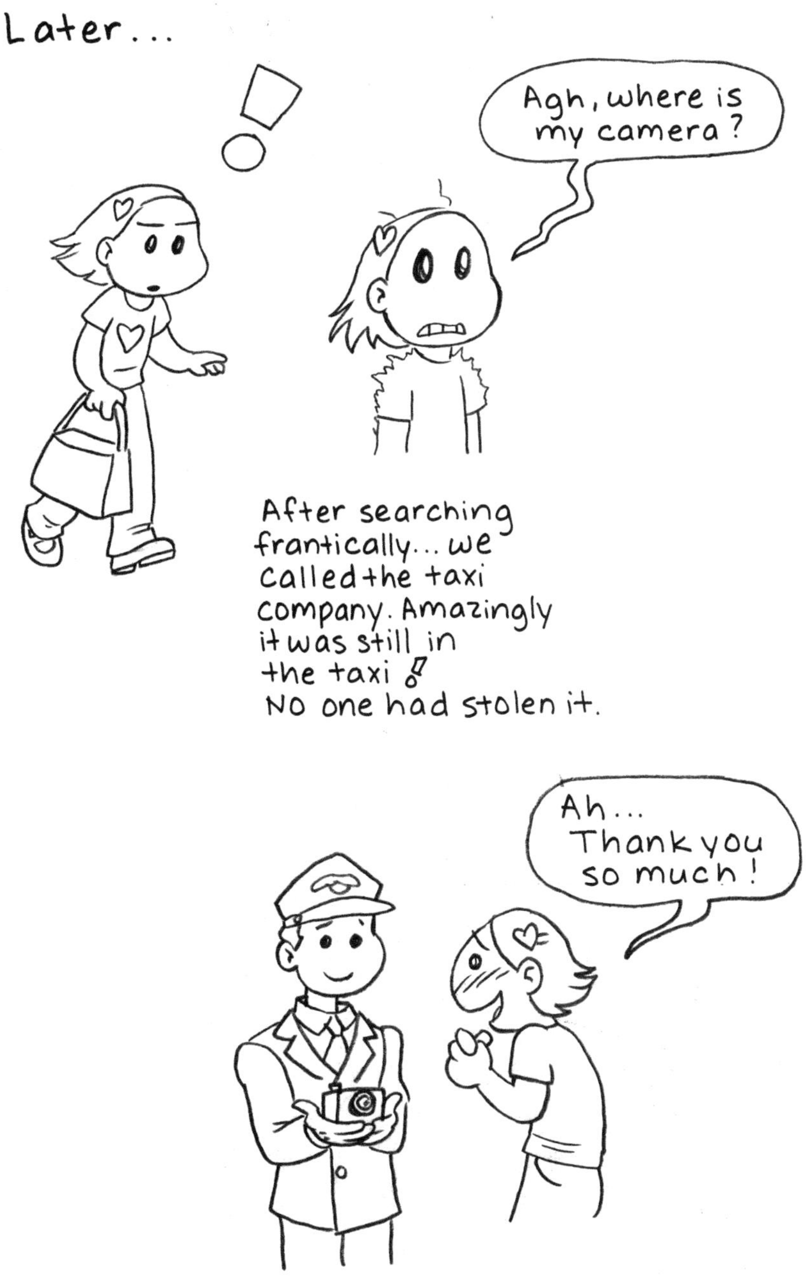
Later...
Agh, where is my camera?
After searching frantically... we called the taxi company. Amazingly it was still in the taxi! No one had stolen it.
Ah... Thank you so much!

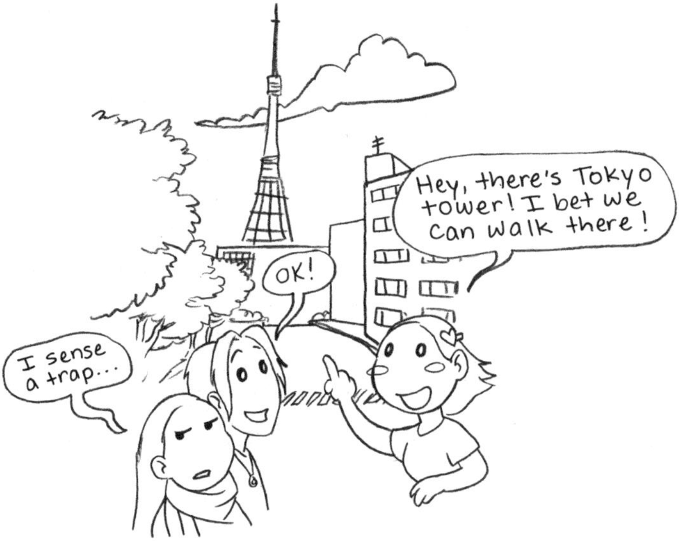
Hey, there's Tokyo tower! I bet we can walk there!
OK!
I sense a trap...

About an hour later...

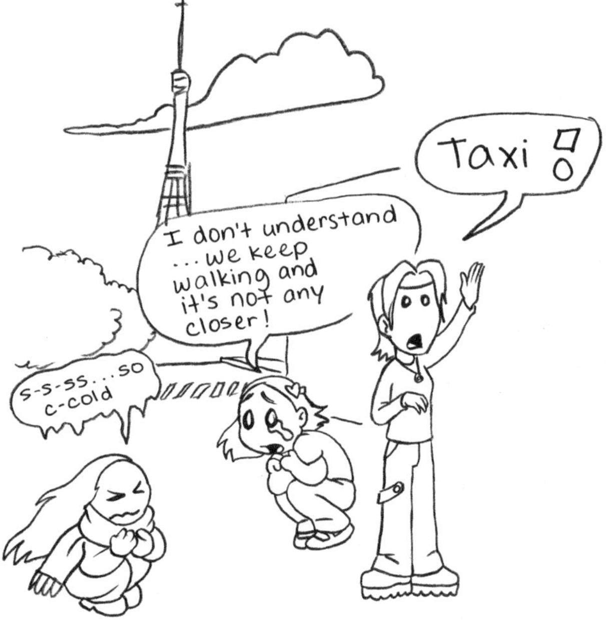
Taxi!
I don't understand ... we keep walking and it's not any closer!
s-s-ss...so c-cold

HOTEL CAPSULE
CAPSULELAND

The title, "Capsuleland," makes it sound like an amusement park, doesn't it?

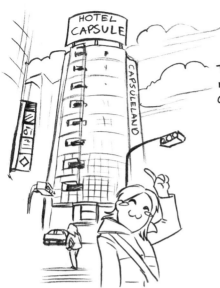

A.J. finds a capsule hotel in Shibuya. These hotels are for salary-men who work too late and miss the last train, so they can't get home. These hotels are "men only".

Welcome to the Borg

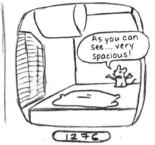

As you can see... very spacious!
1276

Each "room" is only slightly larger than a coffin. They have vents, alarm clock, mattress and TV. That's it.

A friendly face in Japan, the Colonel.

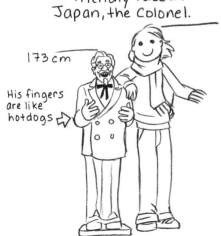

182 cm
173 cm
His fingers are like hotdogs

I've never seen a statue of the KFC mascot in the USA, but every KFC in Japan has one. They get dressed up for holidays too.

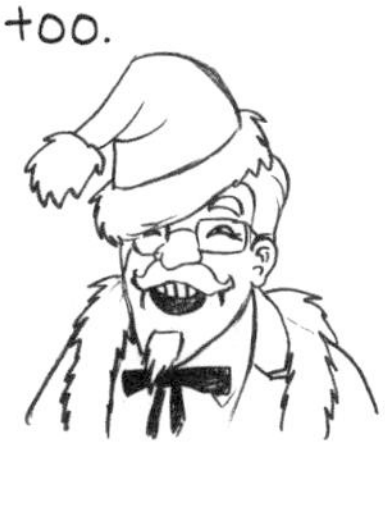

Random Japanese shopping is awesome.

Some gangsters in Japan have boufant hairdos.

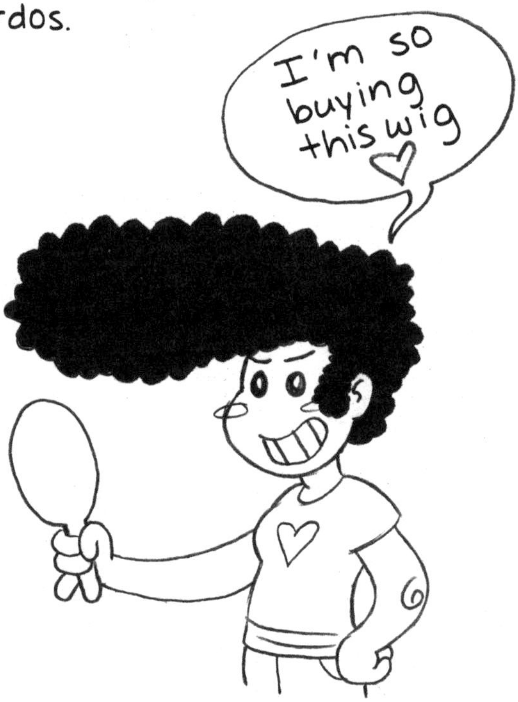
I'm so buying this wig ♡

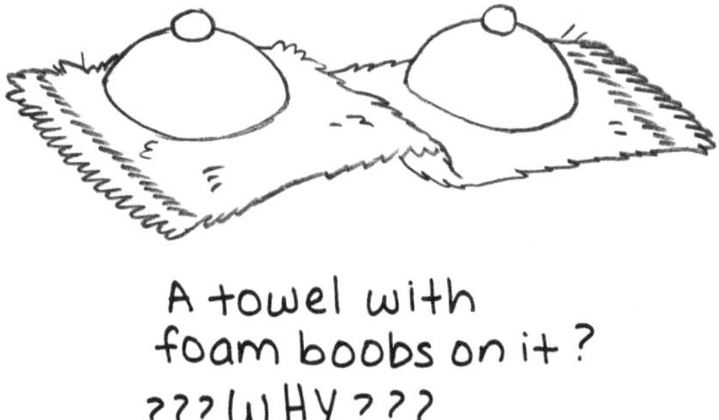

A towel with foam boobs on it?
???WHY???

INTERLUDE:
Itadakimasu!

Average
beer glass

Average
water glass

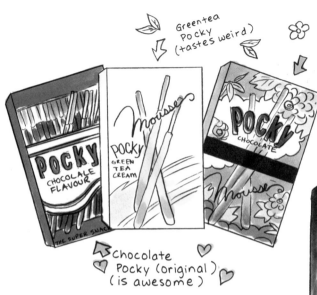

Greentea Pocky (tastes weird)

Pastel purple limited edition pocky made of yams. (They taste weird)

POCKY
CHOCOLALE FLAVOUR
THE SUPER SNACK
Mousse
POCKY
GREEN TEA CREAM
POCKY
CHOCOLATE
Mousse
Men's
POCKY
CHOCOLATE
THE SUPER SNACK

Chocolate Pocky (original) (is awesome)

Apparently men need their own pocky?

(And apparently men's pocky is <u>dark</u> chocolate... my husband doesn't even like dark chocolate.)

It is a mystery...

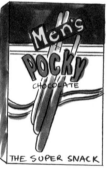

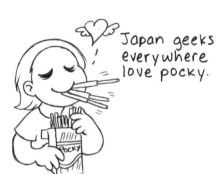

Japan geeks everywhere love pocky.

POCKY

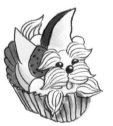

A puppy fruit cup, (with icing)

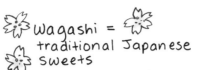

wagashi = traditional Japanese sweets

In nice department stores a whole floor is devoted to gift foods and sweets. Boxes of wagashi are often designed based on the season.

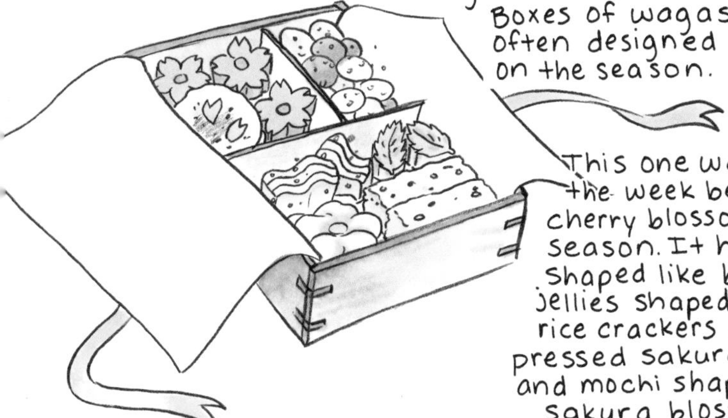

This one was the week before cherry blossom season. It had sugar shaped like blue waves, jellies shaped like leaves, rice crackers with pressed sakura petals, and mochi shaped like sakura blossoms.

my mom had a hard time eating the box I sent her... it was too pretty.

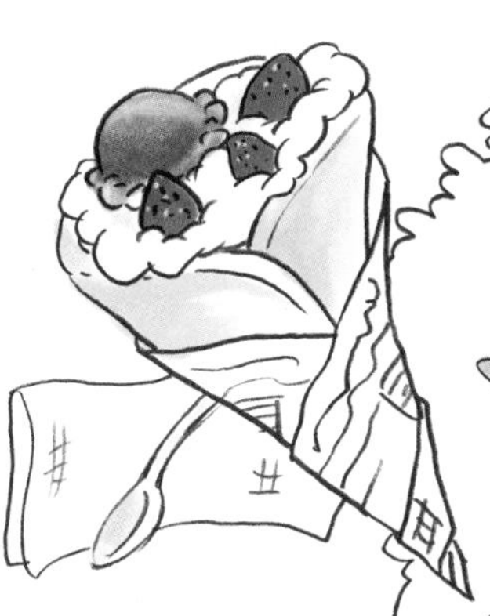

Crepes...
One of the few snacks you will see people eating while walking in Japan ♡♡

filled with whipped cream, ice cream and strawberries

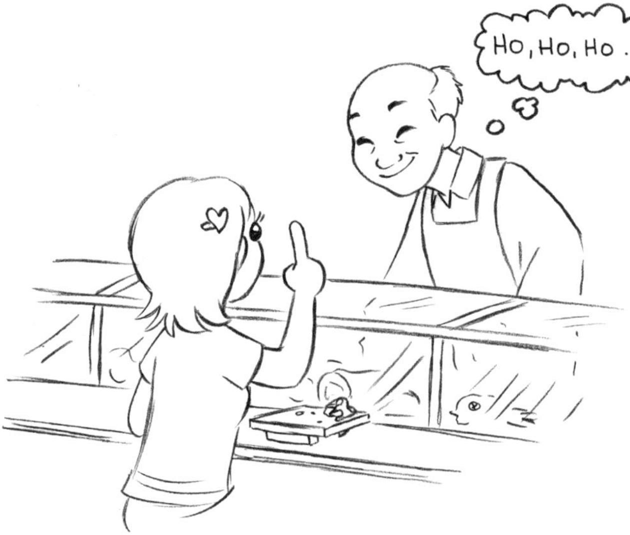
Ho, Ho, Ho . . .

I really like wasabi on sushi. In the USA, wasabi is often diluted. So when we went to a sushi bar in Japan I was disappointed that the chef didn't put much wasabi on my sushi. I think he was afraid that I couldn't handle it (me being American . . .)

So I asked for a little more wasabi!

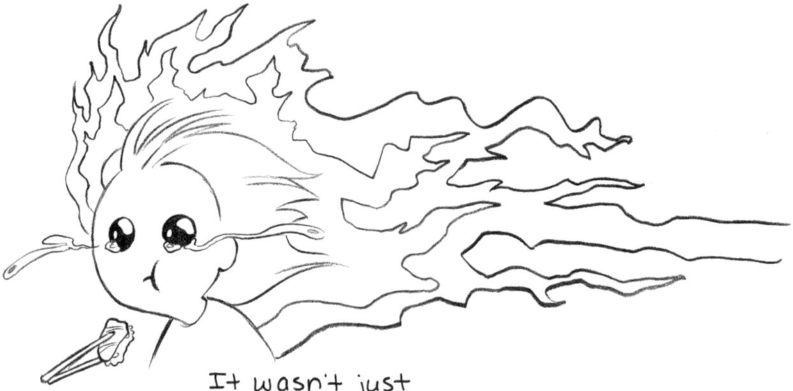

It wasn't just "a little" more wasabi . . .

(still good though)

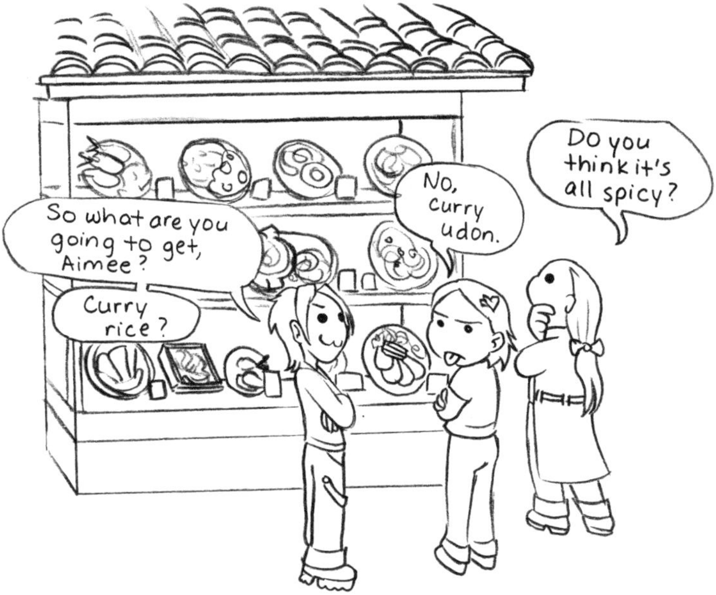
So what are you going to get, Aimee?
Curry rice?
No, curry udon.
Do you think it's all spicy?

Since we couldn't read Japanese, we frequented restaurants with plastic food displays (which, thankfully for us, were plenty)!

Sometimes we had to drag the waitress outside and point to the plastic food display to explain what we wanted.

90% of the time, I ate curry rice, which I adore. ♡

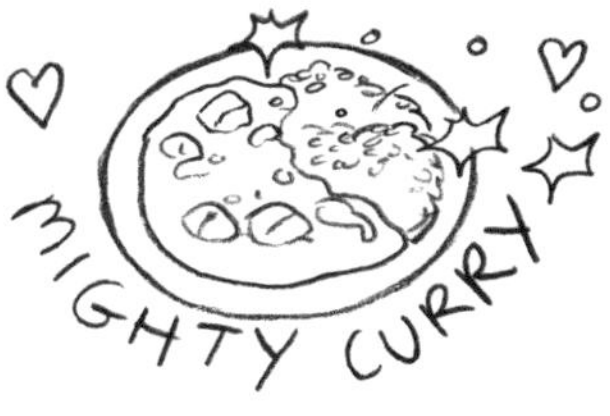
MIGHTY CURRY

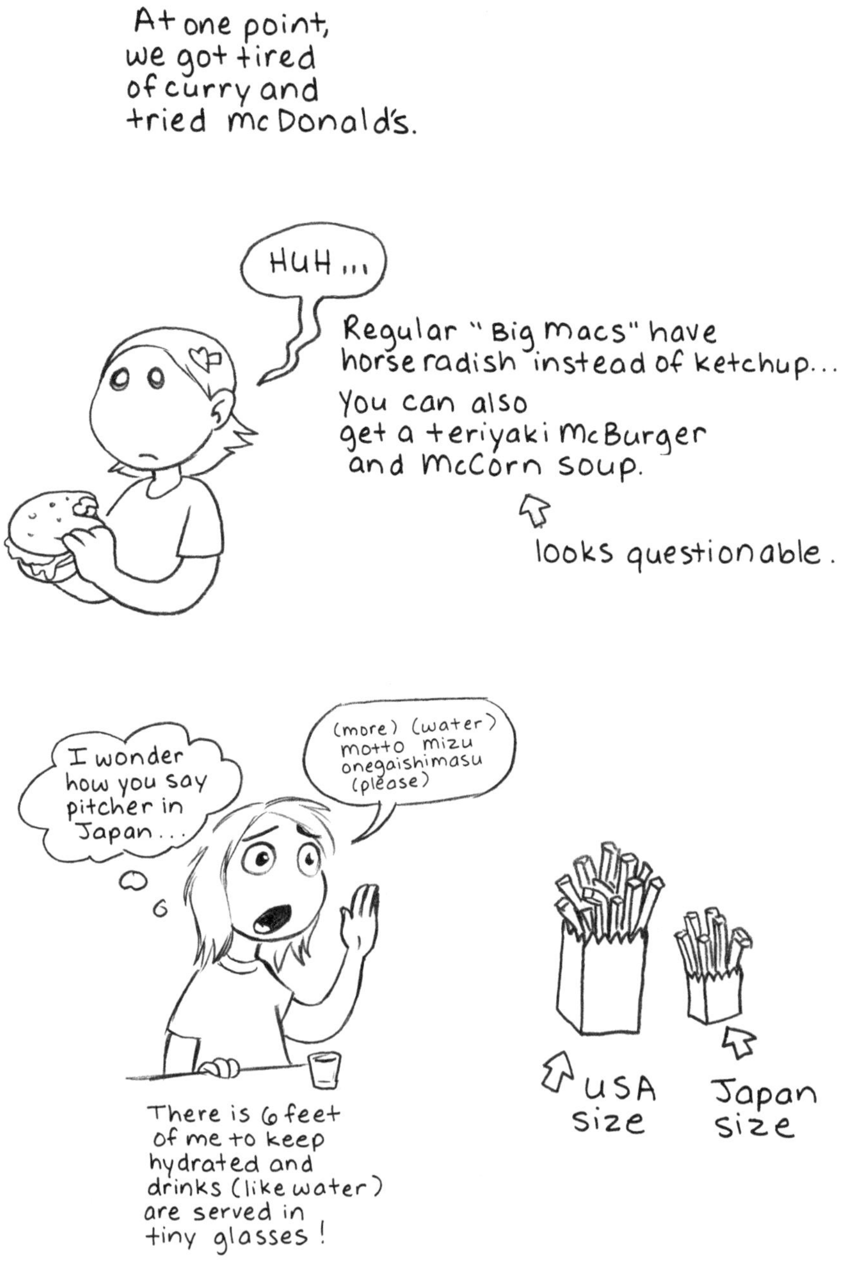
At one point, we got tired of curry and tried McDonald's.
HUH...
Regular "Big Macs" have horseradish instead of ketchup...
You can also get a teriyaki McBurger and McCorn soup.
looks questionable.
I wonder how you say pitcher in Japan...
(more) (water) motto mizu onegaishimasu (please)
There is 6 feet of me to keep hydrated and drinks (like water) are served in tiny glasses!
USA size
Japan size

A.J. fed some birds
at a temple.

Then she went to burn incense.

piyo

piyo

When she came back out...

piyo

piyo piyo

piyo

piyo piyo

The birds remembered her!

Chapter Eight:
Otaku Tokyo

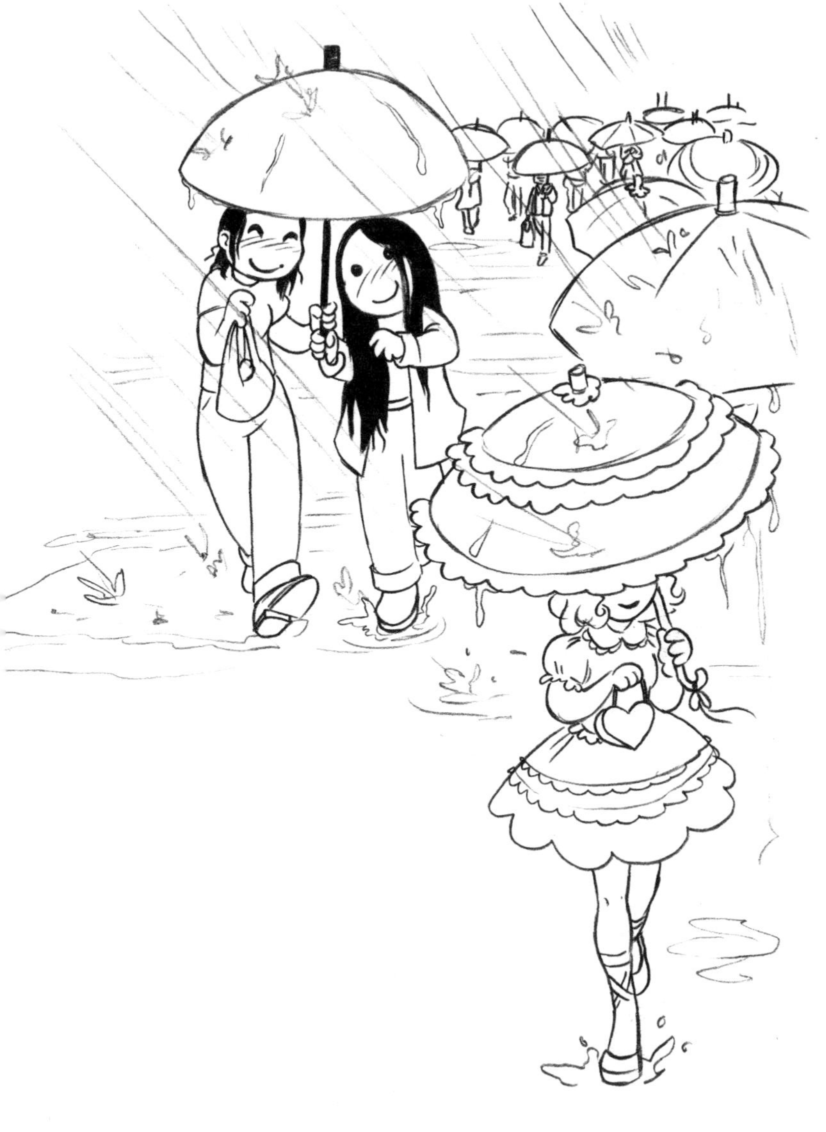

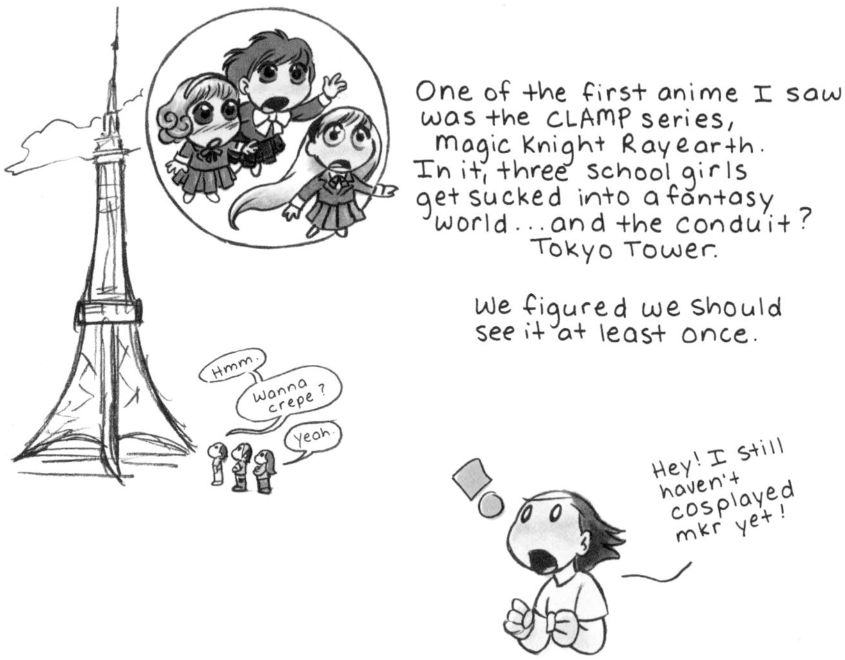
One of the first anime I saw was the CLAMP series, Magic Knight Rayearth. In it, three school girls get sucked into a fantasy world...and the conduit? Tokyo Tower.
We figured we should see it at least once.
Hmm.
Wanna crepe?
Yeah.
Hey! I still haven't cosplayed mkr yet!

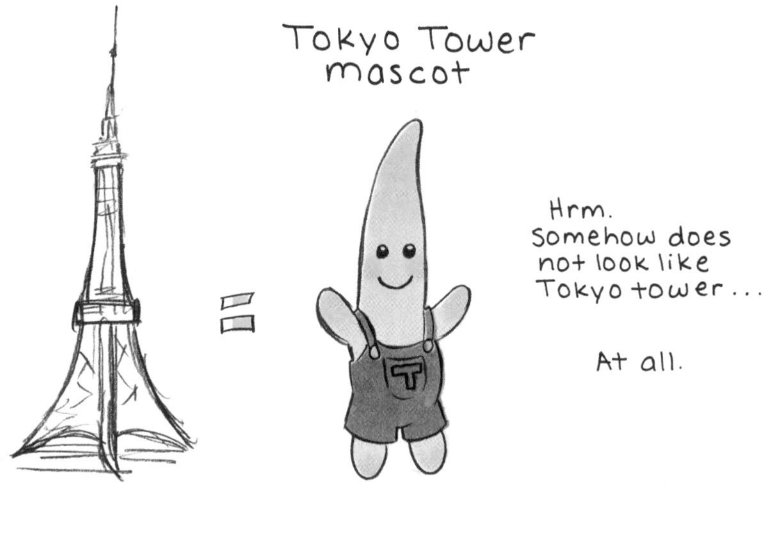
Tokyo Tower mascot
Hrm. Somehow does not look like Tokyo tower...
At all.

Manga/Internet Cafe

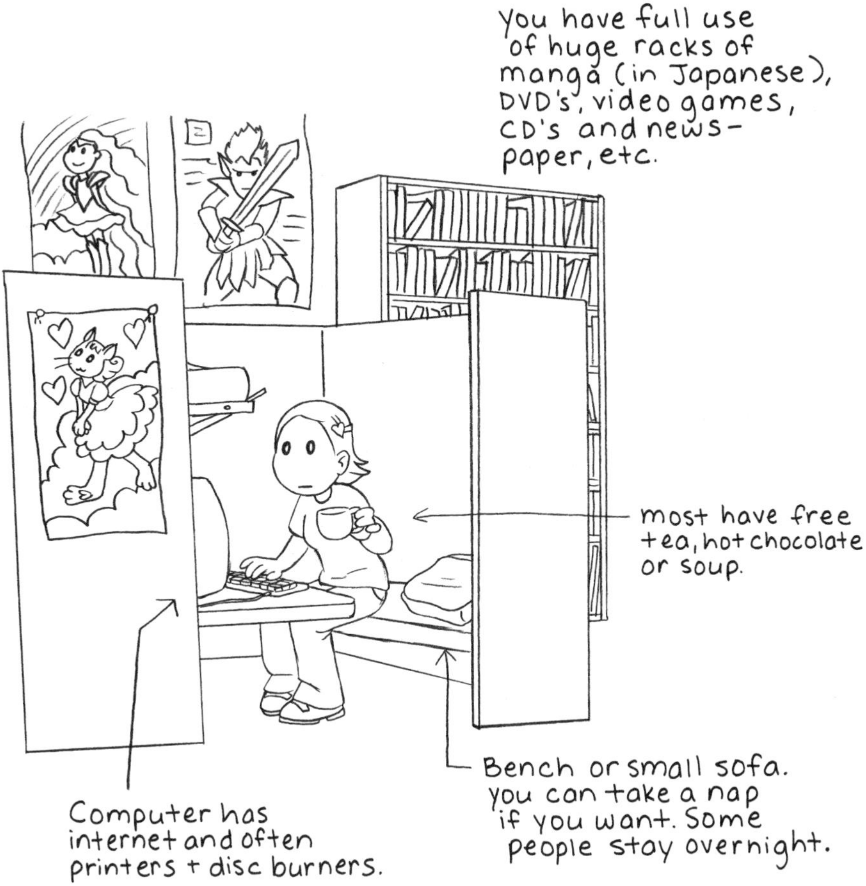
you have full use of huge racks of manga (in Japanese), DVD's, video games, CD's and news-paper, etc.
most have free tea, hot chocolate or soup.
Computer has internet and often printers + disc burners.
Bench or small sofa. you can take a nap if you want. Some people stay overnight.

Nakano Broadway is a mall just minutes from Nakano Train Station. Our Tokyo apartment was almost attached to the mall, so everyday we would walk through the mall and get pastries on the way to the train. On our way home we would get curry, ramen or sushi.

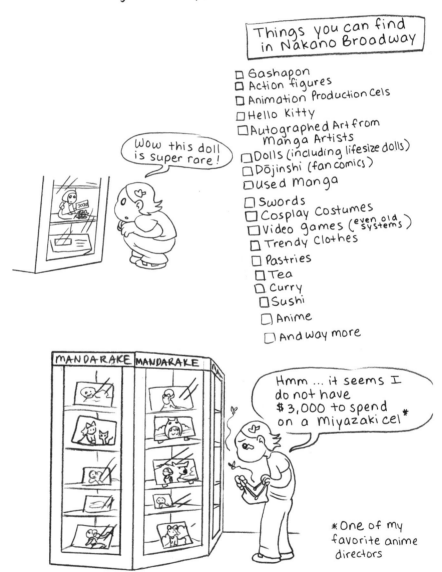

Things you can find in Nakano Broadway

- ☐ Gashapon
- ☐ Action figures
- ☐ Animation Production Cels
- ☐ Hello Kitty
- ☐ Autographed Art from Manga Artists
- ☐ Dolls (including lifesize dolls)
- ☐ Dōjinshi (fan comics)
- ☐ Used Manga
- ☐ Swords
- ☐ Cosplay Costumes
- ☐ Video games (even old systems)
- ☐ Trendy Clothes
- ☐ Pastries
- ☐ Tea
- ☐ Curry
- ☐ Sushi
- ☐ Anime
- ☐ And way more

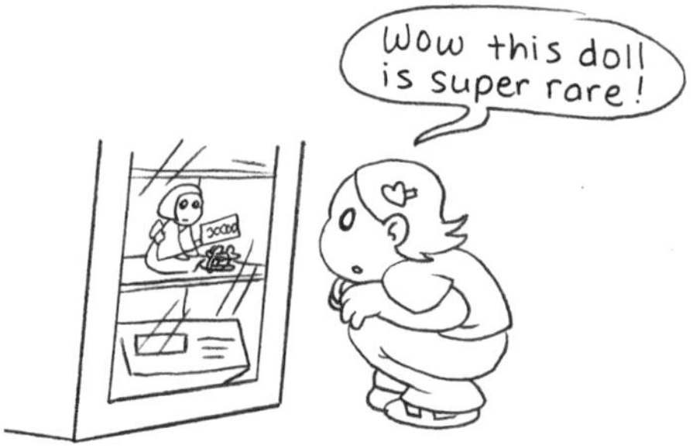
Wow this doll is super rare!

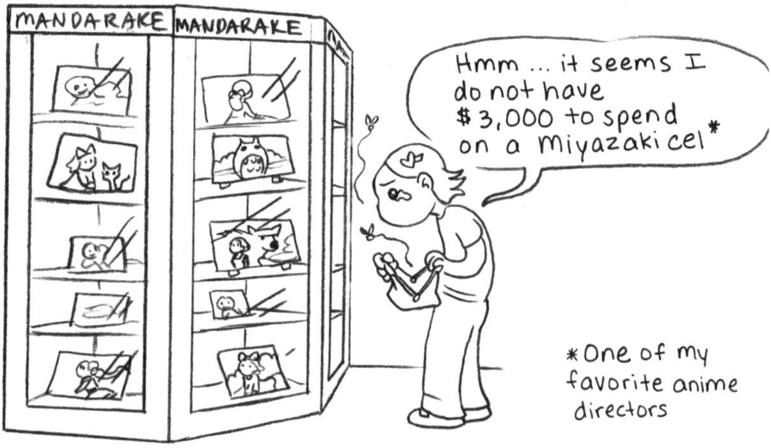
MANDARAKE
MANDARAKE
Hmm ... it seems I do not have $3,000 to spend on a Miyazaki cel*

*One of my favorite anime directors

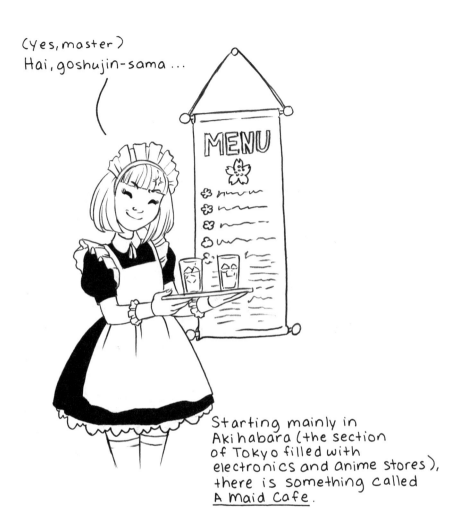

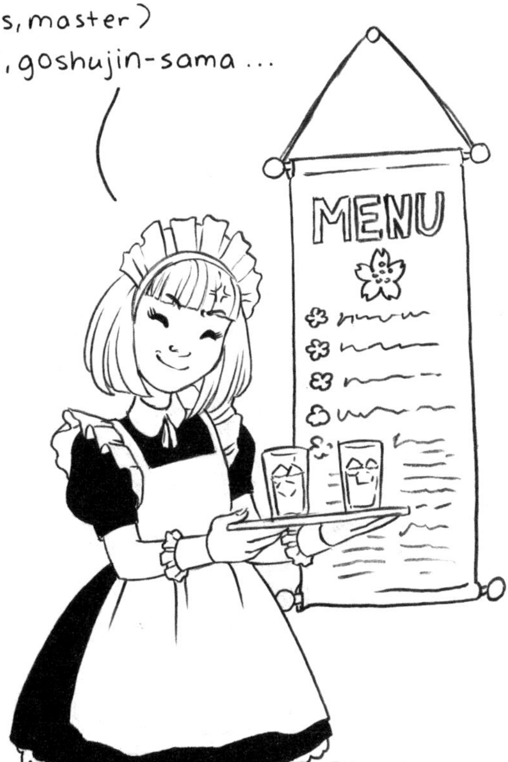
(yes, master)
Hai, goshujin-sama...
MENU

Starting mainly in Akihabara (the section of Tokyo filled with electronics and anime stores), there is something called <u>A Maid Cafe</u>.

Basically, geeky guys who frequent the area really like girls in maid costumes... so they pay to have so-so food served by a maid.

(Lots of anime and games lately feature maids too...)

Sometimes if you pay extra... you get more chatting with cute maids.

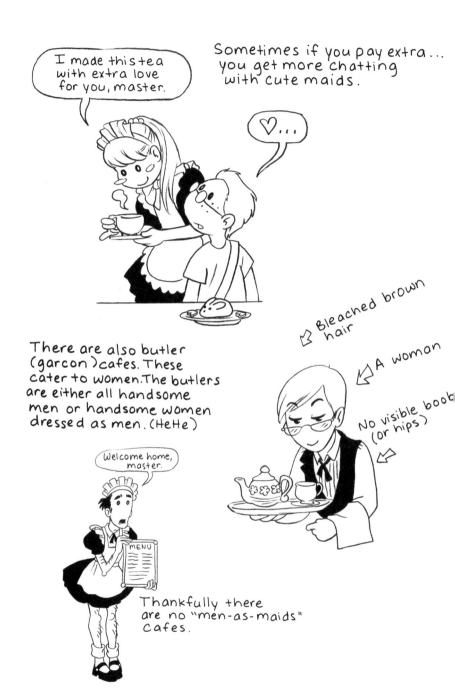

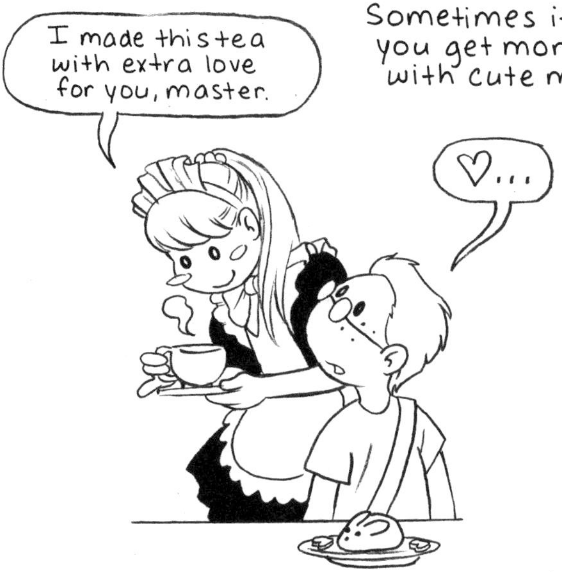
I made this tea with extra love for you, master.
♡...

There are also butler (garcon) cafes. These cater to women. The butlers are either all handsome men or handsome women dressed as men. (HeHe)

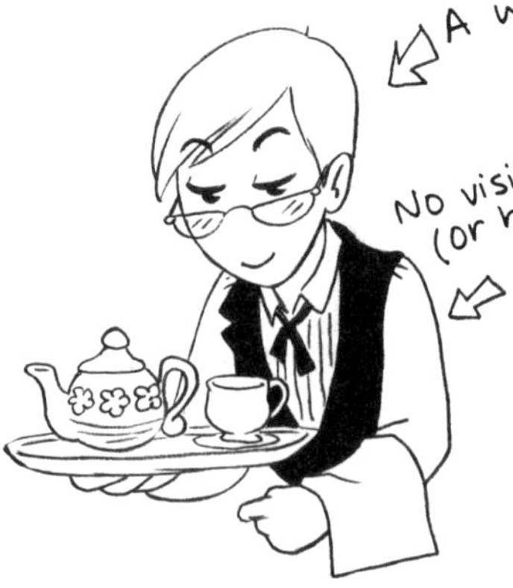
Bleached brown hair
A woman
No visible boob
(or hips)

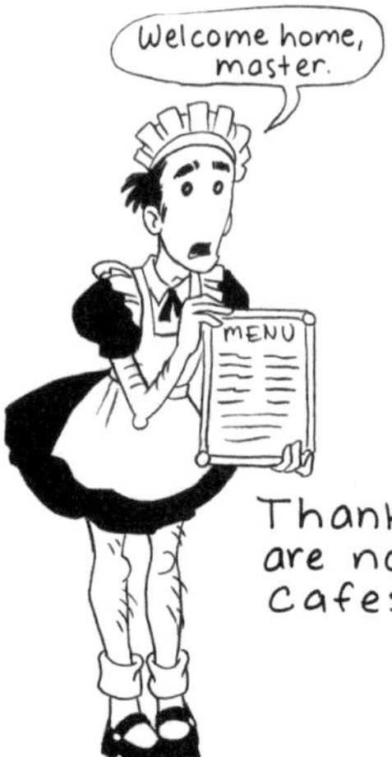
Welcome home, master.
MENU

Thankfully there are no "men-as-maids" cafes.

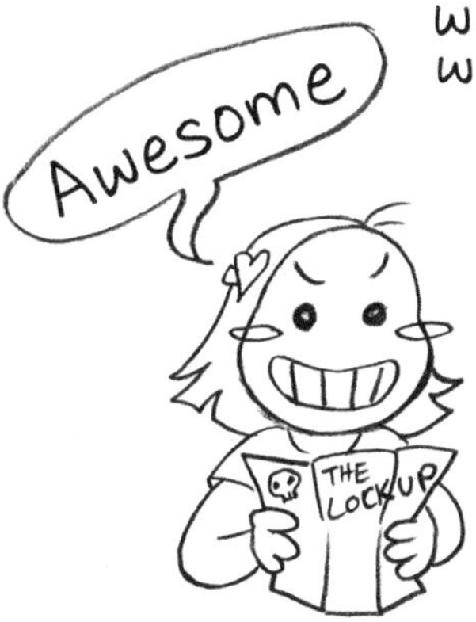
Awesome
THE LOCKUP

One of the things I really wanted to do in Japan was go to a themed cafe. There are tons of them in Tokyo... vampire cafes, maid, Alice... and the one we chose was a monster-prison-themed cafe called

"THE LOCKUP"

We got the address... it was in the basement of a normal dep't store.

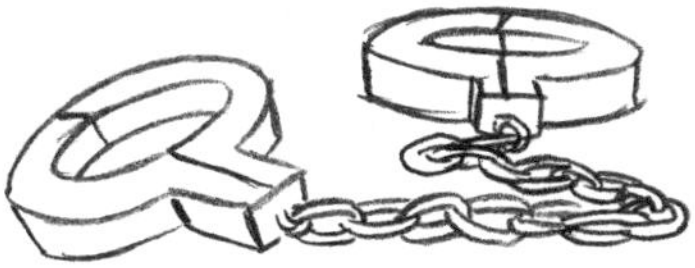

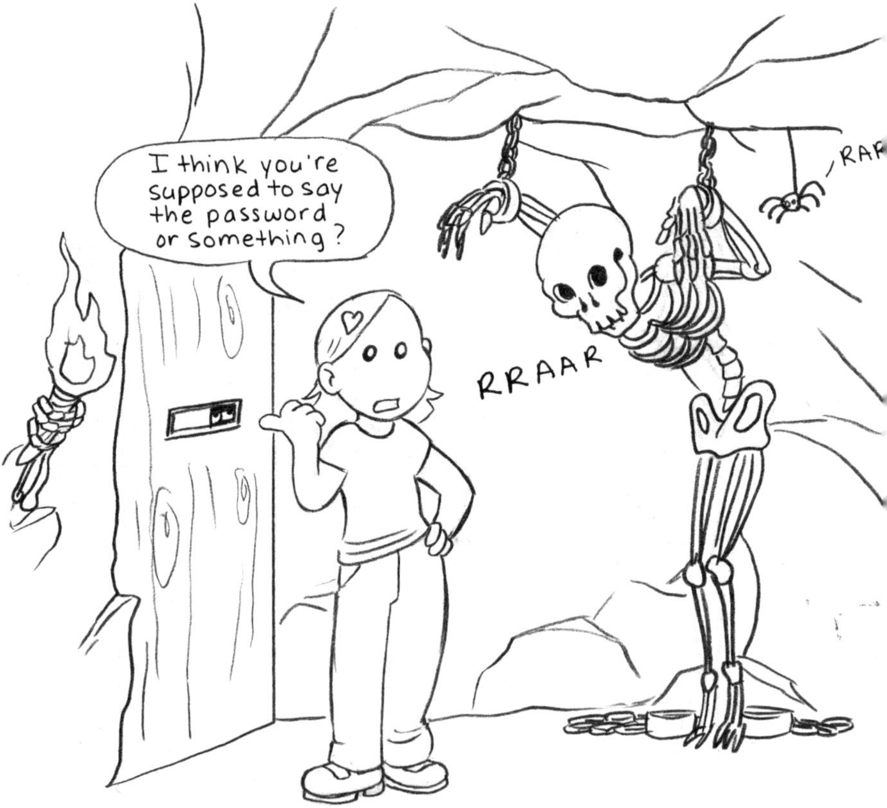
I think you're supposed to say the password or something?
RRAAR
RAR

After tripping down a dark "scary" animatronic-filled hall... we reached a door with a slot.
Somehow we got past...

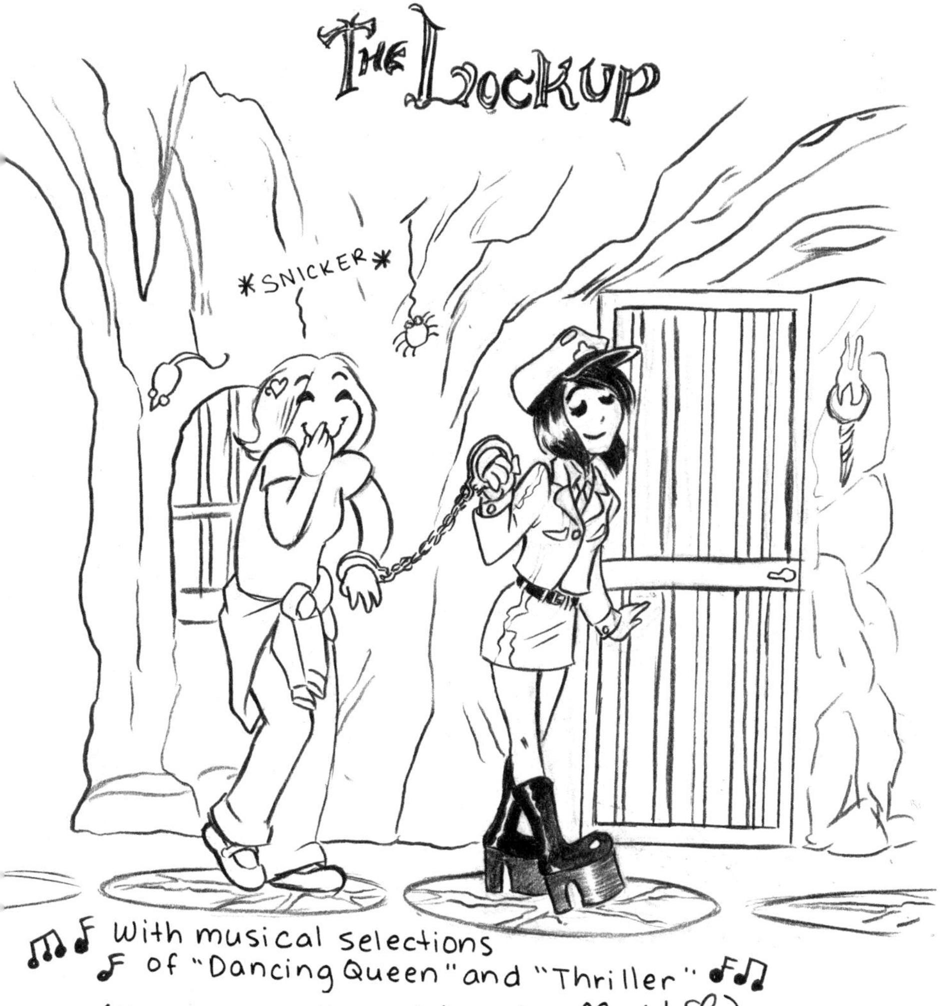
THE LOCKUP
SNICKER

♫♪ With musical selections
♪ of "Dancing Queen" and "Thriller" ♪♫
(yes you really get handcuffed! ♡)

The Lockup is a themed restaurant.
It's like a Disneyland restaurant gone evil.

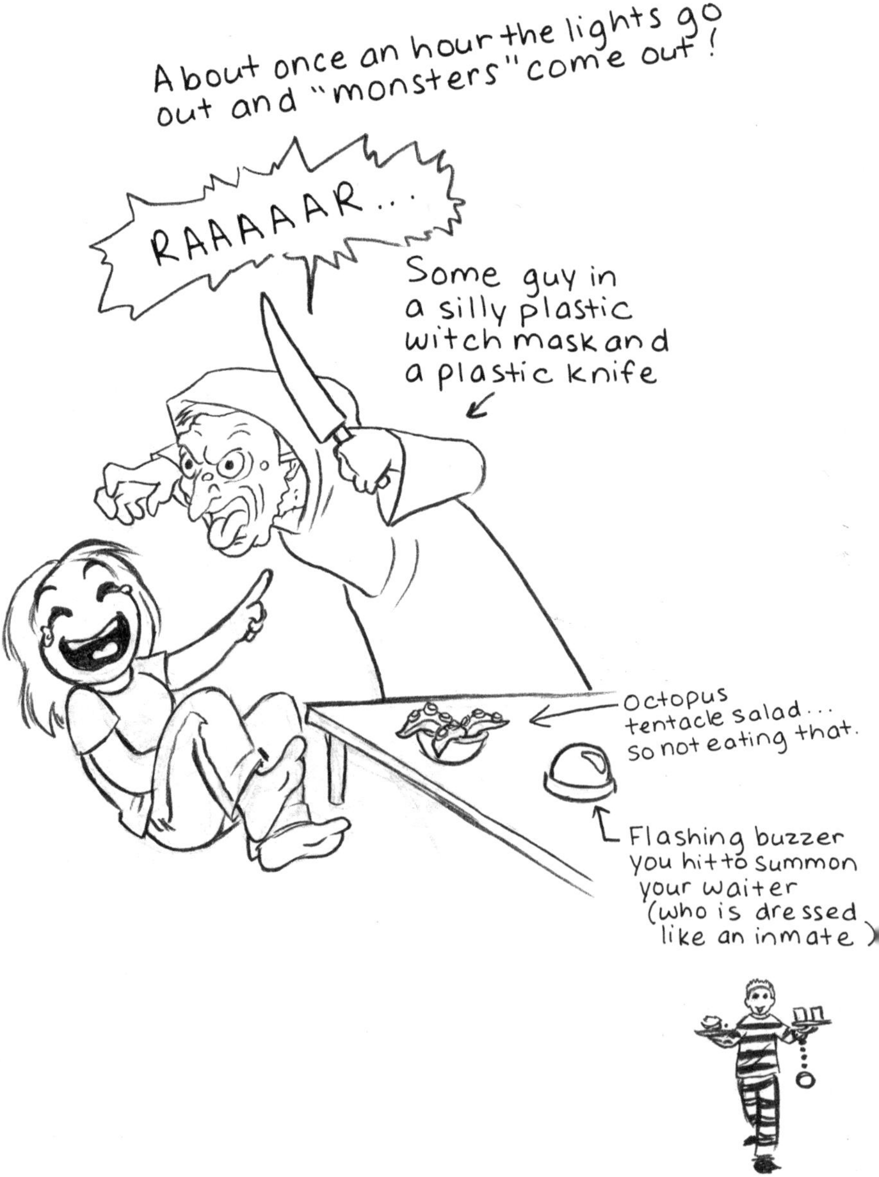
About once an hour the lights go out and "monsters" come out!
RAAAAAR...
Some guy in a silly plastic witch mask and a plastic knife
Octopus tentacle salad... so not eating that.
Flashing buzzer you hit to summon your waiter (who is dressed like an inmate)

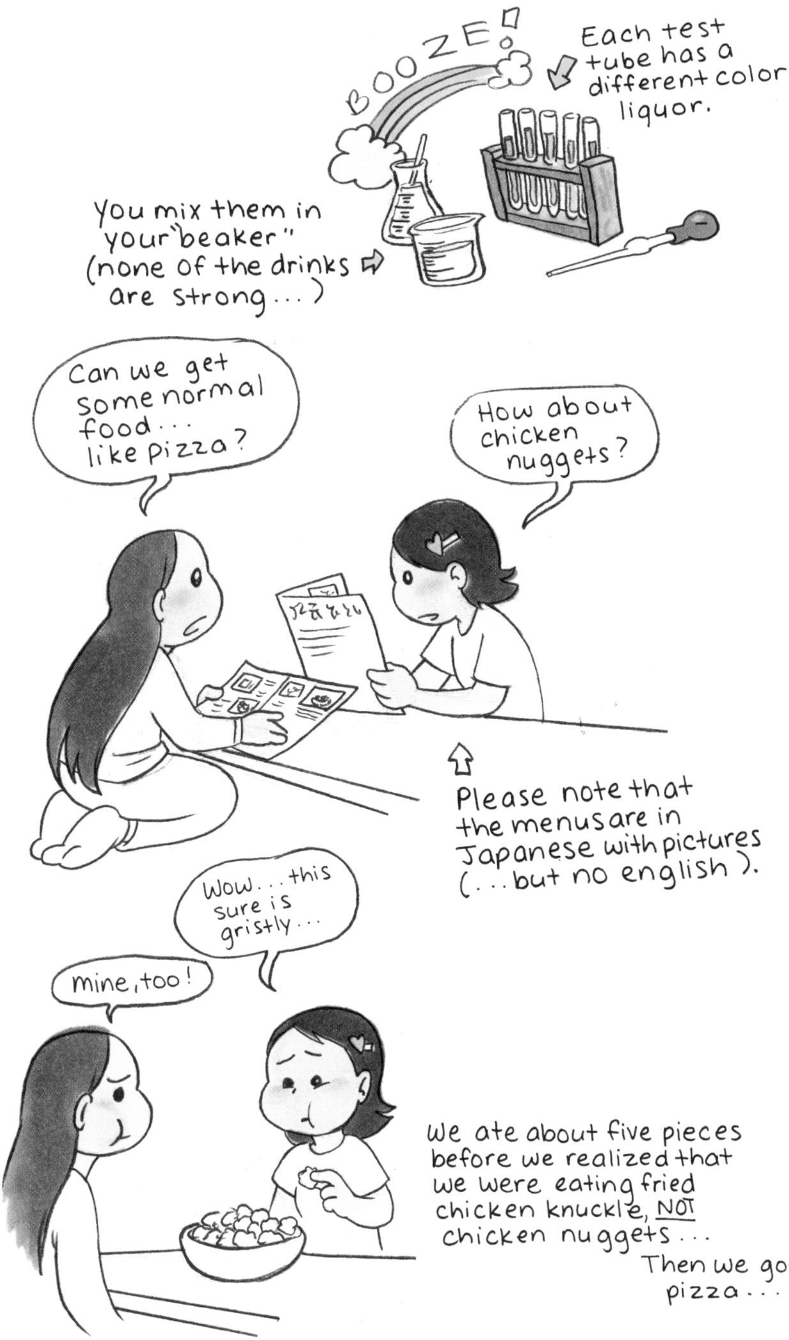
BOOZE!
Each test tube has a different color liquor.
You mix them in your "beaker" (none of the drinks are strong...)
Can we get some normal food... like pizza?
How about chicken nuggets?
Please note that the menus are in Japanese with pictures (...but no english).
Wow...this sure is gristly...
mine, too!
We ate about five pieces before we realized that we were eating fried chicken knuckle, NOT chicken nuggets...
Then we got pizza... ♡

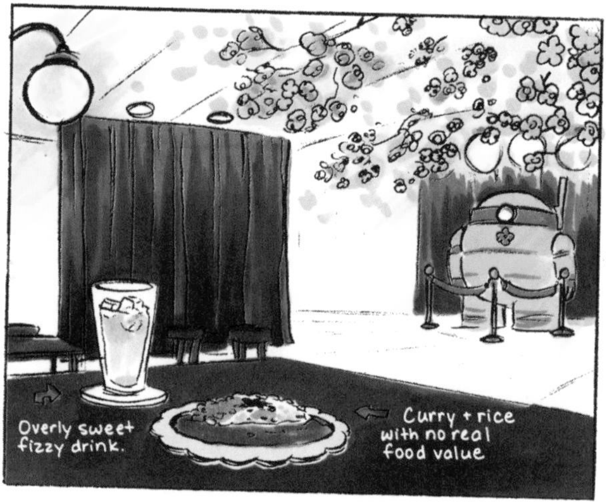
Overly sweet fizzy drink.
Curry + rice with no real food value

Fabric cherry blossoms hung from the ceiling

Giant Pink mecha (robot)

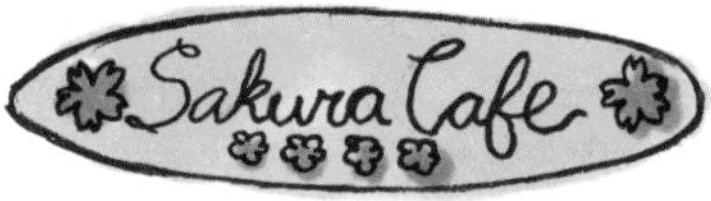
Sakura Cafe

Sakura Cafe is a cafe themed on the series Sakura Taisen (Sakura Wars)... It's a Dating Simulation game turned anime, turned live-action musical (really).

We like the 1920's Japan atmosphere of the series, the spunky personality of the characters and the fabulous music.

By the way, the girls in Sakura Taisen are basically Takarazuka stars. ♡

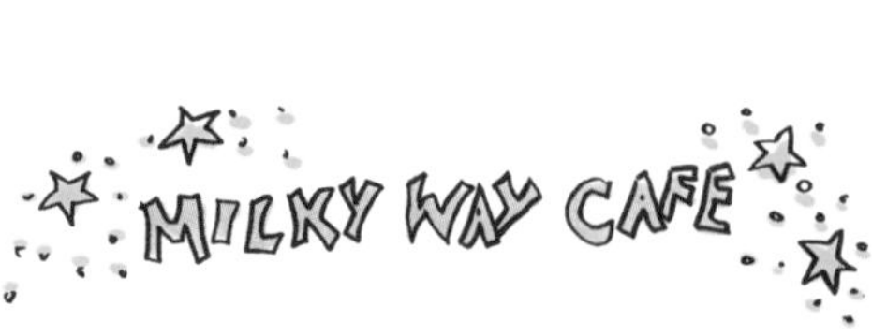
MILKY WAY CAFE

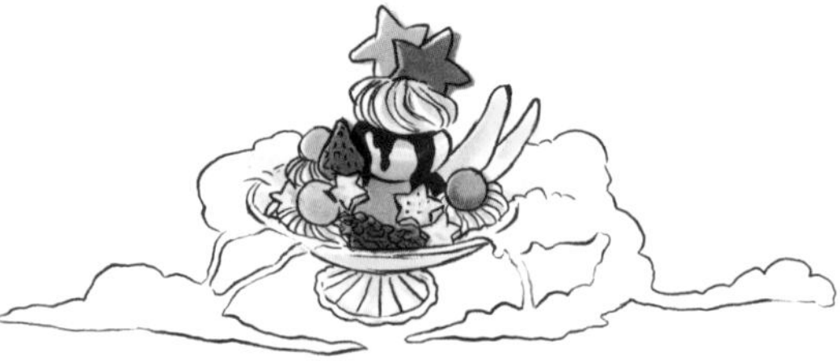

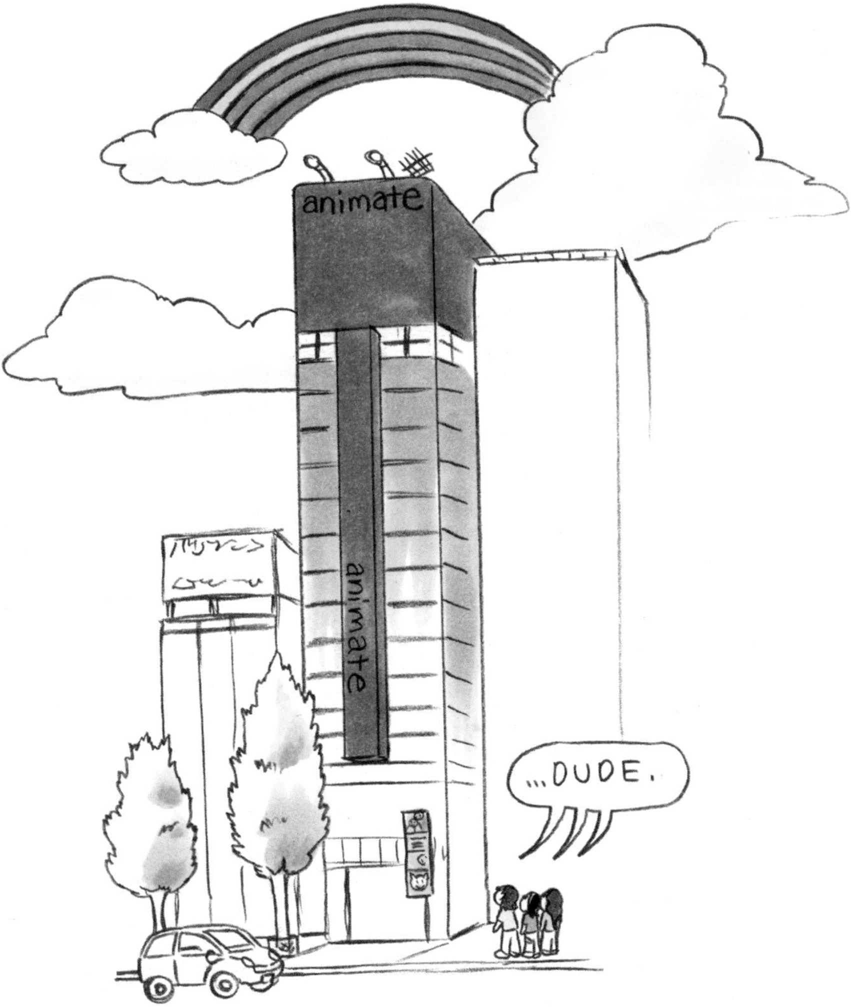
animate
animate
...DUDE.

Animate is a huge store of awesomeness.

It has manga, anime, toys and themed goods. This one is located in Ikebukoro next to a complex called "Sunshine City."

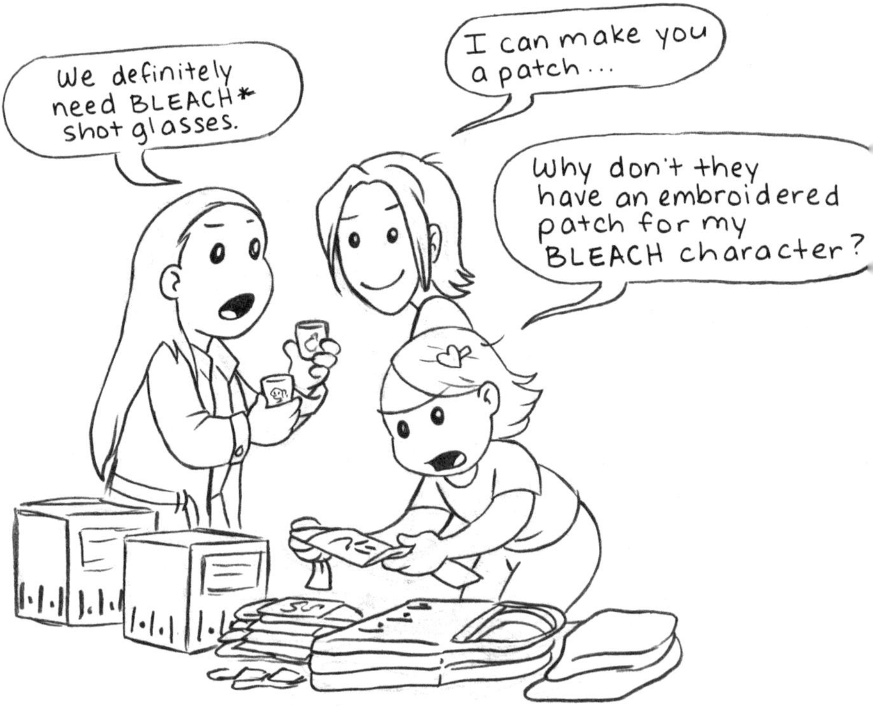
We definitely need BLEACH* shot glasses.
I can make you a patch...
Why don't they have an embroidered patch for my BLEACH character?

*BLEACH is a popular cartoon + comic in Japan. We, of course, as with most cartoons we like... have cosplayed it.

GASHAPON

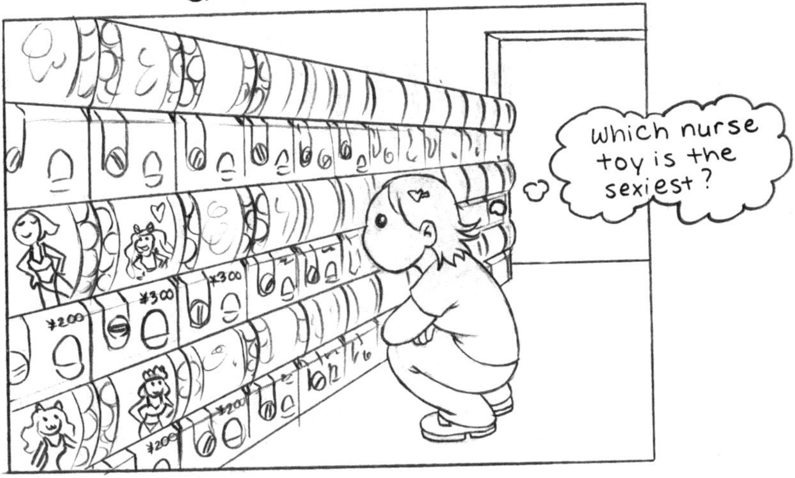
Which nurse toy is the sexiest?

In Japan these type of gumball-like machines are really popular.

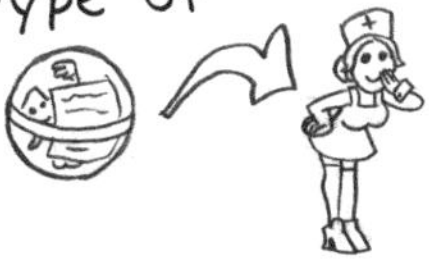

They cost about $2. The toy that pops out is random.

Inside are plastic balls with a partially assembled toy. They quickly snap together to make a very detailed figure.

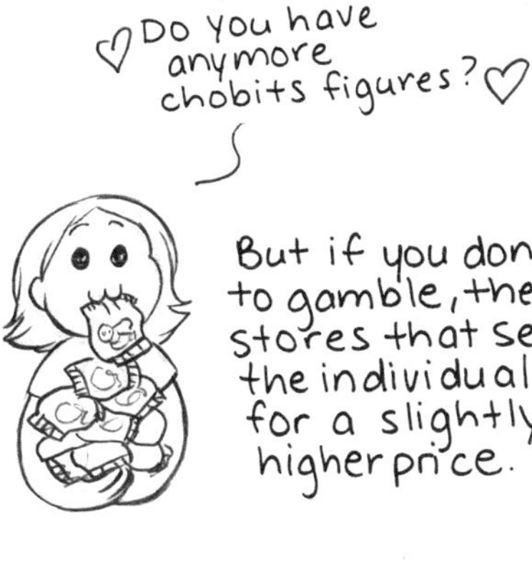
Do you have anymore chobits figures?

But if you don't want to gamble, there are stores that sell the individual toys for a slightly higher price.

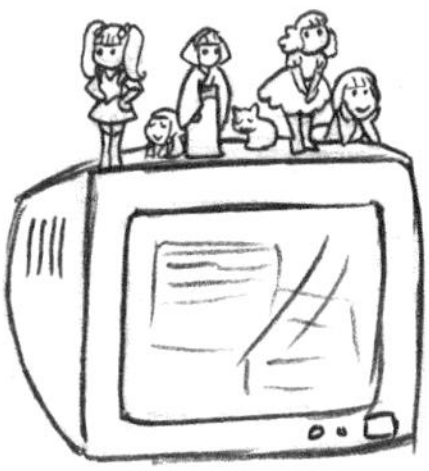

My computer monitor is covered in gashapon.

The sticker booths in Japan are way more advanced than in the USA.

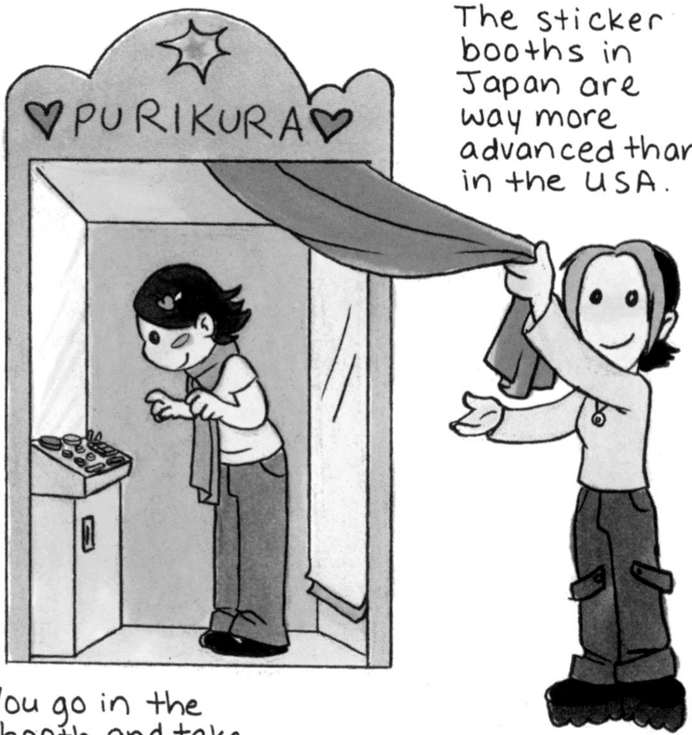
PURIKURA

You go in the booth and take photos with your friends.

You can add:

- Sparkly or themed backdrops
- Frames
- Clipart
- And you can draw on the photo, too!

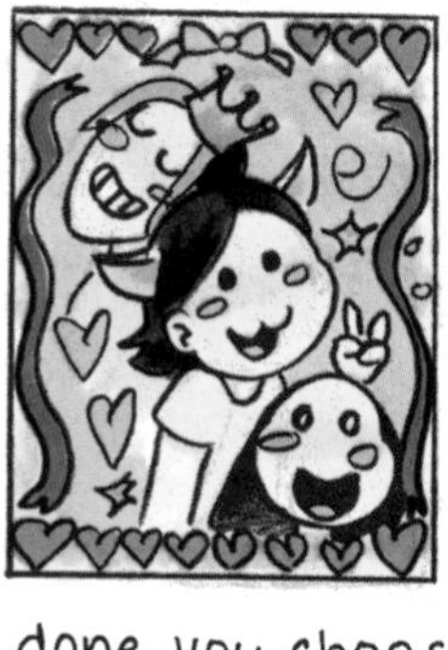

Then you are able to modify the photos.

When you're done you choose the size + layout of your printouts and it prints out stickers!

You can keep some + give some to friends.

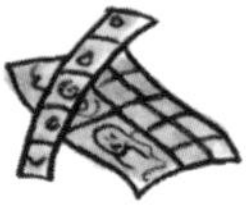

In the 8-story chain store Tokyu Hands...

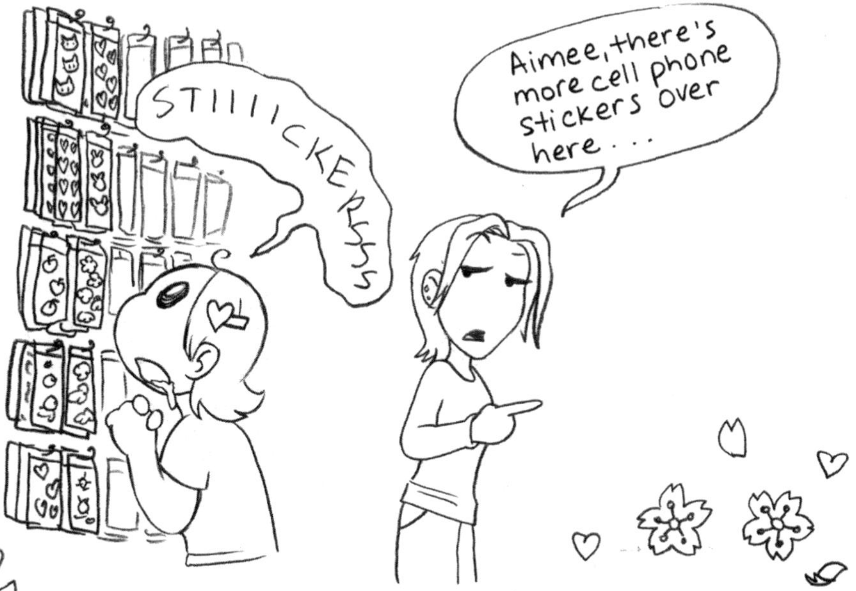
STIIIICKERSSS
Aimee, there's more cell phone stickers over here...

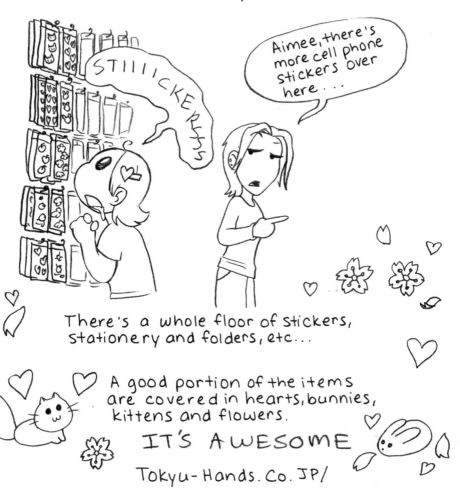

There's a whole floor of stickers, stationery and folders, etc...

A good portion of the items are covered in hearts, bunnies, kittens and flowers.

IT'S AWESOME

Tokyu-Hands.Co.JP/

KARAOKE~

singing along to tracks of your favorite songs

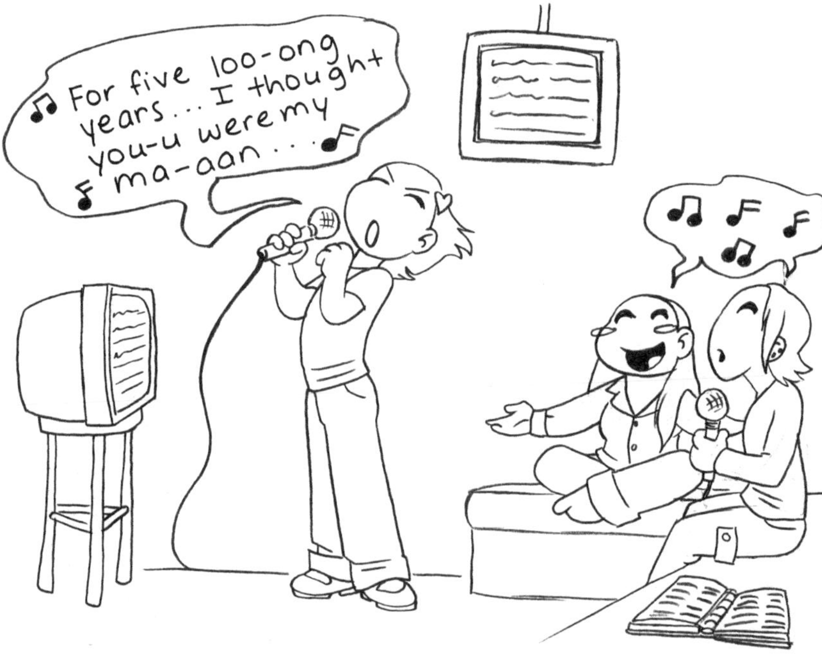
For five loo-ong years... I thought you-u were my ma-aan...

Some karaoke places are public restaurants but many offer private rooms you can sing your heart out in.

Some people love dolls
and some people loooove dolls.

...The monument to
Godzilla in Ginza, Tokyo...
...not very impressive...

Chapter Nine:
Tokyo Fashion

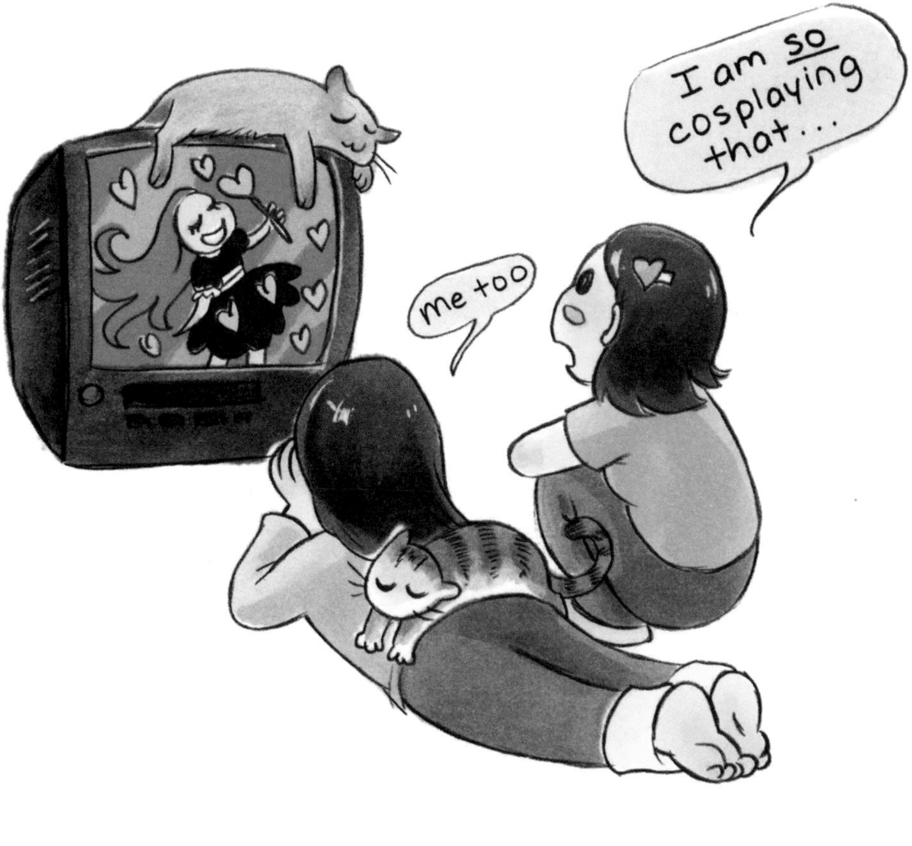
I am so cosplaying that...
me too

In the USA, we cosplay a lot. Cosplay is "costume play"–basically having fun with your friends in costumes, usually from our favorite cartoons.

me being a cartoonist, you can see the attraction. ü

We go to parks and conventions like this... we're used to people staring.

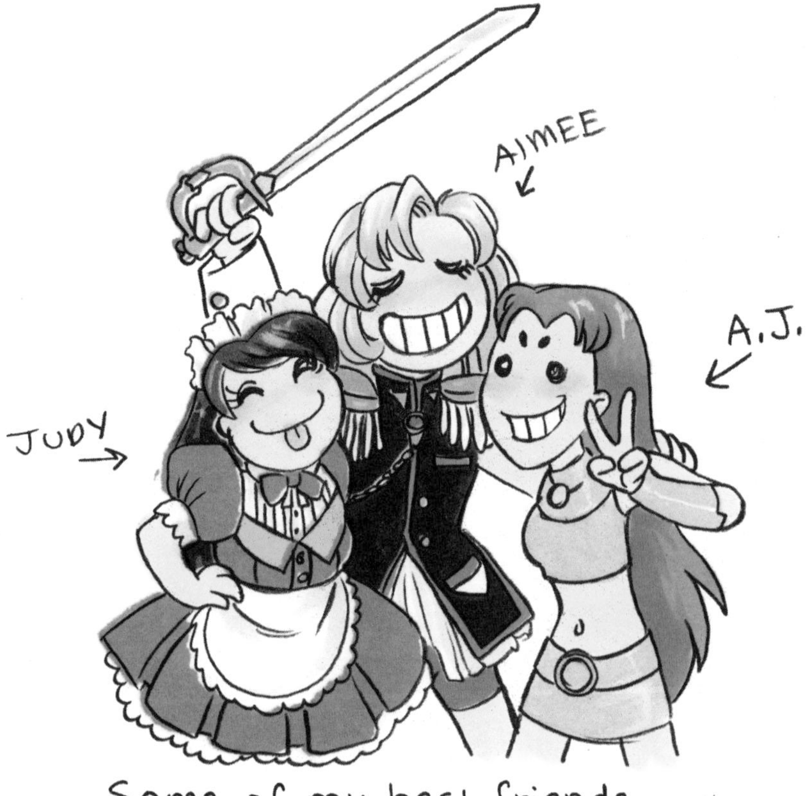
AIMEE
A.J.
JUDY

Some of my best friends I've met through "cosplay."

We heard that on Sundays people dressed up in gothic lolita costumes and rock band outfits go to Harajuku...

We thought we would do like the natives, since we all had our own lolita outfits too...

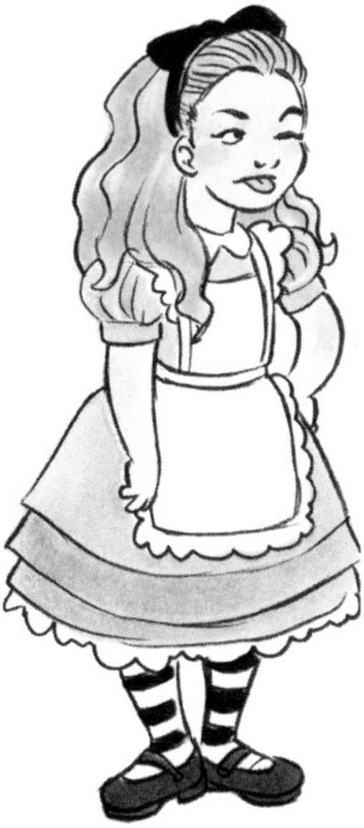

Your typical "Lolita" outfit is actually remarkably similar to classic illustrations of Alice in Wonderland... Complete with:

- puffy sleeves
- Peter Pan collar
- frilly skirt with petticoat
- Mary Jane shoes

... And sometimes a white rabbit...

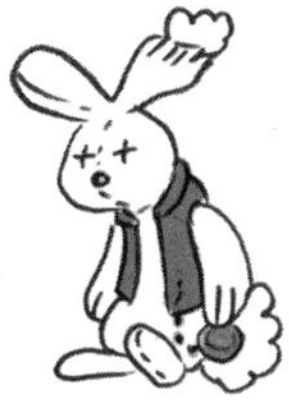

And often a tea party!

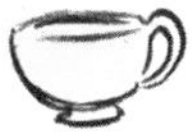

Lolita is all about being adorable and elegant... like a doll or a young girl.

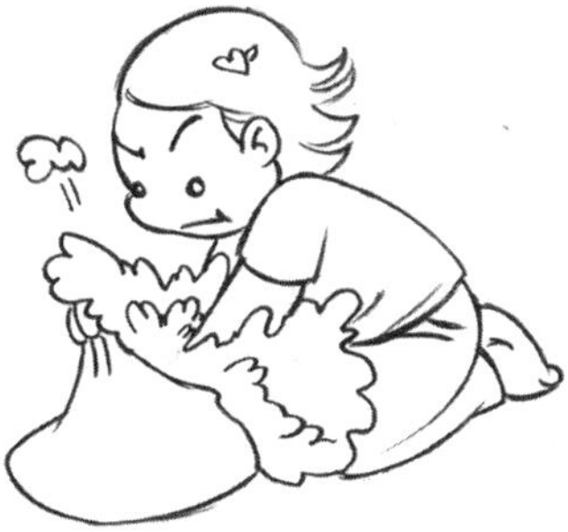

On Sunday morning we shoved our lolita outfits in bookbags (since we were too chicken to wear them on the subway) and made our way to Harajuku.

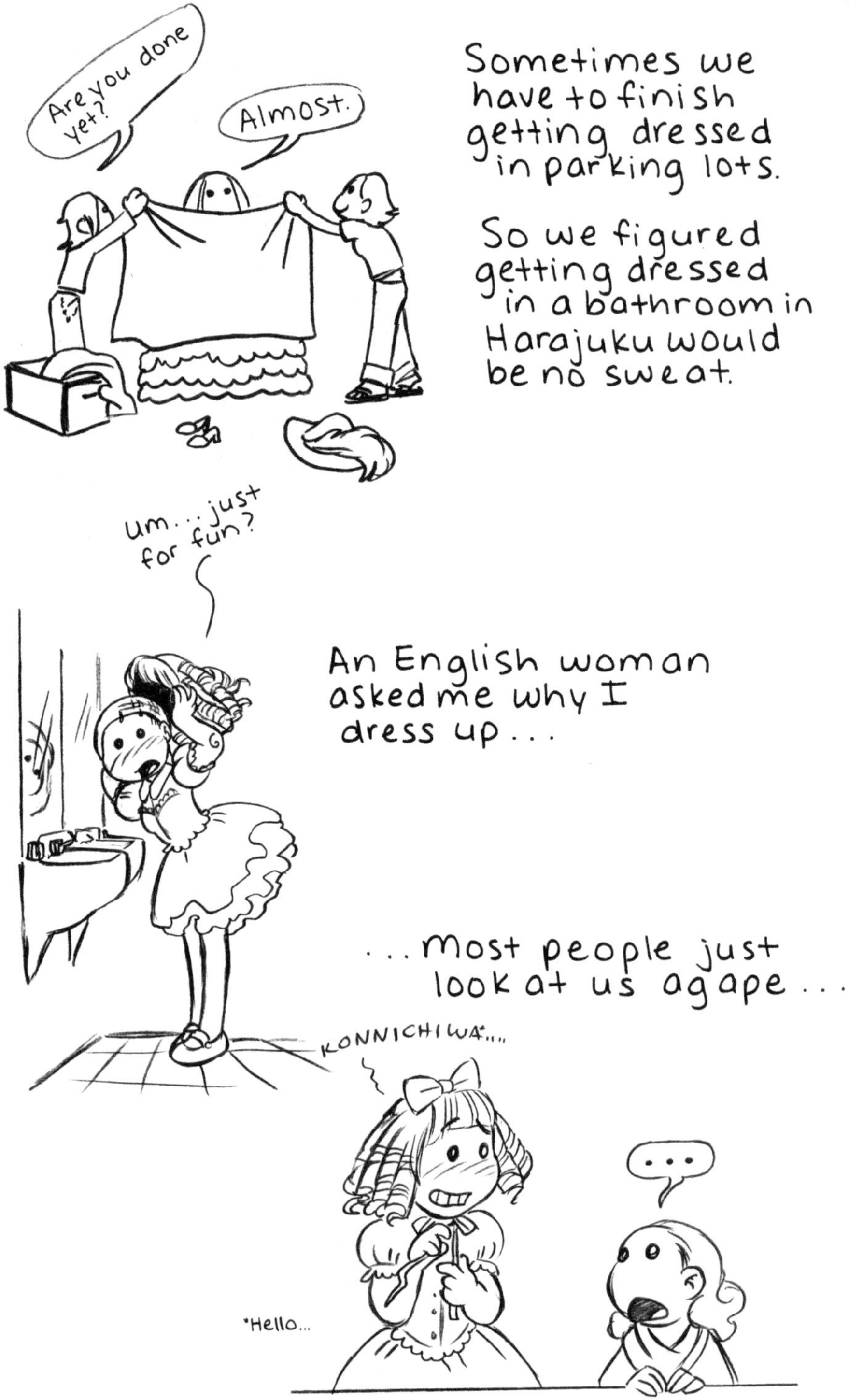
Are you done yet?
Almost.
Sometimes we have to finish getting dressed in parking lots.
So we figured getting dressed in a bathroom in Harajuku would be no sweat.
An English woman asked me why I dress up...
um... just for fun?
...most people just look at us agape...
KONNICHIWA*....
...
*Hello...

Ready to hit Harajuku!

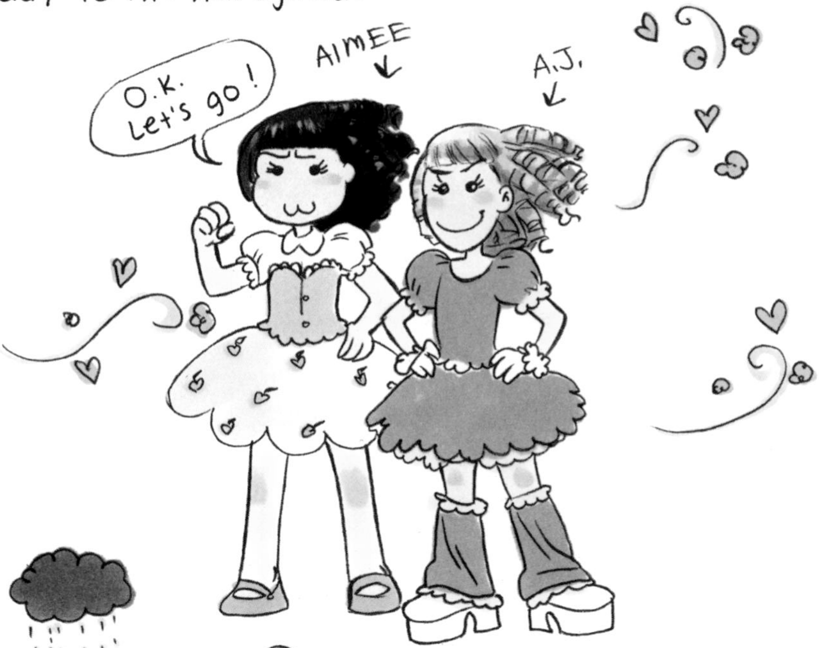
AIMEE
A.J.
O.K. Let's go!

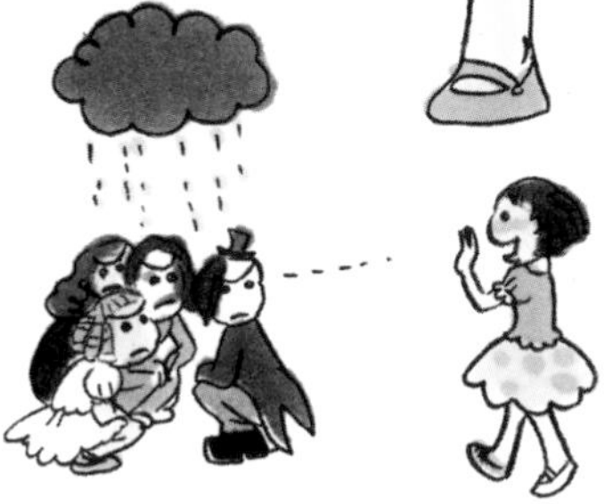

Some people didn't want their picture taken.

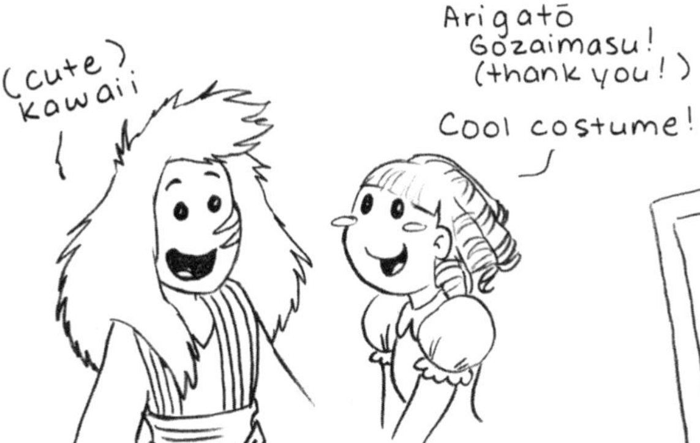
(cute) kawaii
Arigatō Gozaimasu! (thank you!)
Cool costume!

Some people were really friendly though!

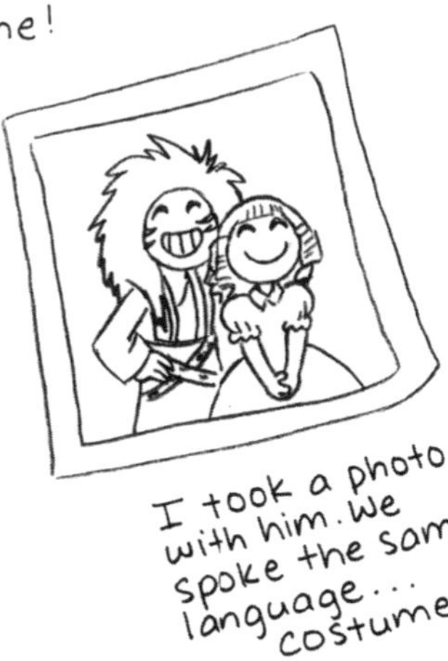

I took a photo with him. We spoke the same language... costumes!

A sullen
cosplayer
in Harajuku

A Victorian-esque
lolita clothes
store

what??

7F Innocent World

6F THANK YOU MART

5F A-TITTY
WEDDING + PARTY

4F LIVE STUDIO

a floor map

AYA from Psycho le Cému

Mana from moi-même-moitié

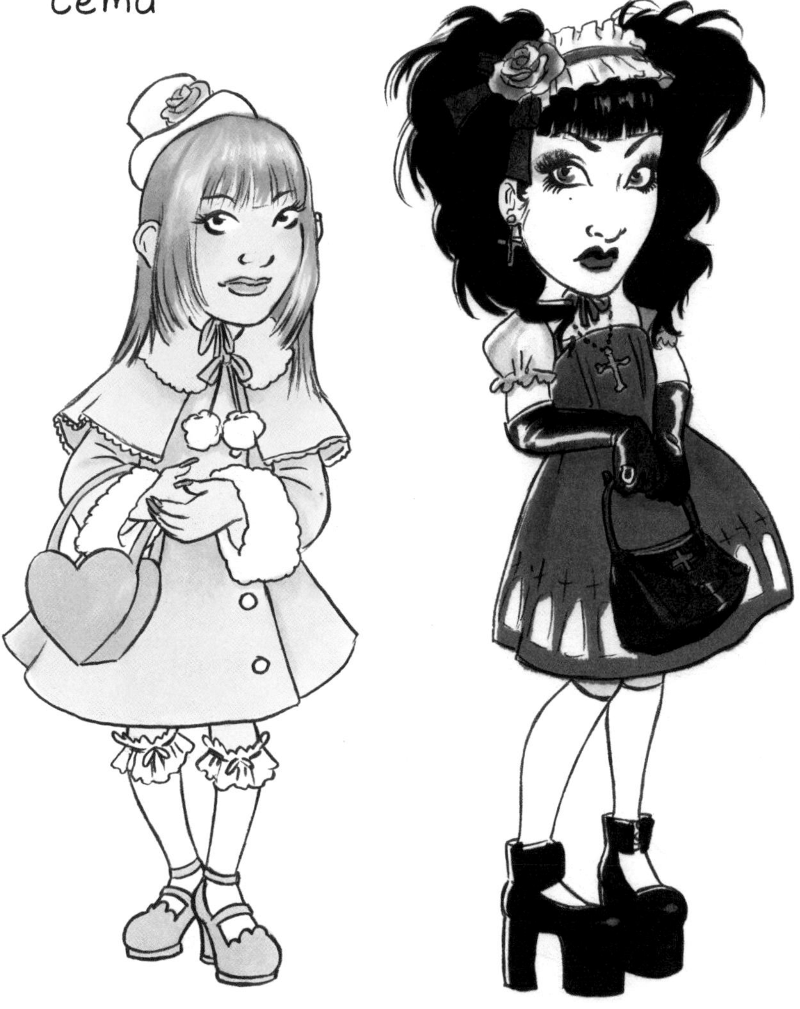

Two of the most famous crossdressers in Japan...
Both men are members of rock bands.
Girls aspire to dress and look like them.

Japanese girl
in hip casual
fashion

ARRR

mostly
random English
words

WILD
THING
REV
BLOOD

Kakkoii =
"cool" or
attractive

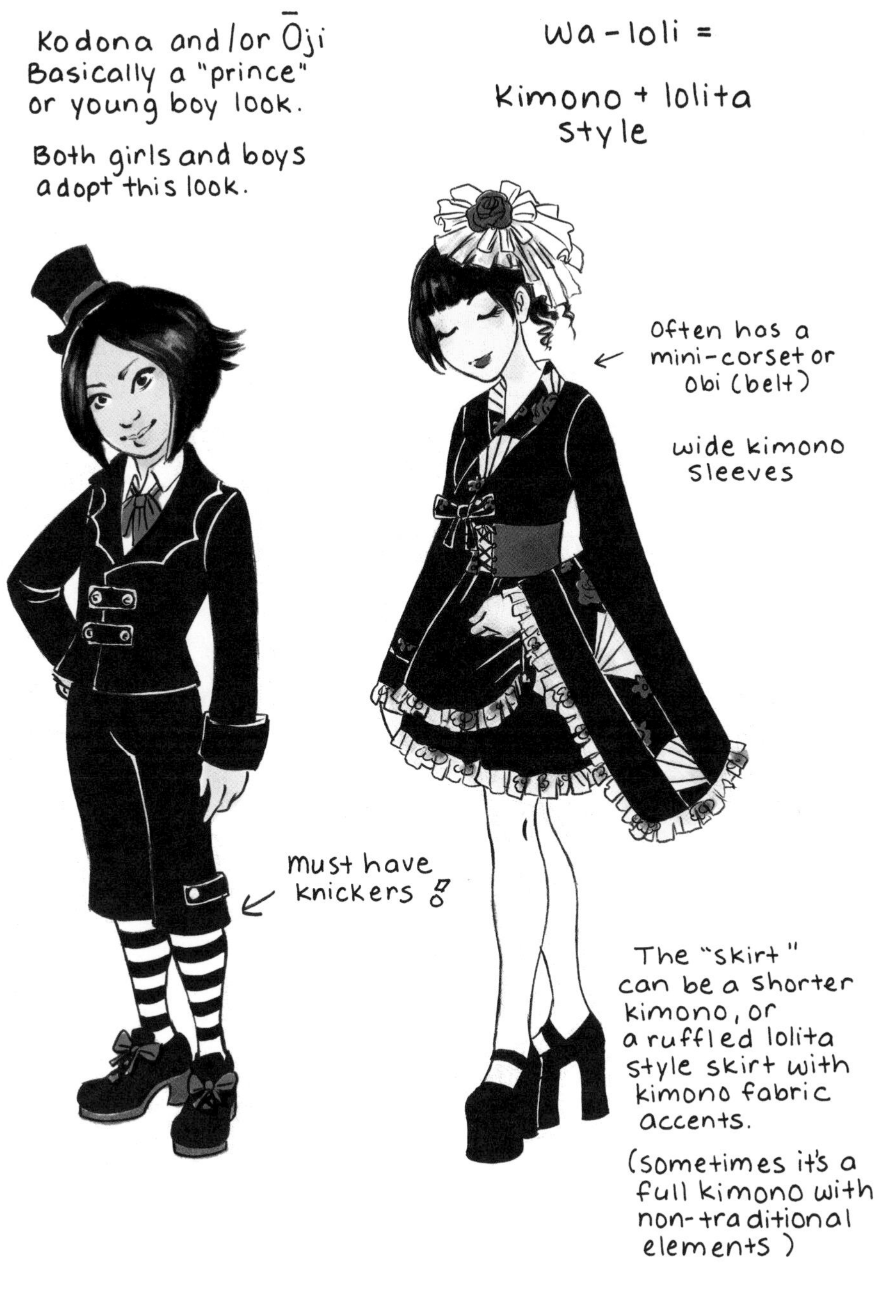
Kodona and/or Ōji
Basically a "prince" or young boy look.
Both girls and boys adopt this look.
Wa-loli =
Kimono + lolita Style
Often has a mini-corset or Obi (belt)
wide kimono sleeves
Must have knickers!
The "skirt" can be a shorter kimono, or a ruffled lolita style skirt with kimono fabric accents.
(sometimes it's a full kimono with non-traditional elements)

You can find more like this in the magazine "EGG"!

LET'S GO CRAZY!

Some wear gems under their eyes. The makeup can become elaborate to the point of war paint!

C'MON! BABY!

I saw some in Ikebukuro...

KOGAL or GANGURO

This is a street fashion trend where teen girls tan their skin...often to the point of being orange. They wear white eye makeup and lipstick. They bleach their hair and wear playful, colorful clothes...rings... tons of flowers + bracelets...platforms. The male version is a "center guy."

Probably about 20 barrettes

← Lots of bracelets + necklaces + rings

Huge furry ← purse

Loud socks →

♥ · ♡ ∘ ♥ · ♡ ∘ ♥
❀ Decorer Style ❀

A street style for girls. Basically they encrust themselves with cute stuff... mostly pink and bright colors... tons of hearts and bows.
Way too many cute hair barrettes is imperative.
One store for it is 6% Doki Doki.

HARAJUKU MAP

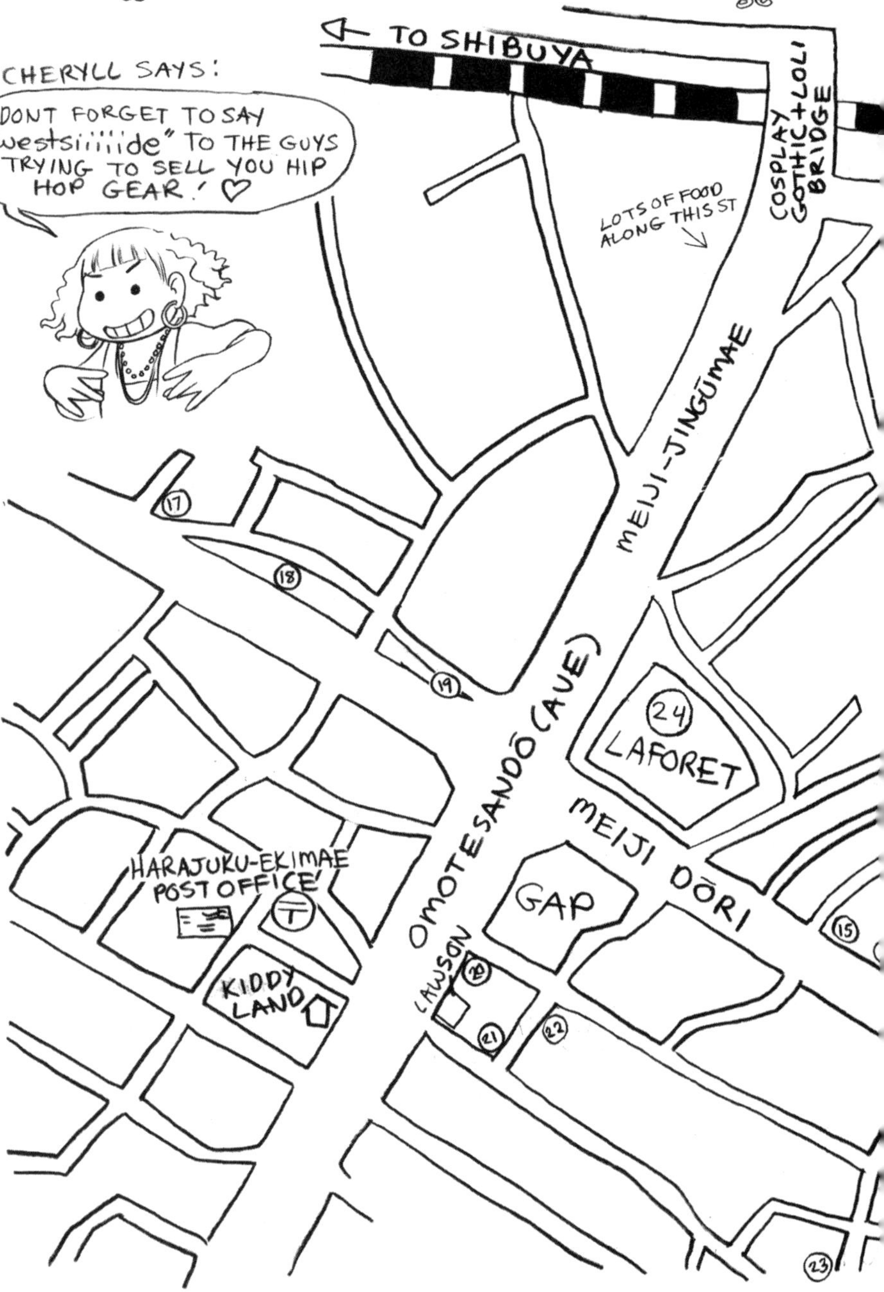
TO SHIBUYA
CHERYLL SAYS:
DONT FORGET TO SAY "westsiiiiiide" TO THE GUYS TRYING TO SELL YOU HIP HOP GEAR! ♡
COSPLAY GOTHIC+LOLI BRIDGE
LOTS OF FOOD ALONG THIS ST
MEIJI-JINGŪMAE
17
18
19
OMOTESANDŌ (AVE)
24
LAFORET
MEIJI DŌRI
GAP
HARAJUKU-EKIMAE POST OFFICE
KIDDY LAND
LAWSON
20
21
22
15
23

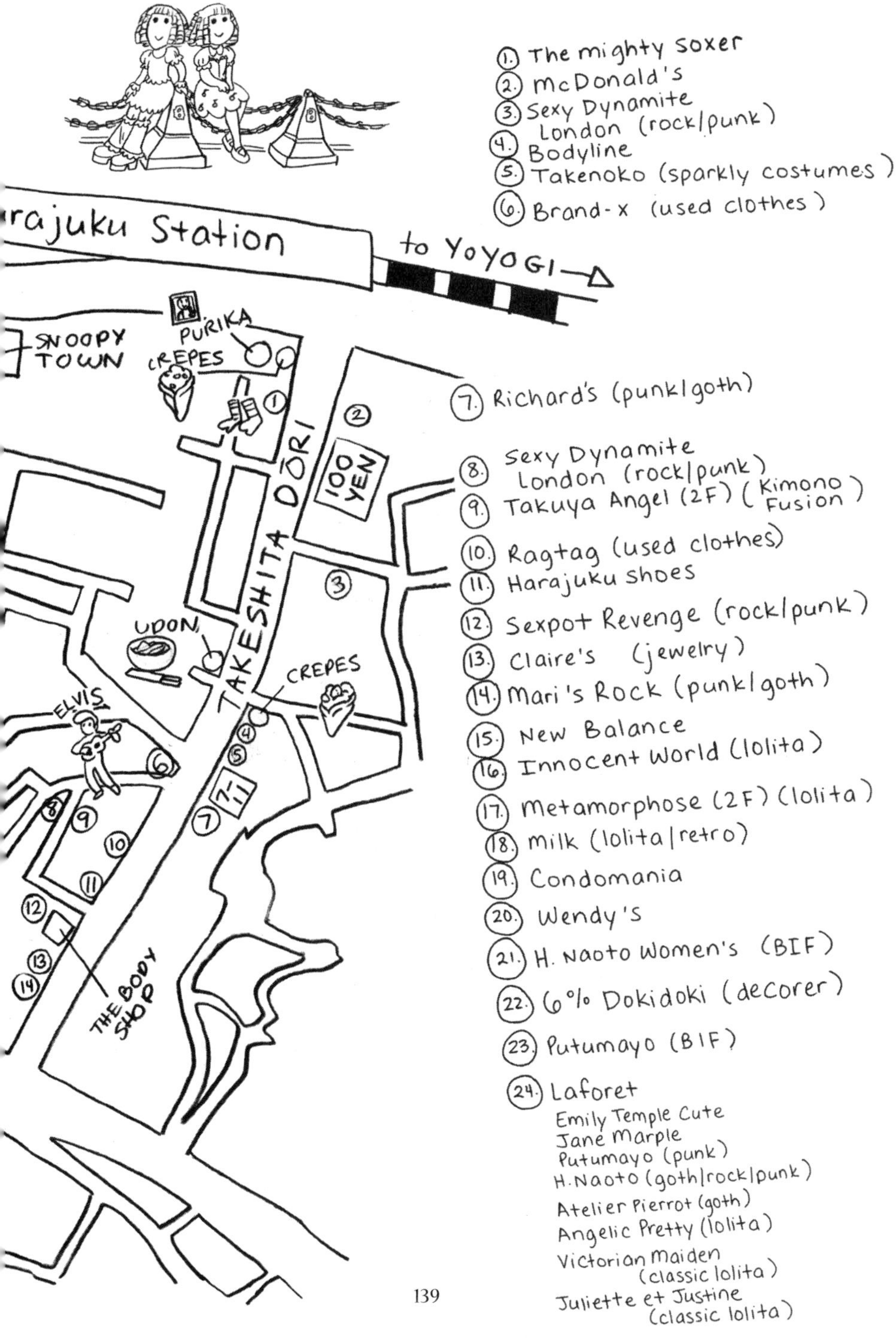
Harajuku Station
to YOYOGI
SNOOPY TOWN
PURIKA
CREPES
TAKESHITA DŌRI
100 YEN
UDON
CREPES
ELVIS
7-11
THE BODY SHOP
1. The mighty soxer
2. McDonald's
3. Sexy Dynamite London (rock/punk)
4. Bodyline
5. Takenoko (sparkly costumes)
6. Brand-x (used clothes)
7. Richard's (punk/goth)
8. Sexy Dynamite London (rock/punk)
9. Takuya Angel (2F) (Kimono Fusion)
10. Ragtag (used clothes)
11. Harajuku shoes
12. Sexpot Revenge (rock/punk)
13. Claire's (jewelry)
14. Mari's Rock (punk/goth)
15. New Balance
16. Innocent World (lolita)
17. Metamorphose (2F) (lolita)
18. milk (lolita/retro)
19. Condomania
20. Wendy's
21. H. Naoto Women's (B1F)
22. 6% Dokidoki (decorer)
23. Putumayo (B1F)
24. Laforet
Emily Temple Cute
Jane Marple
Putumayo (punk)
H.Naoto (goth/rock/punk)
Atelier Pierrot (goth)
Angelic Pretty (lolita)
Victorian Maiden (classic lolita)
Juliette et Justine (classic lolita)

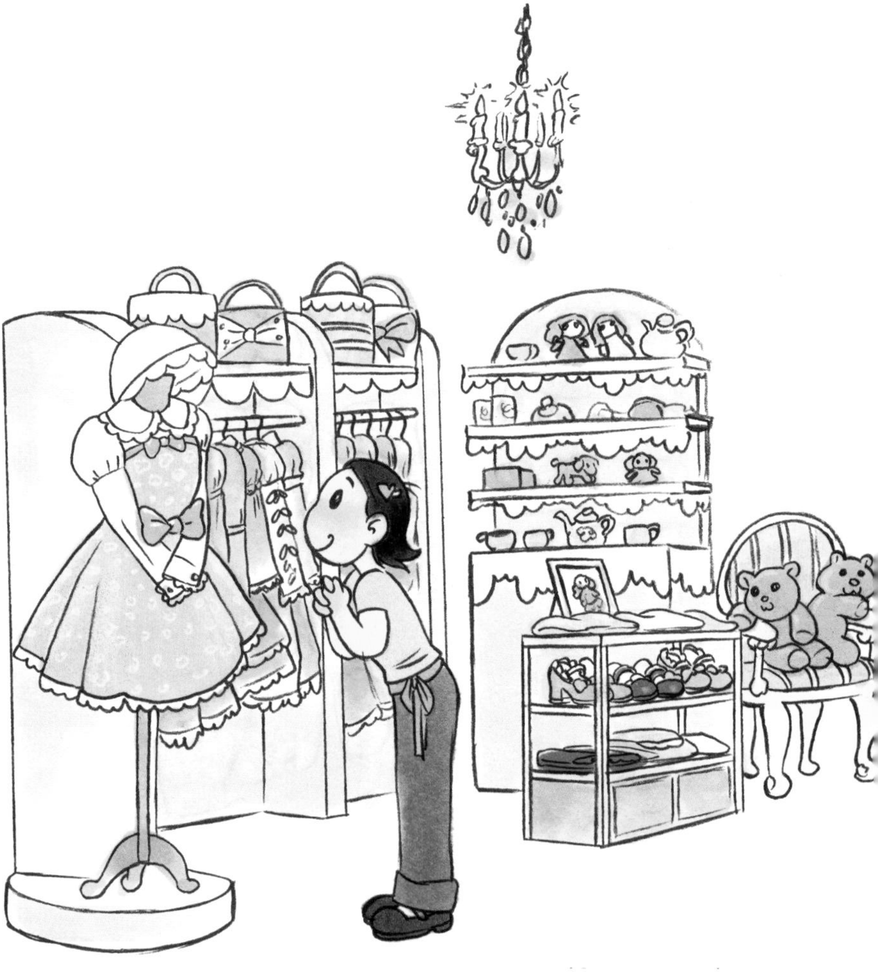

The lolita stores in Japan actually look like this... and everything is in pink... even the walls.

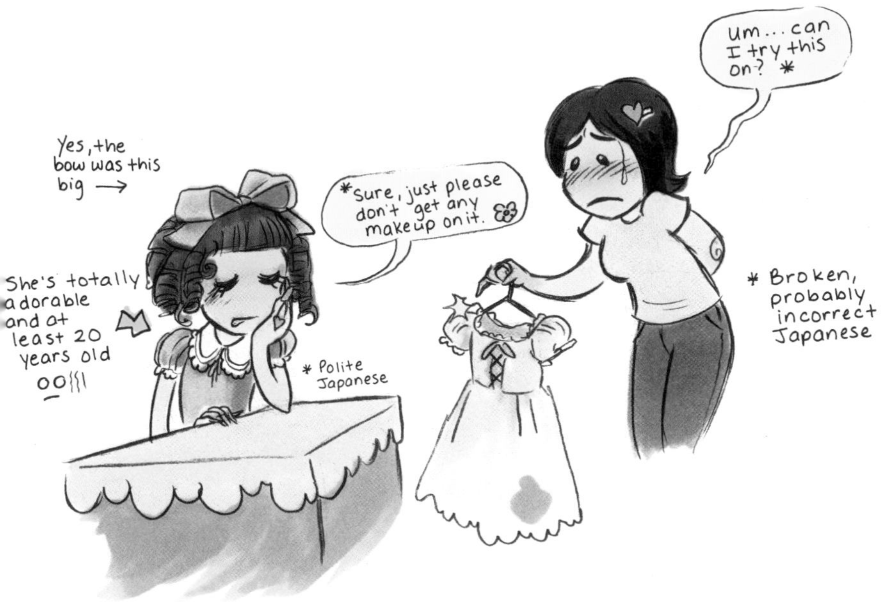
Um... can I try this on? *
*Sure, just please don't get any makeup on it.
Yes, the bow was this big →
She's totally adorable and at least 20 years old
* Polite Japanese
* Broken, probably incorrect Japanese

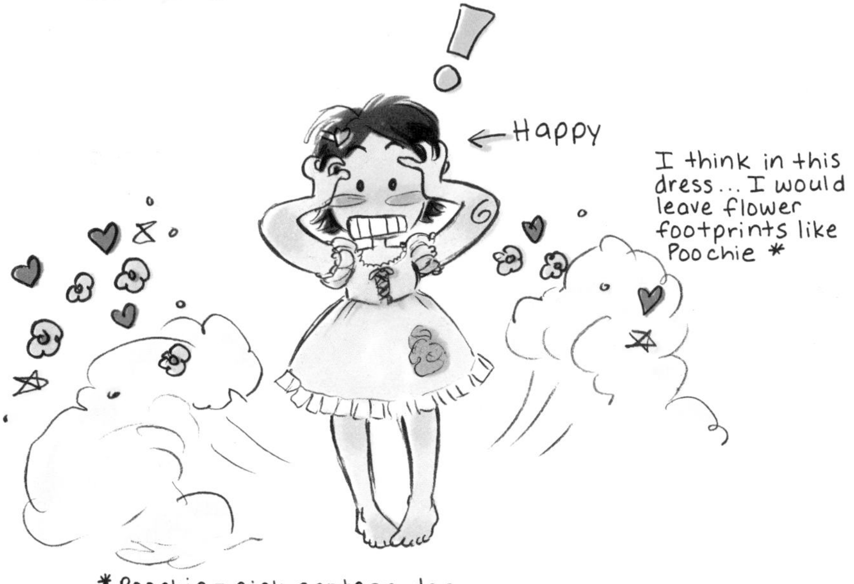
← Happy
I think in this dress... I would leave flower footprints like Poochie *

* Poochie = pink cartoon dog from the `80s that left pink flower footprints

We went to Mana's store which had gorgeous (black) gothic aristocratic clothes.

The outside of the shop is pretty impressive, with glowing blue glass windows + cast iron gates.

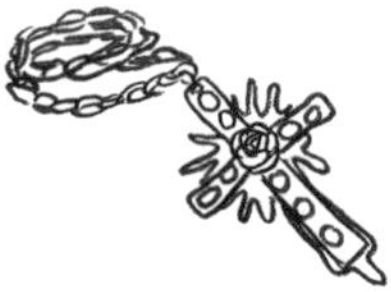

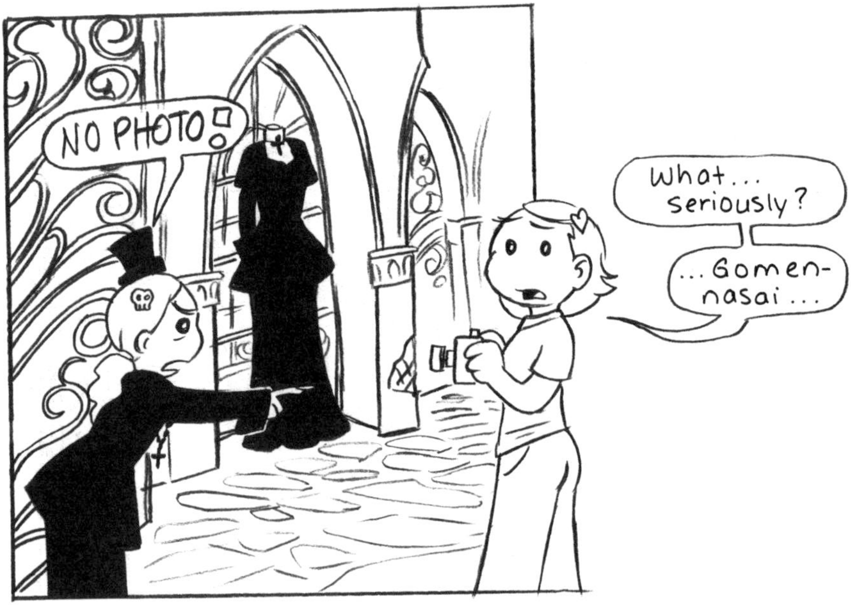
NO PHOTO!
What... seriously?
...Gomen-nasai...

For some reason no stores or restaurants allow you to take photos. (Even if no other people are in the shot...)

The store attendant at the gothic
aristocrat store, Atelier Boz

Is that a
boy or a
girl?

I don't know
but he's prettier
than both of us.

A.J. and I both bought the
coat he was wearing... haha...

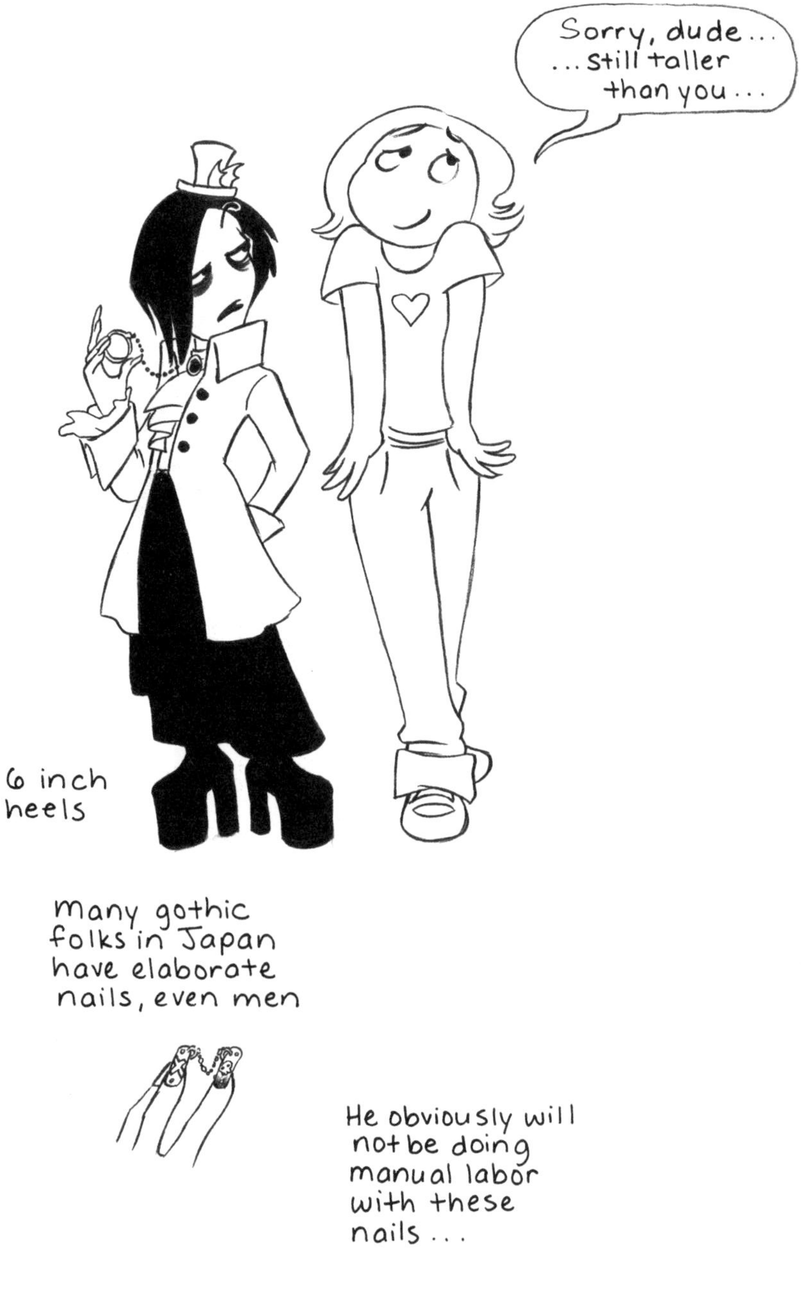
Sorry, dude... ...still taller than you...
6 inch heels
many gothic folks in Japan have elaborate nails, even men
He obviously will not be doing manual labor with these nails...

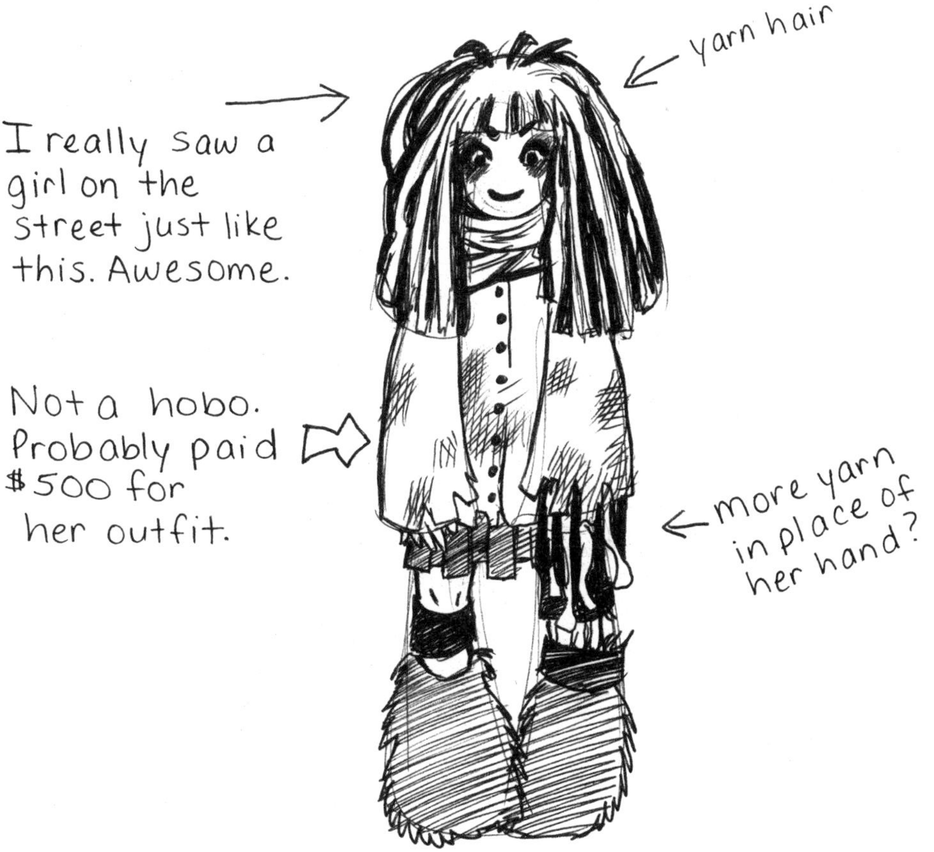
yarn hair
I really saw a girl on the street just like this. Awesome.
Not a hobo. Probably paid $500 for her outfit.
more yarn in place of her hand?

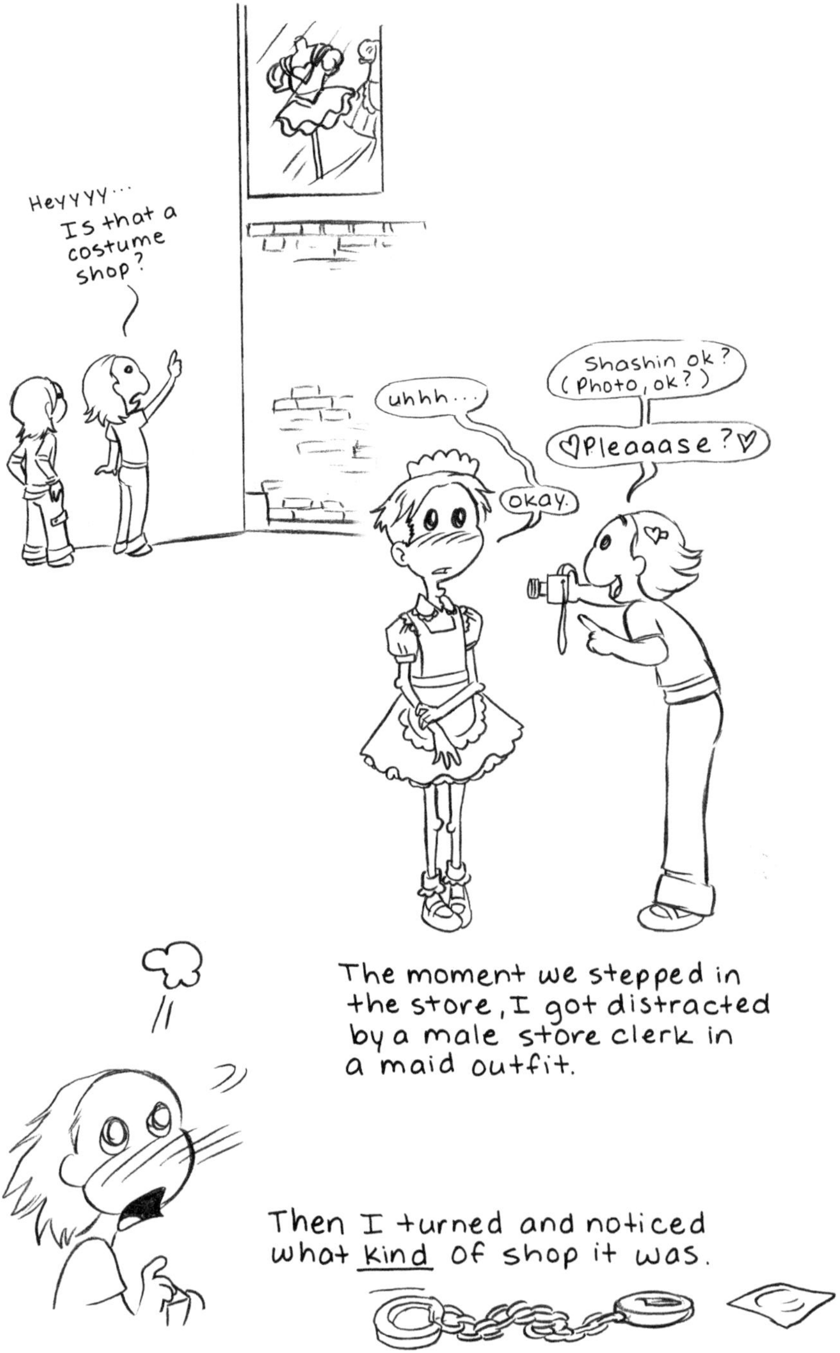
Heyyyy... Is that a costume shop?
Shashin ok? (Photo, ok?)
uhhh...
Pleaaase?
okay.
The moment we stepped in the store, I got distracted by a male store clerk in a maid outfit.
Then I turned and noticed what kind of shop it was.

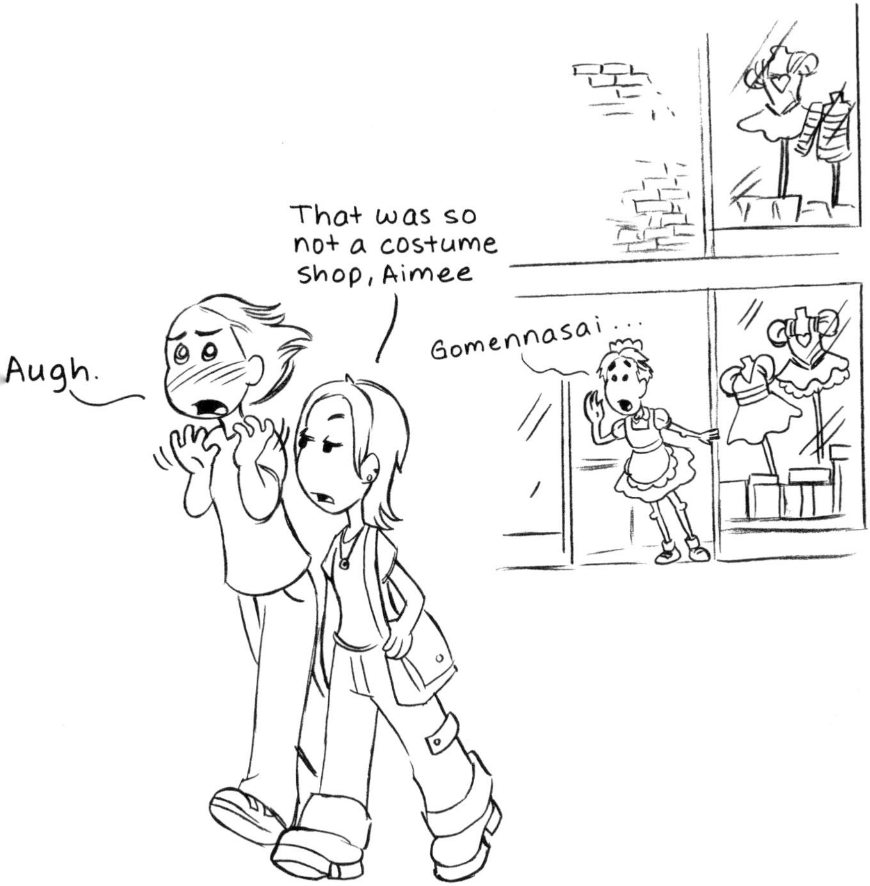
Gomennasai...
That was so not a costume shop, Aimee
Augh.

I got stared at a lot...

... Even when I wasn't in costume.

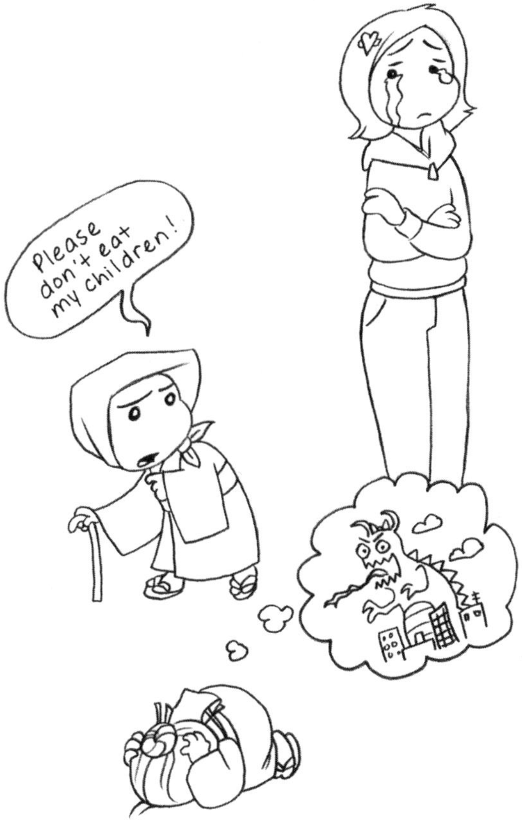
Please don't eat my children!

Once or twice I got fed up and stared back, but most of the time I tried to keep smiling.

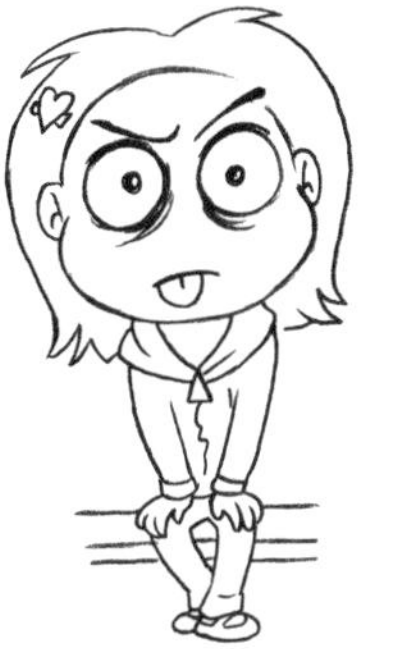

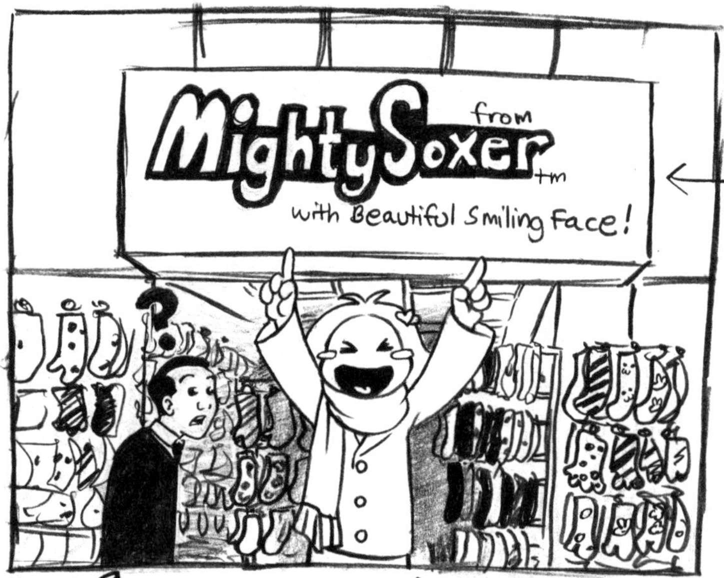
MightySoxer from tm
with Beautiful Smiling Face!

Perfect example of bad English Yay!!

salaryman

me

This is a sock store in Harajuku...
there are stores specializing
in all kinds of socks all over!
(This was my fave.) All colors + designs!
Regrettably, I could buy no
cute Japanese socks.
My feet (US 11) are too
big.

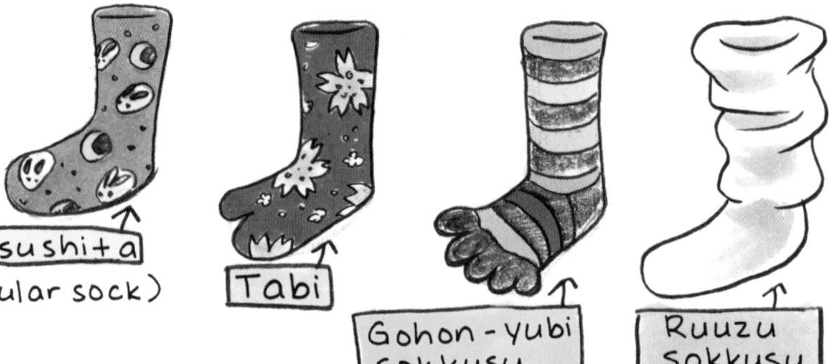

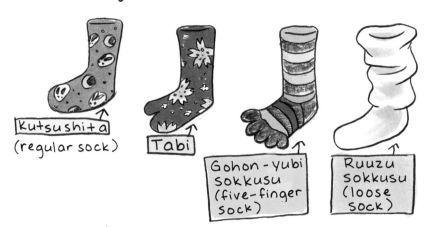

Kutsushita
(regular sock)

Tabi

Gohon-yubi
sokkusu
(five-finger
sock)

Ruuzu
sokkusu
(loose
sock)

Shinjuku Map

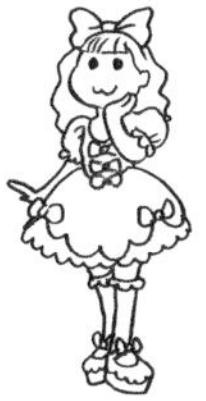

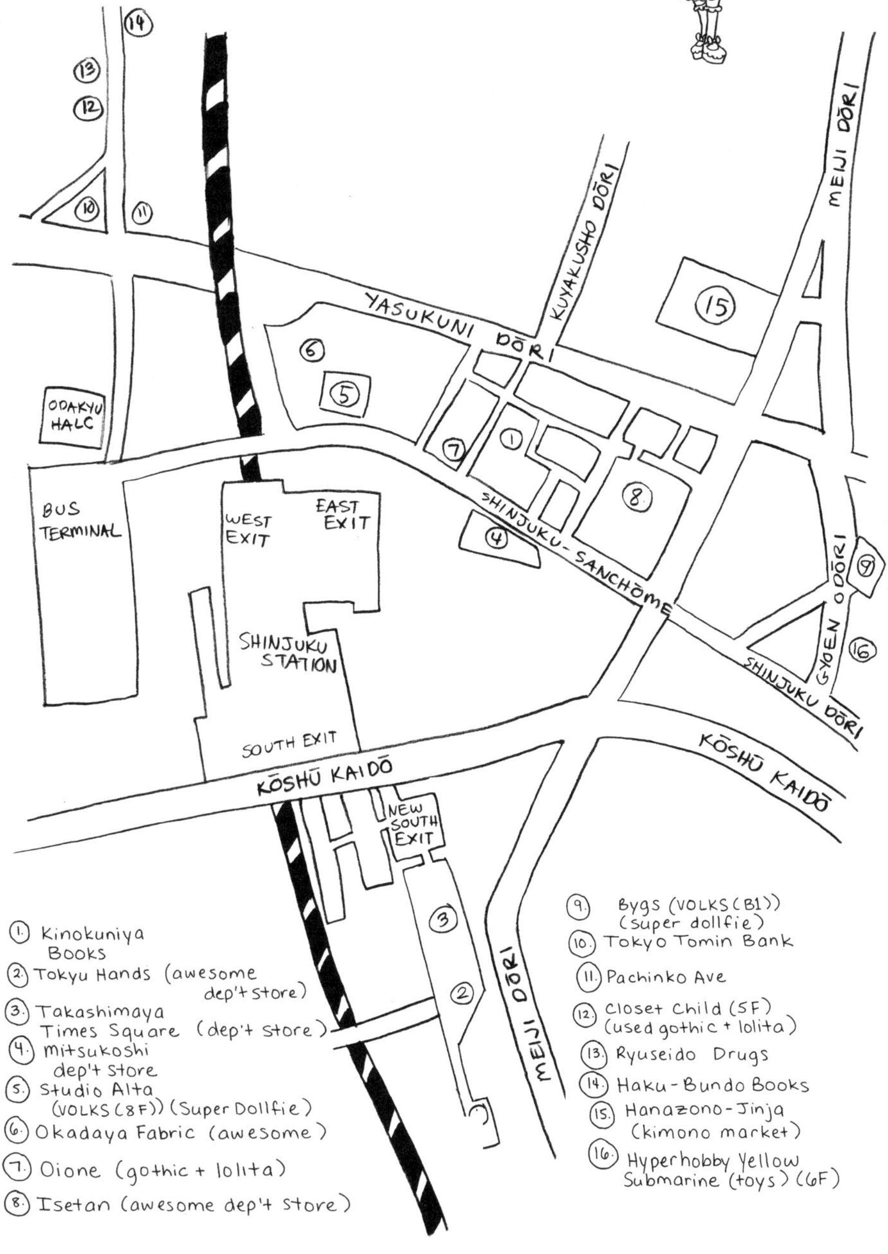
14
13
12
10
11
YASUKUNI DŌRI
KUYAKUSHO DŌRI
MEIJI DŌRI
15
6
5
ODAKYU HALC
7
1
8
BUS TERMINAL
WEST EXIT
EAST EXIT
4
SHINJUKU-SANCHŌME
9
GYOEN ODŌRI
16
SHINJUKU DŌRI
SHINJUKU STATION
SOUTH EXIT
KŌSHŪ KAIDŌ
KŌSHŪ KAIDŌ
NEW SOUTH EXIT
3
2
MEIJI DŌRI
1. Kinokuniya Books
2. Tokyu Hands (awesome dep't store)
3. Takashimaya Times Square (dep't store)
4. mitsukoshi dep't store
5. Studio Alta (VOLKS (8F)) (Super Dollfie)
6. Okadaya Fabric (awesome)
7. Oione (gothic + lolita)
8. Isetan (awesome dep't store)
9. Bygs (VOLKS (B1)) (super dollfie)
10. Tokyo Tomin Bank
11. Pachinko Ave
12. Closet Child (5F) (used gothic + lolita)
13. Ryuseido Drugs
14. Haku-Bundo Books
15. Hanazono-Jinja (kimono market)
16. Hyperhobby Yellow Submarine (toys) (6F)

A blustery day ♡

Chapter Ten:
VOLKS, at Last

The night before going to VOLKS...

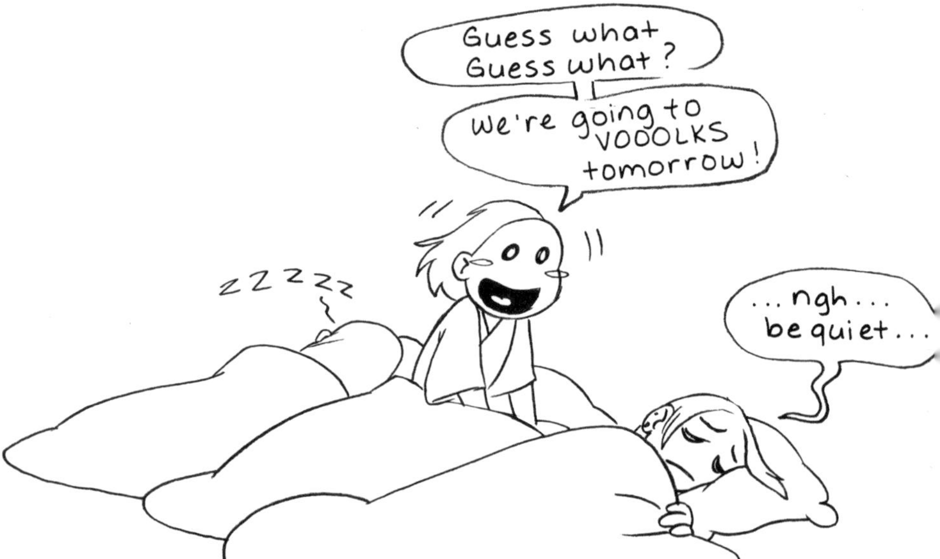
Guess what Guess what?
We're going to VOOOLKS tomorrow!
ZZZZZZ
...ngh... be quiet...

♡ Just like christmas eve ♡

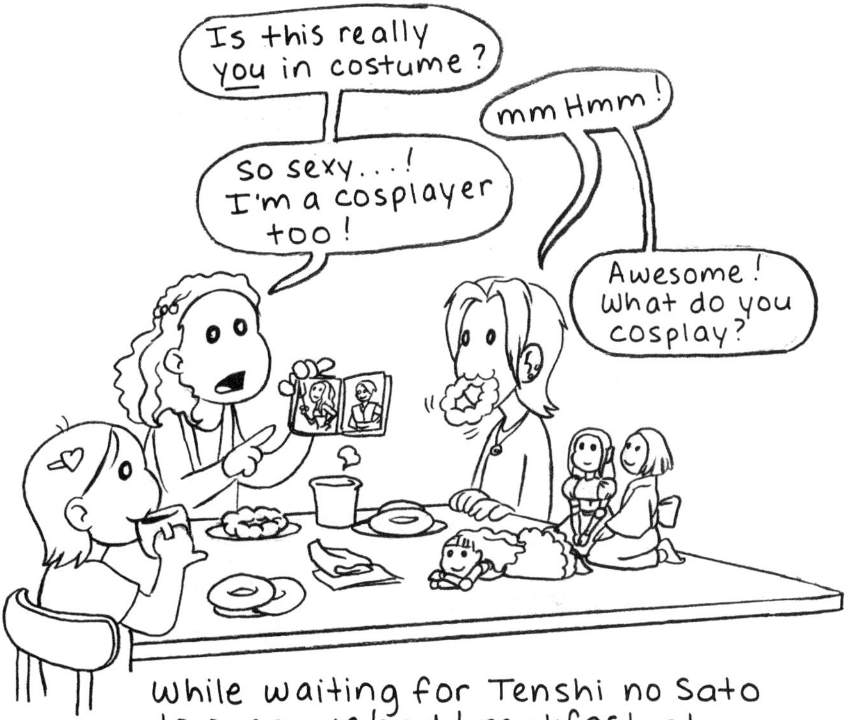
Is this really you in costume?
mm Hmm!
So sexy...! I'm a cosplayer too!
Awesome! What do you cosplay?

While waiting for Tenshi no Sato to open, we had breakfast at Mister Donut. There were other doll fans there, too.

Even though we couldn't speak Japanese, some people were really friendly. We got to know one lady who was a cosplayer, too! Geeks unite!

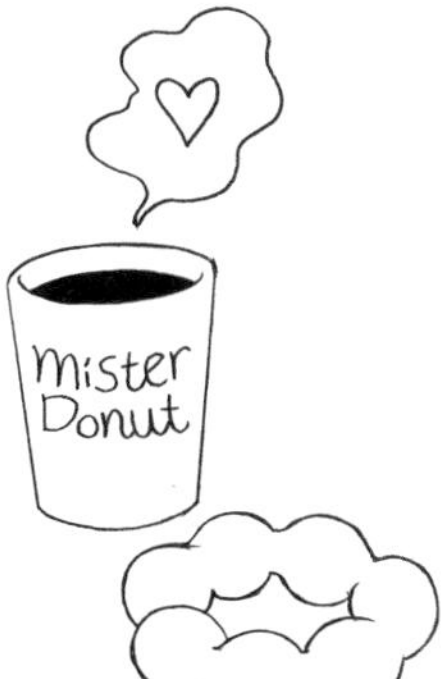
Mister Donut

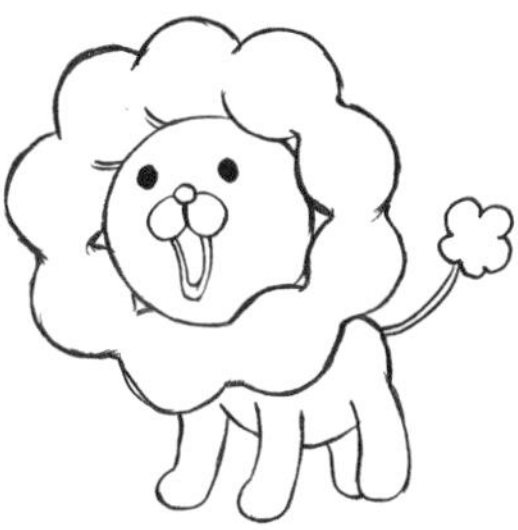

"Super Dollfie Sweet Home
TENSHI NO SATO
This is the place your angels are."

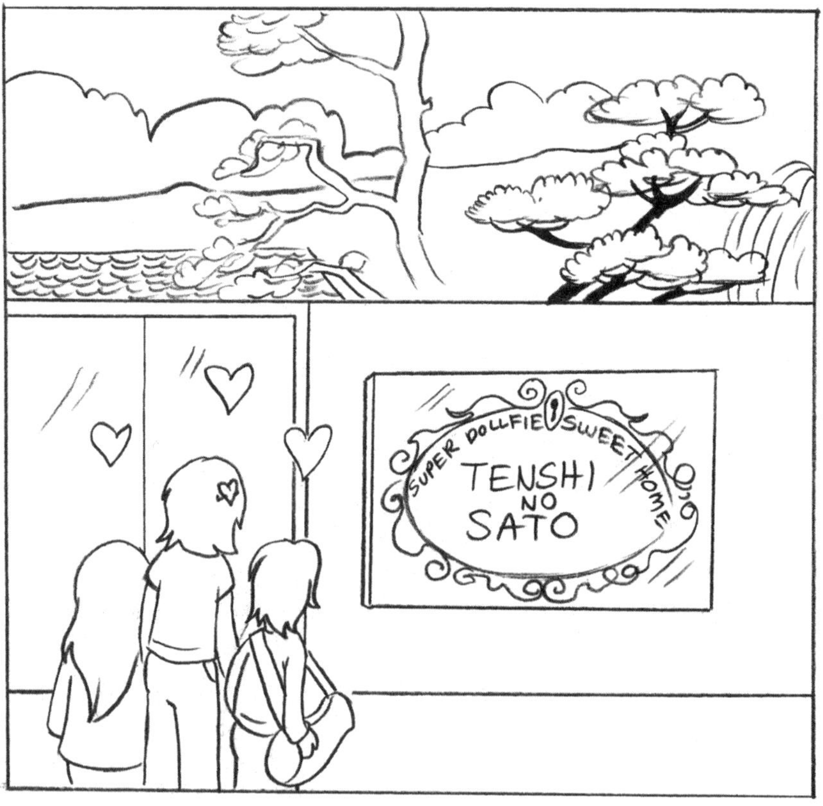
SUPER DOLLFIE SWEET HOME
TENSHI NO SATO

We finally arrived at VOLKS' largest store... Tenshi no Sato. But it's so much more than a "store"!

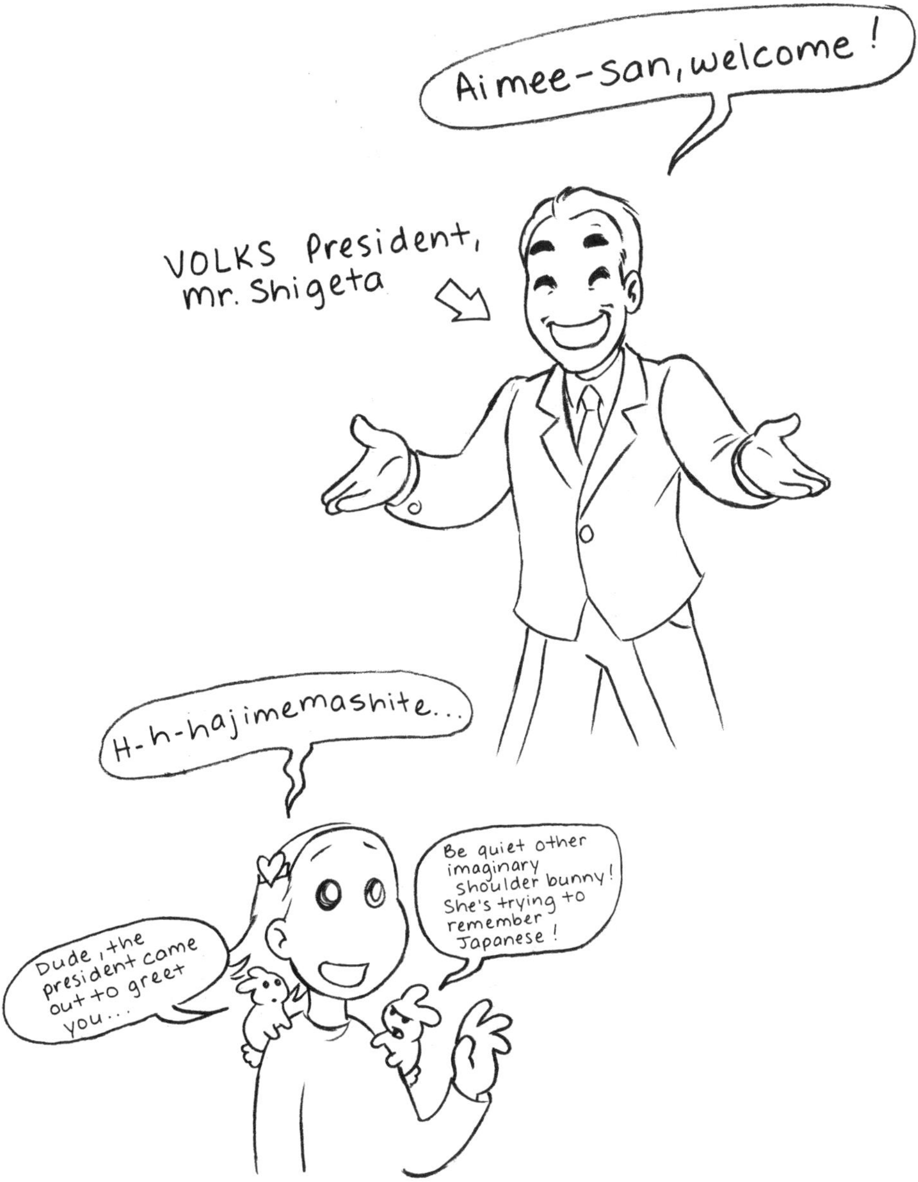
Aimee-san, welcome!
VOLKS President, mr. Shigeta
H-h-hajimemashite...
Dude, the president come out to greet you...
Be quiet other imaginary shoulder bunny! She's trying to remember Japanese!

Map of Tenshi No Sato Main Building

Observation floor
(windows all around!)

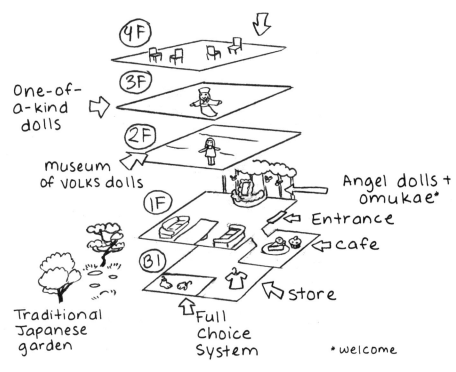

4F

3F

One-of-a-kind dolls ⇨

2F

museum of VOLKS dolls

Angel dolls + omukae*

1F

⇦ Entrance

⇦ cafe

B1

⇦ store

Traditional Japanese garden

Full Choice System

* welcome

1F + 4F Have seats + displays for your dolls, not just sofas for "humans". So you can sit and chat with other doll owners and take photos.

There's also a separate building for classes (How to paint + string dolls, etc.)

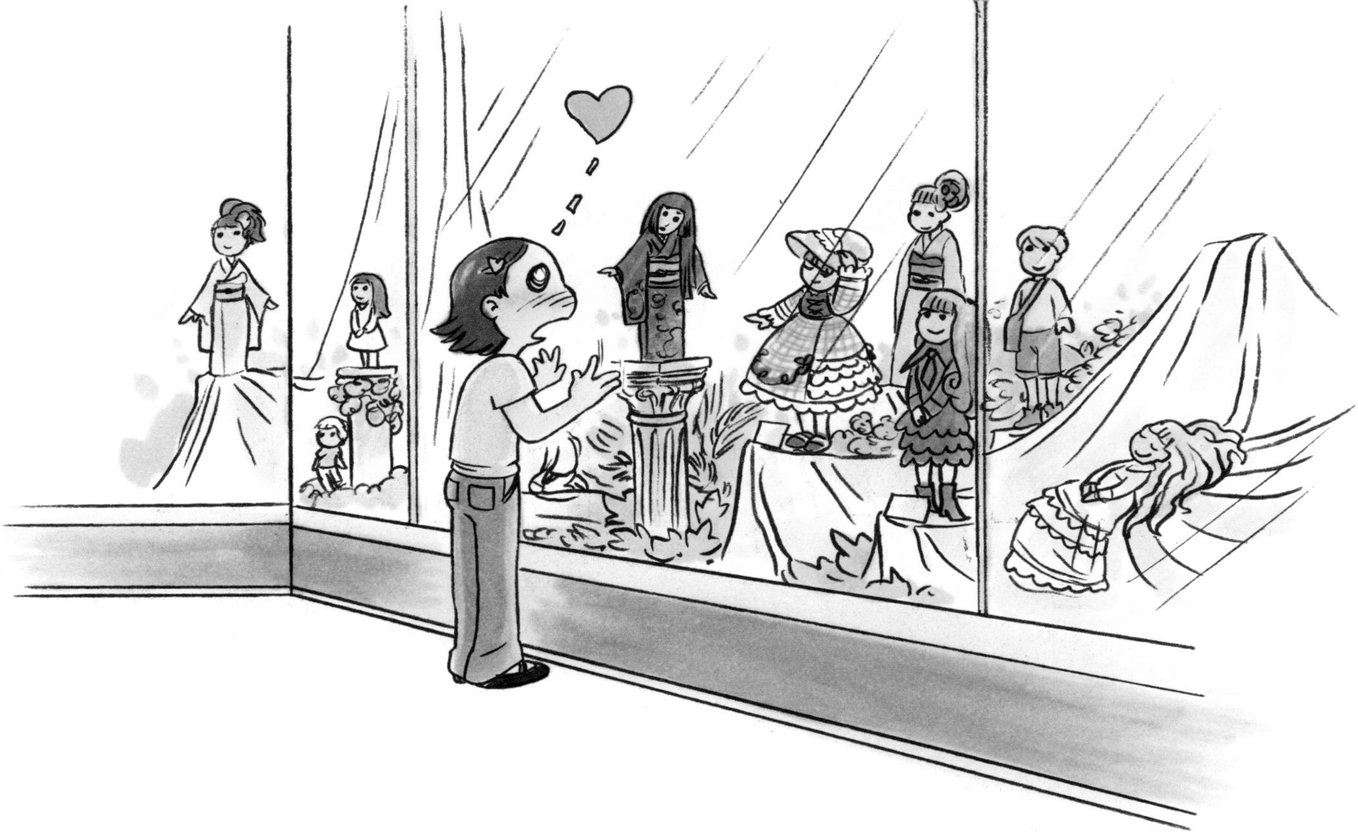

VOLKS has a display of all of the Super Dollfies they have ever made...

Having "cake sets" with dolls

The cafe has huge full-wall windows that look onto a beautiful, manicured Japanese garden.

"Full choice system"

I chose a little
dragon-eared boy
doll

At certain VOLKS stores
you can do "full choice system"
which is where you choose
every part for your doll...
And they make it especially
for you (it even has a
birth certificate... ♡)

∽ VOLKS Omukae Ceremony ∽
(Welcoming Home)

Your friends (and others) can watch

♥ my Doll

Special ceremony velvet cape

Red carpet

The President took photos ⏝⃝

It's basically like a doll adoption, complete with an official certificate.
The text of the ceremony says that VOLKS hopes your doll will bring you peace for the rest of your life together. ♡

♡ It's so sweet. ♡

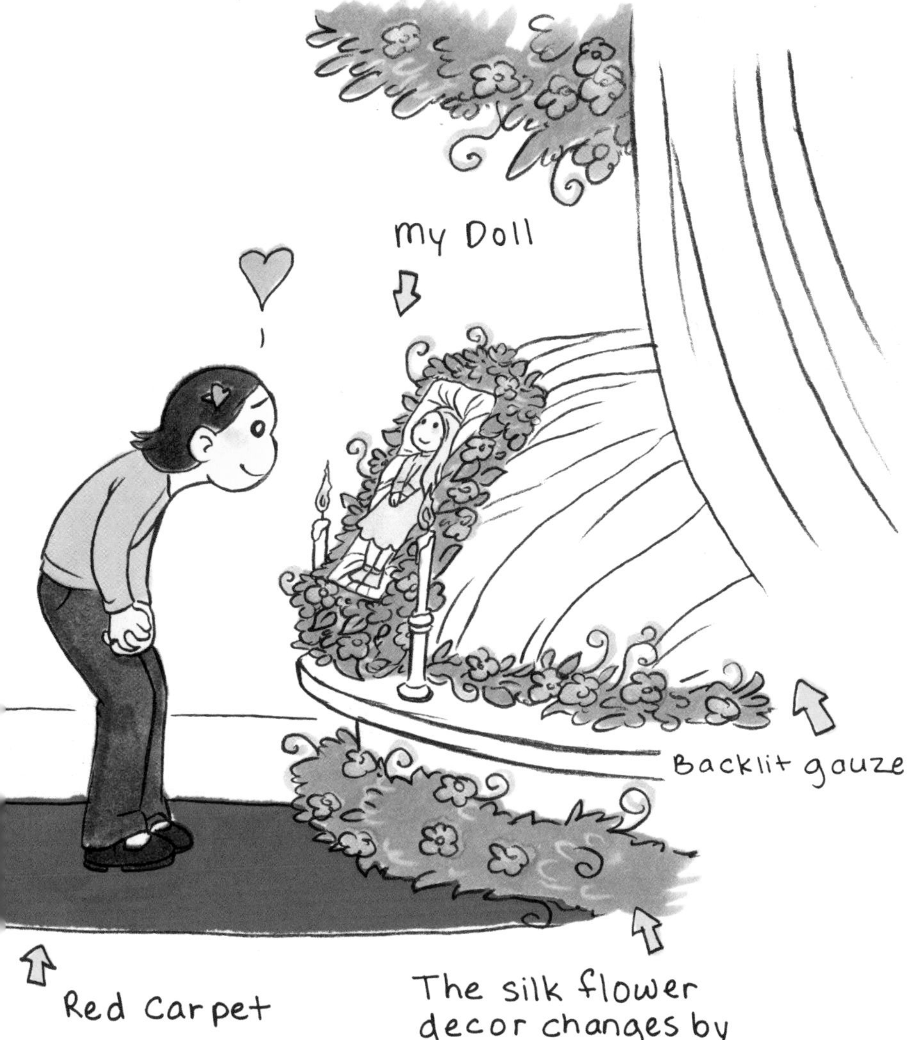
my Doll
Backlit gauze
Red Carpet
The silk flower decor changes by the season

You blow
out the candle
to blow life into
your doll.

And to signify the
start of your life
together. ♡

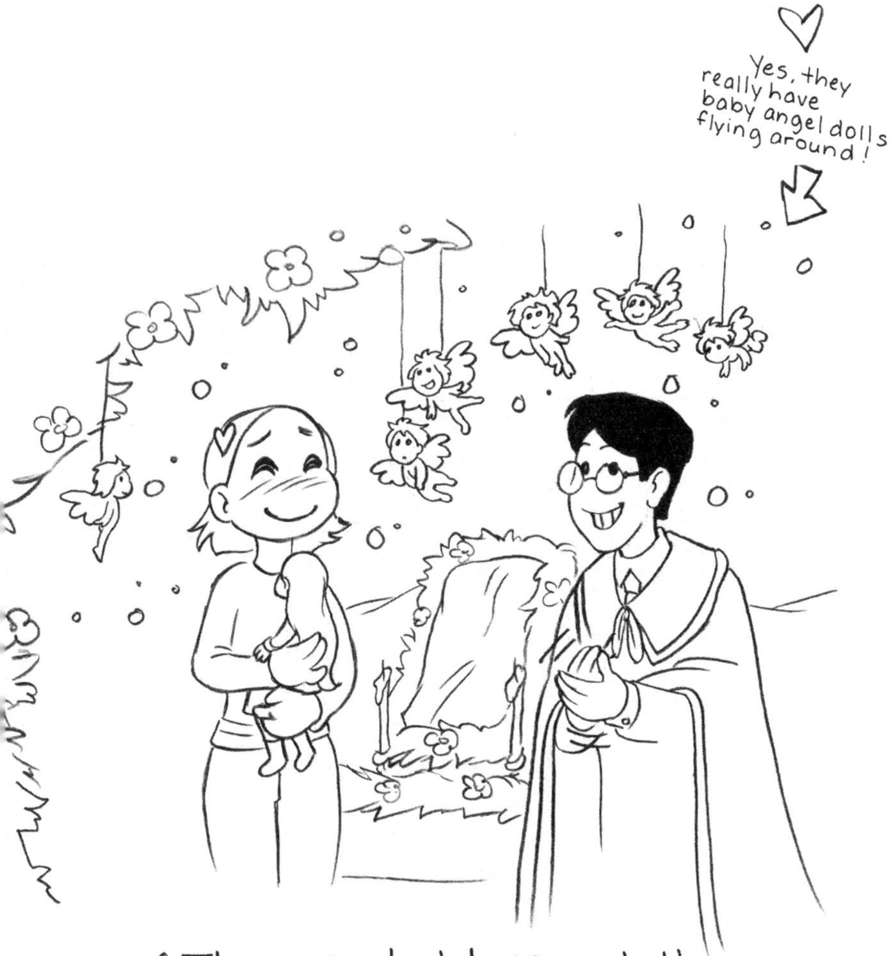
Yes, they really have baby angel dolls flying around!

♡ Then you hold your doll and everyone claps for you. ♡

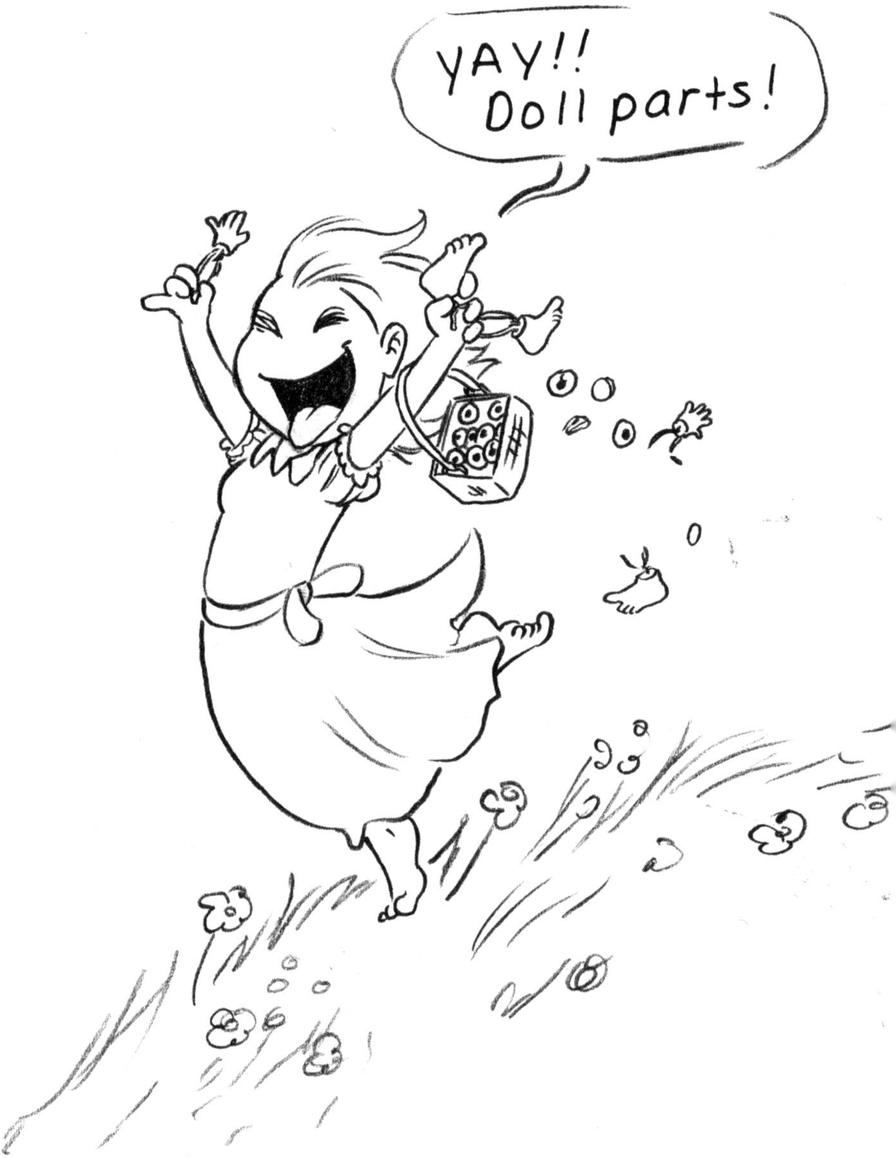
YAY!! Doll parts!

Tenshi (angel) display.

The tenshi are dolls only available at Tenshi No Sato...

I feel like I'm missing something

You can buy wigs, shoes, eyes, clothes and even doll parts (like hands...)

I had dreamt of visiting a VOLKS store for years... now that I'd finally reached it... it was hard to leave. Especially at Tenshi No Sato.

The President then invited us to have dinner with him and his daughters. (It is a family business. ♡)

♡ He took us to a traditional Japanese restaurant. ♡

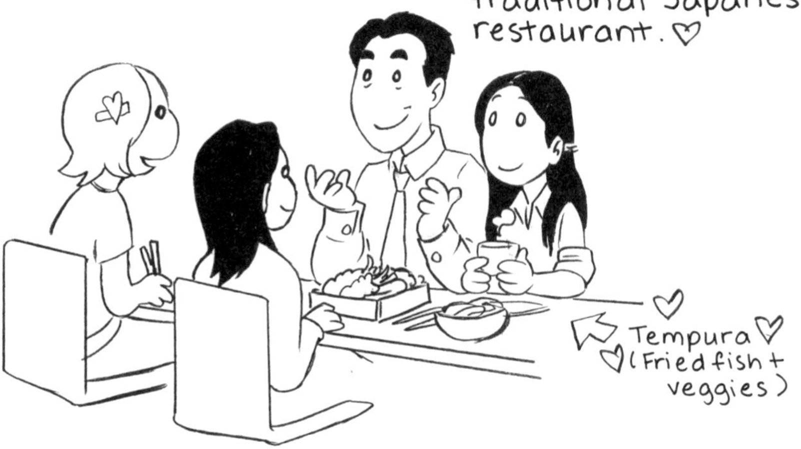
♡ Tempura ♡
♡ (Fried fish + veggies)

We talked about how people in Japan and the U.S.A. feel about dolls... how they make their dolls... and VOLKS' plans for a store in the U.S.A!

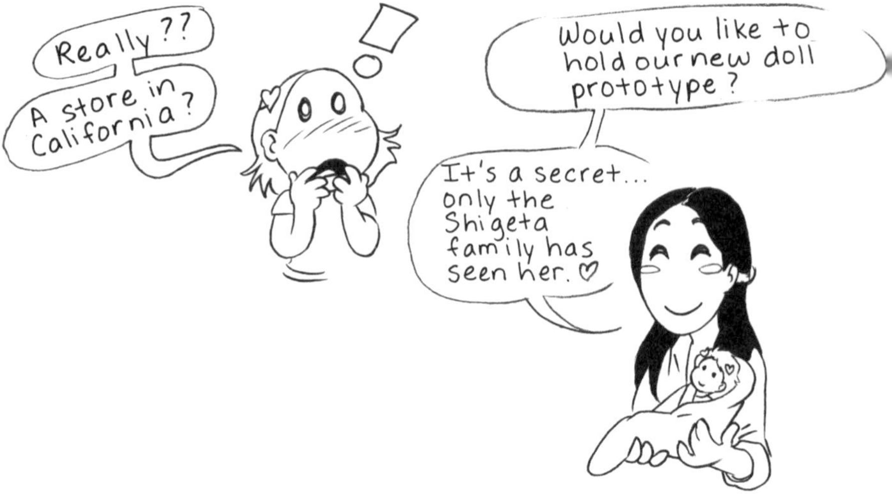
Really??
A store in California?
Would you like to hold our new doll prototype?
It's a secret... only the Shigeta family has seen her. ♡

When I finally got to
visit my first
VOLKS store in Japan...
I kept the plastic bag
my purchases came in.
It was like a culmination
of a quest.

Soon after that wonderful day, it was time to go home to the U. S.

We did everything on our checklist and then some. I'll never forget my wonderful trip with wonderful friends.

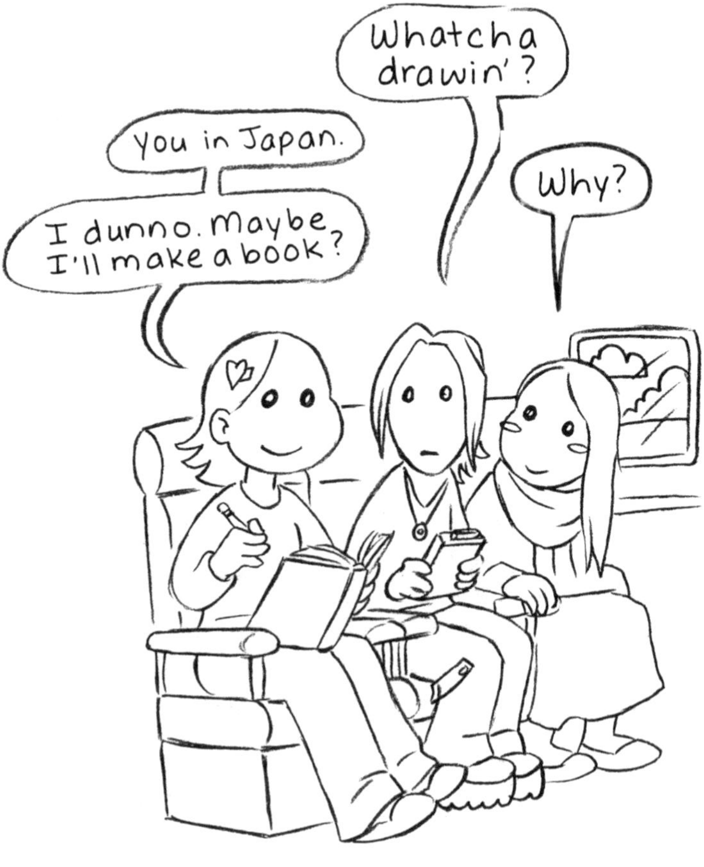
Whatcha drawin'?
You in Japan.
Why?
I dunno. Maybe I'll make a book?

The plane ride home...

As Ferris Bueller Says:
"If you have the means,
I highly recommend it."

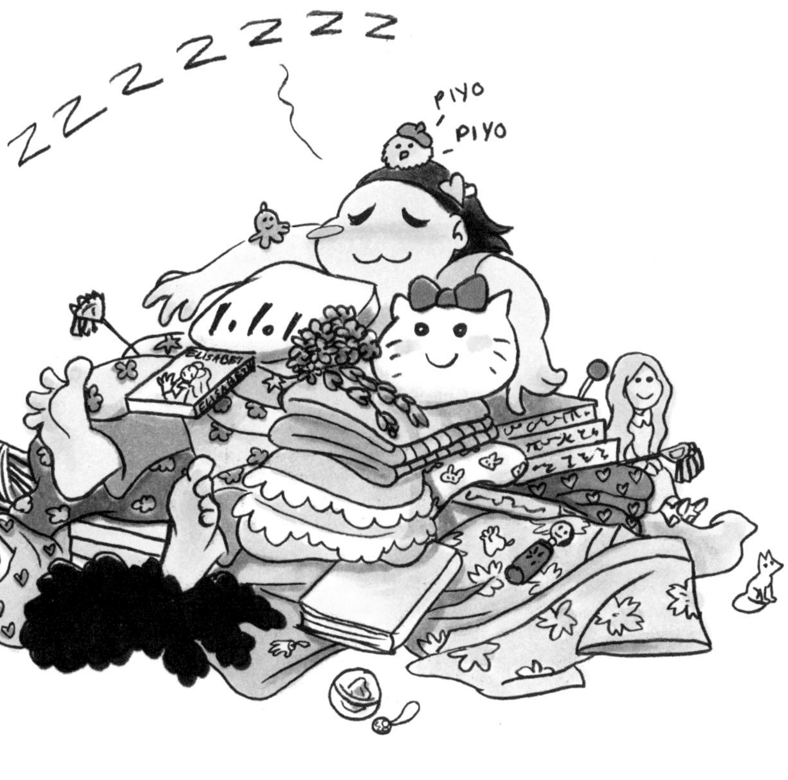
ZZZZZZZZ
PIYO
PIYO
ELISABETH
ELISABETH
POCKY
TEA

GLOSSARY

A

Akihabara — Located less than five minutes by rail from Tokyo Station, Akihabara (also known as Akiba) is best known as one of the largest shopping areas in Tokyo for electronics and computer gear, as well as *anime* and *otaku* merchandise.

Arigatō Gozaimasu — Polite Japanese for "Thank you."

Atelier Boz — An apparel company whose fashion sense runs in the Gothic Aristocrat vein.

B

BLEACH — A popular *shōnen manga* by Tite Kubo about a boy who inadvertently joins the world of Soul Reapers and must fight evil spirits. It's been running in *Shonen Jump Magazine* since 2001, was adapted into an *anime* and a game, and won the 50th Annual Shogakukan *Manga* Award in 2004.

C

Chobits — A *manga* and *anime* series created by CLAMP, Chobits is the story of a shy young man who rescues a pretty female robot from the trash and helps her discover the hidden powers given to her by her creator.

Cosplay — Rumored to have been coined by Nov Takahashi at the 1984 Los Angeles World Science Fiction Convention, this word is a contraction of the English phrase "costume play." In Japan, this sub-culture hobby centers on dressing as characters from *manga, anime* and video games. In America, it can also just mean wearing a costume.

D

Daikaijū — Japanese for "big monster" (such as Godzilla).

Decorer — A street fashion in Japan that is gaudy and overly cute.

Dōjinshi — Self-published Japanese *manga* or novels created by a group of amateurs and/or professionals known as a "circle." The term "*dōjin*" literally means "same person," referring to the fact that the team of creators all share the same interest and passion to publish their work.

E

EGG — A *Kogal*-centric fashion magazine for girls who like to party.

F

Fruits Basket — A *shōjo manga* series which was adapted into a 26-episode *anime*. The story follows an orphan girl named Tohru as she discovers the secret of the family who takes her in: they are possessed by the twelve animal spirits of the Chinese Zodiac.

Furisode — Made of very fine, brightly colored silk, this formal style of kimono is often worn on "Coming of Age Day" (the second Monday of January) by young women who are twenty years old.

G

Gaijin — Japanese for "outsider" or "foreigner."

Ganguro or Kogal — An alternative fashion trend among young Japanese women featuring dyed hair (mostly blonde, but sometimes several colors) and a deep tan. Black and white eyeliner, false eyelashes, platform shoes, tie-dyed sarongs, mini-skirts and a bunch of bracelets, rings and necklaces complete the look. Because the deep tan, use of slang and suspicious hygiene contradict ideals of traditional Japanese beauty, *Ganguro* girls are treated like outcasts by mainstream Japanese society.

Gashapon — This word is made up of two sounds: "*gasha*" (the crank on a toy machine turning) and "*pon*" (the sound of the toy capsule dropping into the dispenser). It refers to both the machines themselves and to the exquisitely detailed and highly collectable little toys they dispense.

Geiko — The Kyoto dialect version of the word "*geisha*."

Geisha — The proper noun for a high-class league of traditional female performers in Japan. The two kanji that make up this noun are "art" and "performer" as these women are trained in the arts of music, dance, and conversation.

Geta — A traditional Japanese wooden clog with a thong that fits between the first two toes, and a pair of transverse supports on the bottom of the sole.

Gomennasai — Polite Japanese for "I'm sorry."

H

Hakama — A type of traditional Japanese garment for men which is tied at the waist and falls to the ankles, resembling a wide, pleated skirt.

Han-eri — In traditional Japanese dress, a protective sheath of cloth sewn into the collar of the main under-kimono (the *juban*). *Han-eri* come in many different colors and patterns and, though small, add a very beautiful touch to a kimono.

Hello Kitty — The best-known of many fictional characters created by the Japanese company Sanrio, Hello Kitty is adored by everyone from little girls to witty goths. Her charming face is recognized all over the world on a host of products.

I

Inuyasha — A popular *shōnen manga* by the prolific *manga-ka* Rumiko Takahashi. The story is about a modern-day girl who falls into the past, where she teams up with the half-demon Inuyasha to find the shards of a magic jewel before they fall into the wrong hands. It was adapted into a 167-episode long *anime* that ran from 2000 to 2004. The *manga* itself is still going as of this writing.

Itadakimasu — The thanks given before a meal in Japanese meaning literally "I humbly receive."

K

Kakkōii — Japanese for "attractive" or "cool."

Kawaii — Japanese for "cute."

Kodona — Inspired by Victorian boys, this Japanese fashion includes masculine blouses and shirts, knickers, short trousers, knee socks, top hats, and newsboy caps. The colors tend to be black, white, blue and burgundy, though the feminine versions have a broader palette. Its name (from *kodomo otona*, literally "child-adult") was coined by Plastic Tree's lead singer Ryūtarō Arimura to describe his fashion sense.

Kogal — see "***Ganguro***"

Konnichiwa — Japanese for "Hello" or "Good afternoon."

L

Lolita — In defiance of the classic definition of "Lolita" created by Vladimir Nabokov's infamous novel of the same name, the term has been transformed into a fashion style, frilly and doll-like, which is meant to brazenly defy the idea of "dressing sexy for your boyfriend" and instead embrace the idea of dressing cute and pretty regardless of whether the look is sexy or not.

M

Magic Knight Rayearth — A popular *shōjo manga* of the magical girl genre created by CLAMP about a trio of high school girls on a quest to save the princess of a magical land. It was also made into an *anime* series and several video games.

Maiko — Apprentices to *geisha*, these girls dress more flamboyantly, with chalk-white face makeup, and elaborate hairdos and kimono.

Mandarake — A used *manga/anime* store chain in Japan which sells *manga*, figures, animation cels, costumes, and other really cool stuff. The HQ of Mandarake is in Nakano, Tokyo where the store envelops three whole floors of the Nakano Broadway strip.

Marie Antoinette — A queen of France guillotined during the French Revolution. She was known for her elaborate wardrobe, excessively complicated wigs and reputed insensitivity to the masses.

Macha — Japanese for a particular kind of powdered green tea used in tea ceremonies.

Moi-même-Moitié — One of the founders of the Gothic and Lolita fashion movement was Mana, the lead guitarist of Malice Mizer. Mana's brand of clothing may be the only brand that can truly be called "Elegant Gothic Lolita" (also known as EGL). His pieces tend to be dark and sophisticated, rather than cute and sweet like other Lolita fashions.

My Neighbor Totoro — A charming and beautiful animated 1988 film written and directed by Hayao Miyazaki. It is the story of two young girls who encounter fanciful forest spirits in postwar Japan.

O

Obi — A wide, often sumptuously embroidered sash which fastens in the back with a large flat bow. This is worn over a kimono by women in Japan as a part of their traditional dress.

Oiran — High-ranking courtesans from the Yoshiwara red-light district in Tokyo who thrived until the *geisha* class replaced them. Now, to preserve this cultural heritage, a celebration in their honor is held through the form of a yearly parade in Niigata prefecture.

Ōji — Japanese for "prince."

Okobo — Traditional high platform wooden sandals worn by *maiko*. The soles of these sandals are made of unfinished wood and are usually quite plain. The straps of the *okobo* vary in color, following a red to yellow progression depending upon the rank of the *maiko*.

Otokoyaku — A combination of the words for "man" and "role" in Japanese, it is the highest and most honored position to gain in the Takarazuka theatre troupe. Playing a lead male role, the actress is idolized by passionate fans.

P

Pocky — A brand of cookie sticks dipped in chocolate and other flavors. This sweet snack has found a home with American *anime* fans and is the perfect energy food at conventions.

Psycho le Cému — A Japanese rock band in the "visual kei" genre, whose image and stage presentation are the main focus of their performance. They are most famous for their over-the-top costumes reminiscent of "magical girl" *anime*.

Purikura — The Japanese combination of the English words "print club," this term refers to special photo booths as well as the small 1"x1" sticker photos they produce. The photo booth allows the user to apply decals and write on the photos taken before printing them, making them very unique mementos.

R

Ramen — In America, this is a very inexpensive package of noodles that comes with powdered sauce packets, but in Japan it can also be a large, fresh bowl of soup filled with thin noodles, fresh vegetables, and juicy meat.

Revolutionary Girl Utena — An *anime* and *manga* about a girl who dresses like a prince and must fight a series of sword duels at her exclusive and mysterious boarding school. The look of this story was clearly influenced by "Rose of Versailles," and it has been made into a number of stage productions, including the "Comedie Musicale Utena la fillette révolutionnaire," which was presented by an all-female Takarazuka-style cast.

Rūzu sokkusu — The Japanese pronunciation of the phrase "loose socks," this footwear is like a regular sock, only with a super long neck that, even when pulled up to the knee, falls in heaps over the wearer's feet. They are popular among school girls as they are believed to make thick legs look thin.

S

Sailor Moon — The famous media franchise created by Japanese *manga* artist Naoko Takeuchi, credited with reviving the "magical girl" genre. The story is about a team of teenage girls in short skirts who battle the evils of the universe with their magical powers.

Sake — Japanese rice wine, also called "*nihonshū*."

Sakura Taisen — Literally "Cherry Battle," this video game was a cross between a tactical war game and a dating sim, which eventually exploded into a widespread media franchise resulting in an animated series, motion picture, and *manga*.

Shōjo manga — Japanese comics aimed specifically at young girls (*shōjo*).

Shōnen manga — Japanese comics aimed specifically at young boys (*shōnen*), though these *manga* are often read by both genders.

Sumimasen — Japanese for "I'm sorry" or "Pardon me."

Super Dollfie — A brand of customizable ball-jointed dolls manufactured by VOLKS. Super Dollfies are known for their beauty, personality and exquisite manufacture. Usually about 22 inches tall, they are made of polyurethane resin and strung together with thick elastic. Unlike most dolls, their hair, eyes, face paint, hands, feet, head, and other body parts can be changed as you like.

T

Takarazuka Revue —An all-female performance troupe founded in 1913. They transform plays, musicals, movies, and even *manga* into glitzy, glamorous stage shows.

Takoyaki —A Japanese dumpling snack, essentially fried octopus (*tako*) balls on a stick.

Tempura — Batter-dipped and deep-fried delicacies, which can be anything from seafood and meat to vegetables, and even ice cream. Though *tempura* in the United States is usually regarded as cheap food, high-quality *tempura* in Japan can be rather expensive.

Tokyu Hands — A chain of craft stores, often several stories high and always brimming with craft supplies.

U

Udon — A type of thick, wheat-based noodle, very popular in Japanese cuisine, and usually served hot in a mildly flavored broth. Common toppings include thinly chopped scallions, tempura shrimp, sugared deep-fried tofu pockets, and a crescent-shaped fish cake.

V

VOLKS — A company that manufactures ball-jointed dolls (including their Super Dollfie brand) of the highest quality.

W

Wasabi — A member of the cabbage family, which grows naturally along stream beds in the mountain river valleys of Japan, this is also known as "Japanese horseradish." The strongly-flavored root is finely grated and sold as a paste, most often used in sushi. The flavor evaporates quickly, which is why sushi chefs put it between the rice and the fish, instead of on top.

Y

Yakuza — Japanese gangsters. The *yakuza* belong to recognized groups, encourage a samurai-esque loyalty, and are fiercely proud of their traditions.

Yukata — Usually made of cotton, linen or hemp, these lightweight summer kimono are worn to festivals, and are provided at *onsen* resorts.

Z

Zōri — Sandals made of cloth, leather or woven grass, these are worn by both men and women and are similar to flip-flops.

APPENDIX

VISITING JAPAN

USING THE JAPAN RAIL:

Japan Guide
http://www.japan-guide.com/e/e2361.html

Kintetsu International
http://www.kintetsu.com/jrpass/
(Purchase a rail pass from abroad.)

Official JR website
http://www.japanrailpass.net/

FINDING CHEAP HOTELS:

Japan National Tourist Organization
http://www.jnto.go.jp/

Japan Youth Hostels, Inc.
http://www.jyh.or.jp/english/

Sakura Hotel
http://www.sakura-hotel.co.jp/
reserve@sakura-hotel.co.jp
2-21-4 Kanda-Jimbocho, Chiyoda-ku,
Tokyo 101-0051
〒101-0051 東京都千代田区神田神保町2-21-4
TEL: 03-3261-3939
(Popular with young, cheap travelers.)

ONLINE GUIDES TO JAPAN:

Japanican
http://www.japanican.com/
(About Japanese tours, hotels, and hot springs.)

Japan Travel and Living Guide
http://www.japan-guide.com

Kyoto City Tourism and Culture Information System
http://kaiwai.city.kyoto.jp/raku/modules/english/index.php

Kyoto Visitor's Guide
http://www.kyotoguide.com

BOOKS ABOUT JAPAN

Cruising The Anime City: An Otaku Guide To Neo Tokyo
Patrick Macias and Tomohiro Machiyama
ISBN-13: 978-1880656884

KYOTO: Seven Paths to the Heart of the City
Diane Durston
ISBN-13: 978-4770028778

Lonely Planet Japan
Chris Rowthorn
ISBN-13: 978-1740599245
http://www.lonelyplanet.com/worldguide/destinations/asia/japan/

Tokyo City Atlas: A Bilingual Guide
Atsushi Umeda
ISBN-13: 978-4770025036

VOLKS DOLLS

ABOUT VOLKS:

VOLKS Websites
http://www.volks.co.jp/en/
http://volksusa.com/

Contacting VOLKS
311 Tsuchiya-cho, Takatsuji-agaru,
Inokuma-dori, Shimogyo-ku, Kyoto 600-8396
〒600-8396 京都府京都市下京区猪熊通高辻上ル
槌屋町311
TEL: 075-813-1171
imos@volks.co.jp

STORE LOCATIONS:

Akihabara Showroom
Radio Kaikan 6th Floor, 1-15-16 Soto-Kanda,
Chiyoda-ku, Tokyo 101-0021
〒101-0021 東京都千代田区外神田1-15-16
ラジオ会館6F
TEL: 03-5295-8160

Ikebukuro Showroom

Kato-Daiichi Bldg. 1st Floor, 3-12-5 Higashi Ikebukuro, Toyoshima-ku, Tokyo 170-0013

〒170-0013東京都豊島区東池袋3-12-5 加藤第一ビル1F

TEL: 03-5957-7356

Kuzuha Shop

2-22-10-106 Kuzuha Namiki, Hirakata City, Osaka 573-1118

〒573-1118大阪府枚方市くずは並木2-22-10-106

TEL: 072-867-1316

Osaka Showroom

4-9-14 Nipponbashi, Naniwa-ku, Osaka City, Osaka 556-0005

〒556-0005大阪府大阪市浪速区日本橋4-9-14

TEL: 06-6648-6832

Shinjuku Showroom

Bigs Shinjuku Basement Lv. 1, Shinjuku 2-19, Shinjuku-ku, Tokyo 160-0022

〒160-0022東京都新宿区新宿2-19

ビッグス新宿B1F

TEL: 03-5269-8518

Tachikawa Showroom

From Nakatake Bldg. 7th Floor, 2-11-2 Akebono-cho, Tachikawa City, Tokyo 190-0012

〒190-0012東京都立川市曙町2-11-2 フロム中武7F

TEL: 042-527-0931

TENSHI NO SATO:

Tenshi No Sato website

http://www.volks.co.jp/en/volks/tenshinosato/

Store Location

Tenshi-no-Sato Kachu-an 天使の里　霞中庵

12 Wakamiya-cho, Saga Tenryu-ji, Ukyo-ku, Kyoto 616-8371

〒616-8371京都府京都市右京区嵯峨天竜寺若宮町12番地

TEL: 075-872-3100

Daily: 11am – 5pm

Wed: Closed

Yuzuko's Tenshi no Sato Walking Guide

http://www.honey-drop.net/work/sato/intro.htm

MORE DOLLS

GENERAL:

Den of Angels

http://denofangels.com/

(Online community and website about dolls.)

http://www.denofangels.com/forums/showthread.php?t=114662

(The thread for doll events in Japan.)

Haute Doll Magazine

http://hautedoll.com

(The magazine I write for, which covers all types of popular dolls from Barbie and Gene Marshall to Pinky:st, Blythe and VOLKS Super Dollfie.)

STORES & MUSEUMS:

DollyTeria

http://closetchild-doll.ocnk.net/

info@closet-child.com (Email for ordering from abroad.)

(An online store that sells dolls from all sorts of companies.)

Junie Moon

http://www.juniemoon.jp/index_e.cgi

Suzuen Daikanyama Bldg. 1st Floor, 4-3 Sarugaku-cho, Shibuya-ku, Tokyo 150-0033

〒150-0033 東京都渋谷区猿楽町4-3

鈴円代官山ビル1F

jm@juniemoon.jp

Tues-Sat: 12pm – 10pm • Sun+Hol: 12pm – 6pm

Mon: Closed

http://www.juniemoon.jp/eng/access/index.html

(You can make up a short set of directions to the store using this uber helpful website!)

Kobayashi Doll Museum 小林人形資料館

6-31-2 Yahiro, Sumida-ku, Tokyo 131-0041

〒131-0041東京都墨田区八広6-31-2

TEL: 03-3612-1644

Sat, Sun: 10am – 5pm

Admission: Free, but reservations are required.

Maria Cuore - A "Rockin' Doll Museum"

http://www.mariacuore.com/
Parkway Building Basement Lv. 1, 1-20-9 Jinnan,
Shibuya-ku,Tokyo 150-0041
〒150-0041東京都渋谷区神南1-20-9パークウェイビルB1
TEL: 03-3780-9818
info@mariacuore.com
Daily: 1pm – 7pm • Tues: Closed
1000 yen for adult admission
500 yen for Children 12 and under
Three blocks from the Shibuya station on the
JR line.

Nakanishi Toku Shoten 中西徳商店

Antique doll museum
359 Moto-cho, Yamatooji Higashiiri, Furumonzen-
dori, Higashiyama-ku, Kyoto 605-0089
〒605-0089京都市東山区古門前通大和大路東入元町359
TEL: 075-561-7309
Daily: 10am – 5pm

Tanka 丹嘉

Focuses on Fushimi dolls (伏見人形)
22-504 Hon-cho, Higashiyama-ku, Kyoto 605-
0981
〒605-0981 京都市東山区本町22-504
TEL: 075-561-1627

Toy Museum おもちゃ美術館

http://www.toy-art.co.jp/museum.html
2-12-10 Arai, Nakano-ku, Tokyo 165-0026
〒165-0026東京都中野区新井2-12-10
TEL: 03-3387-5461
Daily: 10:30am – 4pm • Closed: Tues, Fri
Admission: 500 yen

DOLL EVENTS

Doll 1/6

http://doll-onesixth.office-crea.jp/
Yamaguchi Chuo Bldg. Art Space 201 5th Floor,
West 1-7-8, South 2, Chuo-ku, Sapporo City 060-0062
〒 060-0062 札幌市中央区南2条西1-7-8 山口中央ビル
アートスペース201 5F
Admission: FREE

Doll Show

http://dollshow.hp.infoseek.co.jp/
Tokyo Trade Center (Hamamatsu-cho Bldg.), 1-7-
8 Kaigan, Minato-ku, Tokyo 105-0022
〒105-0022 東京都港区海岸1-7-8東京都立産業貿易
センター　浜松町館
Admission: 1000 yen
Held every Spring and Fall.

Doll's Myth

http://dolls-myth.com/
New Osaka Sunny City, Bldg. 2, 5th Floor, 2-2-17
Nishimiyahara, Yodogawa-ku, Osaka 532-0004
〒532-0004大阪市淀川区西宮原 2-2-17 新大阪センイシテ
ィ2号館 5F
Admission: 500 yen

Dolpa

(Short for "Dolls Party.")
http://www.volks.co.jp/en/index.aspx (Scroll down
to "Event Schedule." Some events are held in the
U.S., including L.A.)

iDoll

http://www.youyou.co.jp/idoll/
Tokyo Event held in the Tokyo Ryutsu Center.

NEAT STORES

Animate

http://www.animate-world.com/ (English)
http://www.animate.co.jp/ (Japanese)
The branch featured in this book is in Ikebukuro
across the street from the building complex
known as Sunshine City. It's part of a row of
manga, anime, cosplay, J-Pop, and dōjinshi stores
which include a yaoi-themed Mandarake and a
yellow BL store called Character Queen.

Azone Geestore / Cospa

http://geestore.com/real_gee/nagoya/
http://www.cospa.com/
3-11-34 Osu, Naka-ku, Nagoya City, Aichi 460-0011
〒460-0011 愛知県名古屋市中区大須 3-11-34
TEL: 052-242-3181
Daily: 10:30am – 8pm

Decks Nostalgia Mall (1cho-me Shotengai)
デックス東京ビーチーお台場
http://www.odaiba-decks.com/floor/4f/
1-6-1 Daiba, Minato-ku, Tokyo 135-0091
〒135-0091東京都港区台場1-6-1
TEL: 03-3599-6500

Kiddy Land
http://www.kiddyland.co.jp/
6-1-9 Jingumae, Shibuya-ku, Tokyo 150-0001
〒150-0001東京都渋谷区神宮前6-1-9
Omotesando Street, Harajuku
TEL: 03-3409-3431
Daily: 10am – 9pm • Tues: Closed

Kinokuniya Bookstore 紀伊國屋書店
3-17-7 Shinjuku, Shinjuku-ku, Tokyo 163-8636
〒163-8636新宿区新宿3-17-7
TEL: 03-3354-0131
Daily: 10am – 9pm
The Shinjuku branch is next to Takashimaya (and has a great doll book section).

Nomura Taylor Fabrics ノムラテーラー
http://nomura-tailor.co.jp/
Higashi-iru, Fuya-cho, Shijo-dori, Shimokyo-ku, Kyoto 600-8004
〒600-8004 京都市下京区四条通麩屋町東入ル
TEL: 075-221-4679
Daily: 10am – 7:30pm

Okadaya オカダヤ
Two buildings, one with crafts and the other with fabrics.
http://www.okadaya.co.jp/
3-23-17 Shinjuku, Shinjuku-ku, Tokyo 160-0022
〒160-0022東京都新宿区新宿3-23-17
TEL: 03-3352-5411
Located in Shinjuku near Alta Plaza.

Tokyu Hands 東急ハンズ
http://www.tokyu-hands.co.jp/
5-24-2 Sendagaya, Shibuya-ku, Tokyo 151-0051
〒151-0051東京都渋谷区千駄ヶ谷5-24-2
TEL: 03-5361-3111
The Shinjuku branch is in the same building as Takashimaya.

YumeKoubou, The Maiko Salon
http://www.yumekoubou.info/english/
JKK Bldg. 2nd Floor, 45 Kitanouchi-cho, 9 Minami-ku, Kyoto 608-8411
〒601-8411 京都市南区西九条北の内町45JKKビル2F
TEL: 075-661-0858

FOOD

FOOD MENTIONED IN JAPAN AI:

Sakura Taisen Café
http://www.sakura-taisen.com/romando/
Ikebukuro Gigo TECH 35 Bldg. 7th Floor, 1-21-1 Higashi Ikebukuro, Toyoshima-ku, Tokyo 170-0013
〒170-0013東京都豊島区東池袋1-21-1 TECH35ビル 池袋ギーゴ 7階
TEL: 3-3981-3603

The Lockup
http://r.gnavi.co.jp/k175602/
Mimatsu World Basement Lv. 1, 583-2 Nakano-cho, Shijo-agaru, Shinkyogoku, Nakagyo-ku, Kyoto 604-8042
〒604-8042 京都府京都市中京区新京極四条上る中之町 583-2 ミマツワールドB1
TEL: 075-212-7223

OTHER THEMED RESTAURANTS:

Alice Cafe
http://www.diamond-dining.com/alice/
Taiyo Bldg. 5th Floor, 8-8-5 Ginza, Chuo-ku, Tokyo 104-0061
〒104-0061東京都中央区銀座8-8-5 太陽ビル 5F
TEL: 03-3574-6980
alice@diamond-dining.com

Vampire Cafe
http://www.diamond-dining.com/vampire/
La Paix Bldg. 7th Floor, 6-7-6 Ginza, Chuo-ku, Tokyo 104-0061
〒104-0061東京都中央区銀座6-7-6 La Paix BUILDING 7F
TEL: 03-3289-5360
vampire@diamond-dining.com

TAKARAZUKA

Salon De Takarazuka
http://kageki.hankyu.co.jp/salon/

SkyStage (Takarazuka TV)
http://www.skystage.net/

Takarazuka Grand Theatre Bow Hall
http://kageki.hankyu.co.jp/english/
1-1-57 Sakaemachi, Takarazuka City,
Hyogo 665-8558
〒665-8558 兵庫県宝塚市栄町1-1-57
TEL: 057-000-5100

Takarazuka Wikipedia
http://www.takarazuka-revue.net/takawiki/

Takarazuka (the town)
http://www.hyogo-tourism.jp/english/takarazuka/

FASHION

GENERAL GUIDES:

Avant Gauche
http://www.avantgauche.co.uk/

Gothic & Lolita Bible
http://www.indexcomm.co.jp/kera/mook_01.html
(Monthly Japanese publication which can be
found at most Japanese bookstores.)

Kera
http://www.indexcomm.co.jp/kera/
(Popular fashion magazine with some gothic &
lolita along with punk and fusion.)

Morbid Outlook: "What is Gothic & Lolita?"
http://www.morbidoutlook.com/fashion/
articles/2002_07_gothiclolita.html

Sumire's Tokyo Gothic & Lolita Shopping Guide
http://hillieras.ld.infoseek.co.jp/gothloli/
shopguide.html

Zipper
http://www.zipper.jp/
(Another popular fashion magazine similar in nature
to Kera.)

KIMONO:

Azabu-Ya
http://www.azabu-ya.com/cgi-bin/webc.cgi/
home.html
(Fun Japanese fabric store.)

Fabric TALES
http://www.fabrictales.com/
(Another fun Japanese fabric store.)

Kimono Flea Market Ichiroya
http://www.ichiroya.com/
(A fabulous online kimono and accessory store.)

Mamechiyo's Official Site
http://mamechiyo.jp/
(Mamechiyo-san is famous for making the kimono
more hip and playful. She's made several books
illustrating how to "pop" kimonos up and also has
her own store with Mamechiyo designed shoes,
kimonos and accessories.)

LOLITA:

6% DokiDoki
http://www.dokidoki6.com/
TX101 Bldg. 2nd Floor, 4-28-16 Jingumae,
Shibuya-ku, Tokyo 150-0001
〒150-0001東京都渋谷区神宮前4-28-16 TX101ビル2F
TEL: 03-3479-6116
Daily: 12pm - 8pm
doki6@mb.infoweb.ne.jp

Angelic Pretty
http://www.angelicpretty.com/
La Foret Harajuku Basement Lv. 1.5, 1-11-6
Jingumae, Shibuya-ku, Tokyo 150-0001
〒150-0001東京都渋谷区神宮前1-11-6　ラフォーレ原宿B1.5
TEL: 03-3478-0860
Daily: 11am – 8pm

Baby, the Stars Shine Bright
http://www.babyssb.co.jp/
Daikanyama Tokyu Apt. 1st Floor, 20-23
Daikanyama-cho, Shibuya-ku, Tokyo 150-0034
〒150-0034東京都渋谷区代官山町20-23 代官山東急アパートメント1F
TEL: 03-5459-6687

Innocent World (Classic Lolita)
http://www.innocent-w.jp/
Coxy188 7th Floor, 1-8-8 Jingumae, Shibuya-ku, Tokyo 150-0001
〒150-0001 東京都渋谷区神宮前1-8-8 COXY188 7F
TEL: 03-3403-6018
Daily: 11am – 8pm

Juliette et Justine (Classic Lolita)
http://www.juliette-et-justine.com/
La Foret, Atelier Pierrot Basement Lv. .5, 1-11-6 Jingumae, Shibuya-ku, Tokyo 150-0001
〒150-0001東京都渋谷区神宮前1-11-6 ラフォーレ原宿 B0.5 アトリエピエロ
TEL: 03-3475-0463

Metamorphose
http://www.metamorphose.gr.jp/
Scenic Sekine Bldg. 2nd Floor, 6-28-4 Jingumae, Shibuya-ku, Tokyo 150-0001
〒150-0001 東京都渋谷区神宮前6-28-4 SCENIC関根ビル2F
TEL: 03-3406-6978
Daily: 11am – 8pm • Tues: Closed

Victorian Maiden (Classic Lolita)
http://www.victorianmaiden.com/
La Foret, Atelier Pierrot Basement Lv. 1.5, 1-11-6 Jingumae, Shibuya-ku, Tokyo 150-0001
〒150-0001東京都渋谷区神宮前1-11-6 ラフォーレ原宿 B1.5アトリエピエロ
TEL: 03-3475-0463

GOTHIC LOLITA:

Atelier Boz (Gothic Aristocrat)
http://www.boz.ne.jp/
Kuramochi Bldg. 1st Floor, 1-14-12 Tomigaya, Shibuya-ku, Tokyo 151-0063
〒151-0063 東京都渋谷区富ヶ谷1-14-12クラモチビル1F
TEL: 03-5738-3501

Atelier Pierrot
http://www.netlaputa.ne.jp/~pierrot-/
La Foret, Atelier Pierrot Basement Lv. 1.5, 1-11-6 Jingumae, Shibuya-ku, Tokyo 150-0001

〒150-0001東京都渋谷区神宮前1-11-6 ラフォーレ原宿 B1.5アトリエピエロ
TEL: 03-3475-0463 • Daily: 11am – 8pm

Black Peace Now/ Peace Now
http://www.peacenow.net/
La Foret, Basement Lv. 1.5, 1-11-6 Jingumae, Shibuya-ku, Tokyo 150-0001
〒150-0001東京都渋谷区神宮前1-11-6 ラフォーレ原宿B1.5
TEL: 03-3401-2067
Daily: 11am – 8pm

BodyLine
http://bodyline.co.jp
http://www.rakuten.co.jp/bodyline/
Harajuku Jeunesse Bldg. 2nd Floor, 1-6-15 Jingumae, Shibuya-ku, Tokyo 150-0001
〒150-0001 東京都渋谷区神宮前1-6-15 原宿ジュネスビル2F
TEL: 03-5410-6665 • Daily: 11am – 8pm

h. NAOTO
http://eng.s-inc.com/hnaoto/
Basement Lv. 1, 4-28-12 Jingumae, Shibuya-ku, Tokyo150-0001
〒150-0001東京都渋谷区神宮前 4-28-12 B1
TEL: 03-3478-6466
Mon-Sat: 12pm – 9pm • Sun+Hol: 12pm – 8pm

Moi-même-Moitié (Elegant Gothic Lolita)
http://www.rakuten.co.jp/moi-meme-moitie/
3-18-15 5th Floor, Shinjuku, Shinjuku-ku, Tokyo 160-0022
〒160-0022東京都新宿区新宿3-18-1 5F
TEL: 03-3441-0667
Mon-Sat: 11:30am – 9pm • Sun+Hol: 11:30am – 8:30pm

OTHER & MIXED FASHIONS:

Closet Child (Gothic/Lolita/Punk USED clothing)
http://www.closet-child.com/
Waseda ST Bldg. 5th Floor (lolita) & 6th Floor (gothic/punk), 7-10-20 West Shinjuku, Shinjuku-ku, Tokyo 160-0023
〒160-0023東京都新宿区西新宿7-10-20 ワセダSTビル 5F (ロリータ)/6F(ゴス・パンク)
TEL: 03-3365-6361 (5th Floor)
03-3365-6317 (6th Floor) • Daily: 11am – 9pm

Excentrique (corsets)

http://www.excentrique.biz/

Marui Young Bldg. 5th Floor, 3-18-1 Shinjuku, Shinjuku-ku, Tokyo 160-0022

〒160-0022 東京都新宿区新宿3-18-1　マルイヤング館5F

TEL: 03-3352-0771

Daily: 11am – 9pm • Mon+Hol: 11am – 8:30pm

Wed: Closed

Jane Marple (Lolita, retro, etc)

http://www.janemarple-stmm.co.jp/

La Foret 2nd Floor, 1-11-6 Jinguumae, Shibuya-ku, Tokyo150-0001

〒150-0001東京都渋谷区神宮前1-11-6　ラフォーレ原宿2F

TEL: 03-3408-5119

MA/MAM (Gothic, Punk, Lolita)

http://www.maxicimam.com/

La Foret, Basement Lv. 1.5, 1-11-6 Jingumae, Shibuya-ku, Tokyo 150-0001

〒150-0001東京都渋谷区神宮前1-11-6　ラフォーレ原宿B1.5

TEL: 03-3405-8870

Daily: 11am – 8pm

Mari's Rock (Gothic/Punk)

http://www.maris-rock.co.jp/

1st Floor, 1-8-3 Jingumae, Shibuya-ku, Tokyo 150-0001

〒150-0001東京都渋谷区神宮前1-8-3 1F

TEL: 03-3423-0069

Putumayo (Punk/Lolita)

http://www.putumayo-home.com/putumayo.html

La Foret, Basement Lv. 1.5, 1-11-6 Jingumae, Shibuya-ku, Tokyo 150-0001

〒150-0001東京都渋谷区神宮前1-11-6　ラフォーレ原宿B1.5

TEL: 03-3404-3627

Daily: 11am – 8pm

Sex Pot Revenge (Gothic/Punk)

http://www.sexpot-revenge.com/

Ranzan Annex 1st Floor and Basement, 1-8-25 Jingumae, Shibuya-ku, Tokyo 150-0001

〒150-0001 東京都渋谷区神宮前1-8-25ランザン・アネックス 1F-B

TEL: 03-3796-8939

Daily: 11am – 8pm

Takuya Angel (Kimono/Punk/Fusion)

http://homepage.mac.com/takuya_angel/

COXY 176 Bldg. 203 2nd Floor, 1-7-10 Jingumae, Shibuya-ku, Tokyo 550-0014

〒550-0014東京都渋谷区神宮前1-7-10 COXY 176 ビル203 2F

TEL: 03-3478-5867

Daily: 12pm – 7pm

Too tall for Torii!

Aimee Major Steinberger grew up in Charleston, South Carolina. She is a professional animator and layout artist whose work can be seen on *The Simpsons* and *Futurama*, as well as in Disney's Three Caballeros ride at Epcot and the Warner Bros. film *Looney Tunes Back in Action*. She is well-known in the doll world as a staff writer for Haute Doll Magazine and an administrator for denofangels.com, the largest English-language Asian ball-jointed doll website and forum in the world. Her passion for costumes has earned her multiple cosplaying awards, including Best in Show at several of the world's largest conventions. She currently lives in California.

ACKNOWLEDGEMENTS

My deepest gratitude to my editors and publisher, Go! Comi, for helping me to find a coherent voice within my scattered journal pages.

Thank you to VOLKS' Shigeta family for showing me amazing kindness.

Thank you to Heather Russel, Susan Goldberg, Cheryll DelRosario, Charlene Ingram and the members of the Takarazuka, EGL and denofangels.com forums for their invaluable advice.

Thank you to my parents and my husband for putting up with my obsessions and supporting me always.

Lastly, thank you to my travel companions, A.J. Wu and Judy Grivich. I knew we would have fun no matter what because we were together. Thank you, ladies, for getting gloriously lost with me.

And dear reader, when you visit Japan, I hope you get gloriously lost, too!

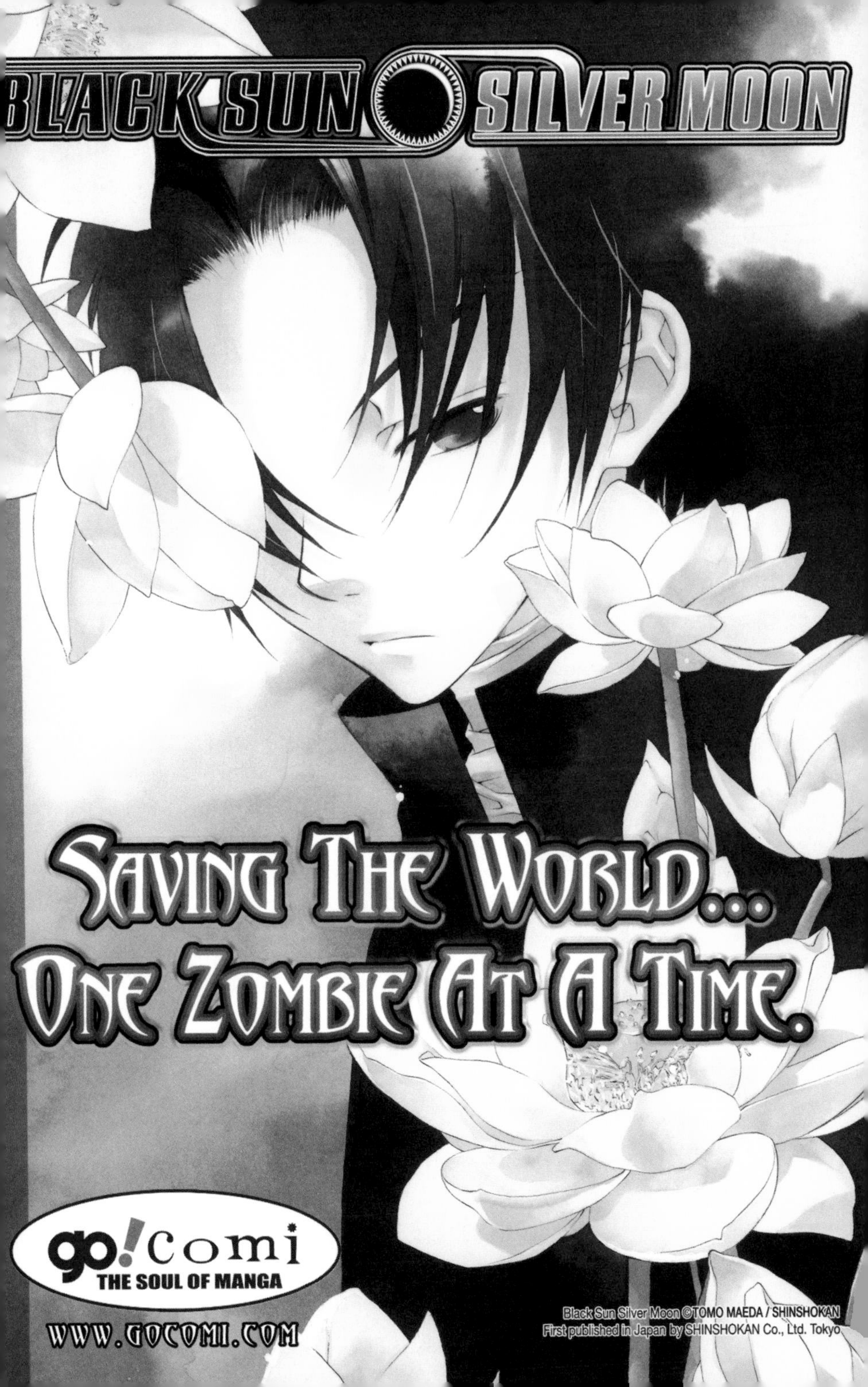

BLACK SUN SILVER MOON
SAVING THE WORLD...
ONE ZOMBIE AT A TIME.
go!comi
THE SOUL OF MANGA
WWW.GOCOMI.COM
Black Sun Silver Moon ©TOMO MAEDA / SHINSHOKAN
First published in Japan by SHINSHOKAN Co., Ltd. Tokyo.

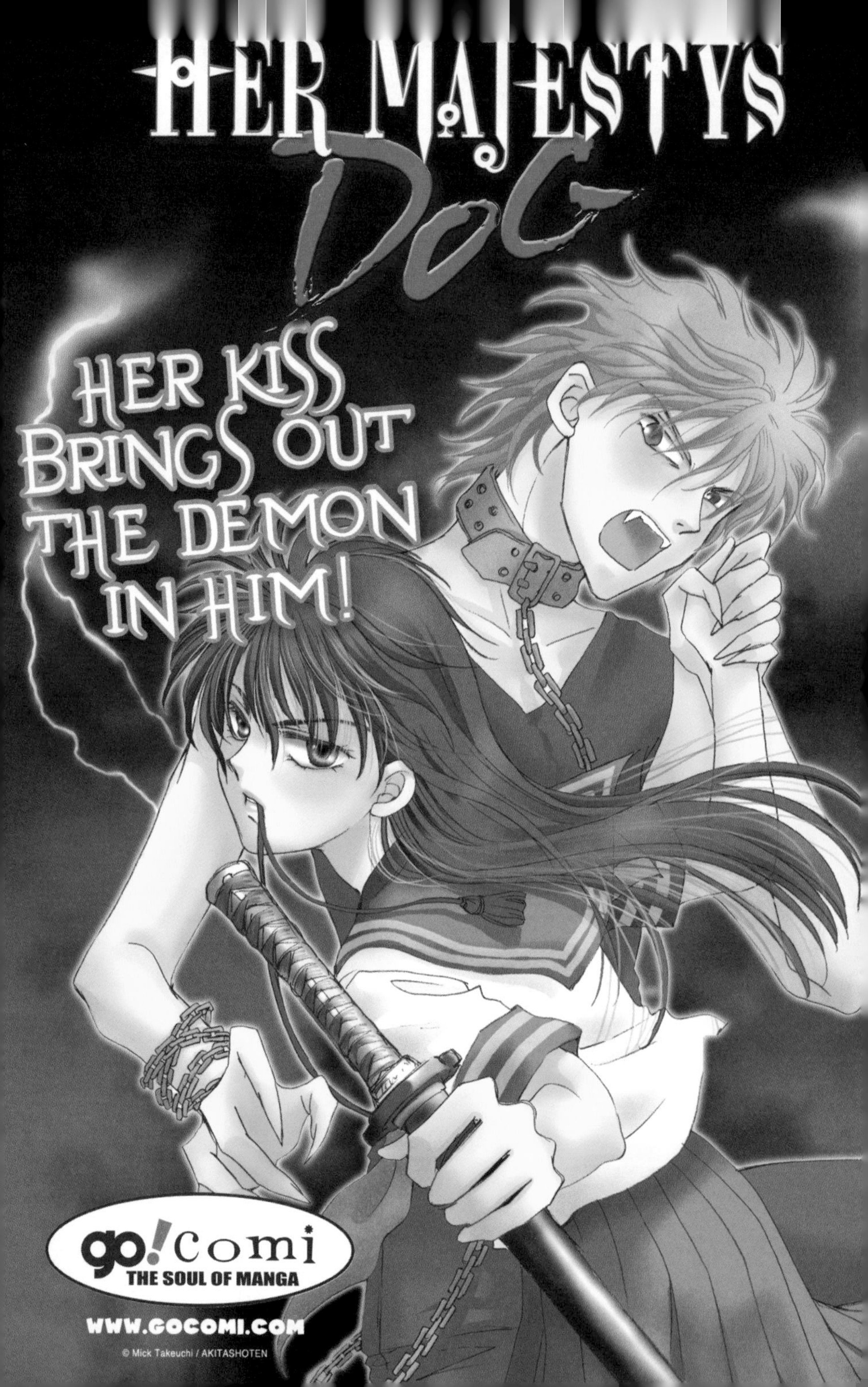
HER MAJESTY'S DOG
HER KISS BRINGS OUT THE DEMON IN HIM!
go!comi
THE SOUL OF MANGA
WWW.GOCOMI.COM
© Mick Takeuchi / AKITASHOTEN

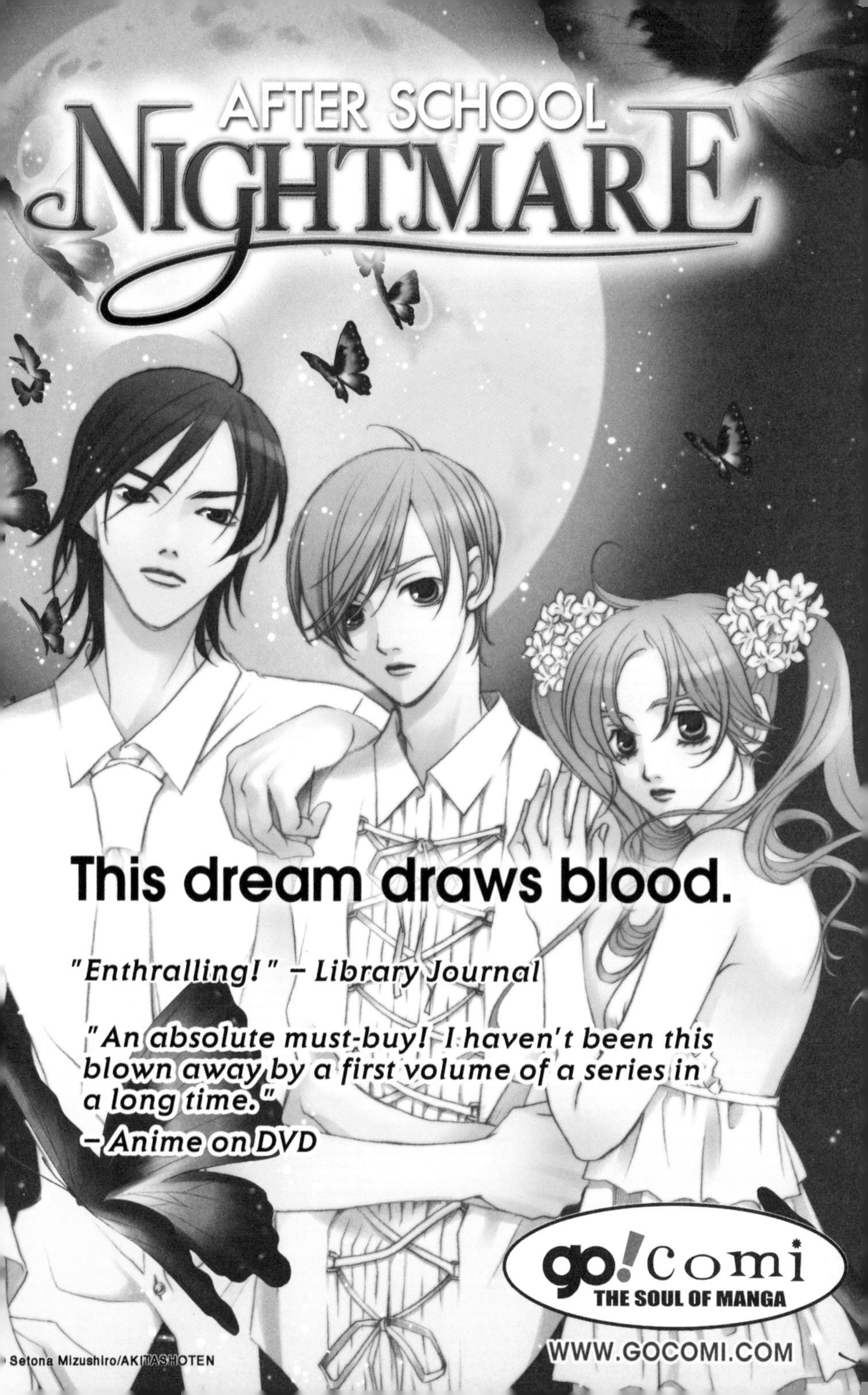
AFTER SCHOOL
NIGHTMARE
This dream draws blood.
"Enthralling!" – Library Journal
"An absolute must-buy! I haven't been this blown away by a first volume of a series in a long time."
– Anime on DVD
go!comi
THE SOUL OF MANGA
WWW.GOCOMI.COM
Setona Mizushiro/AKITASHOTEN

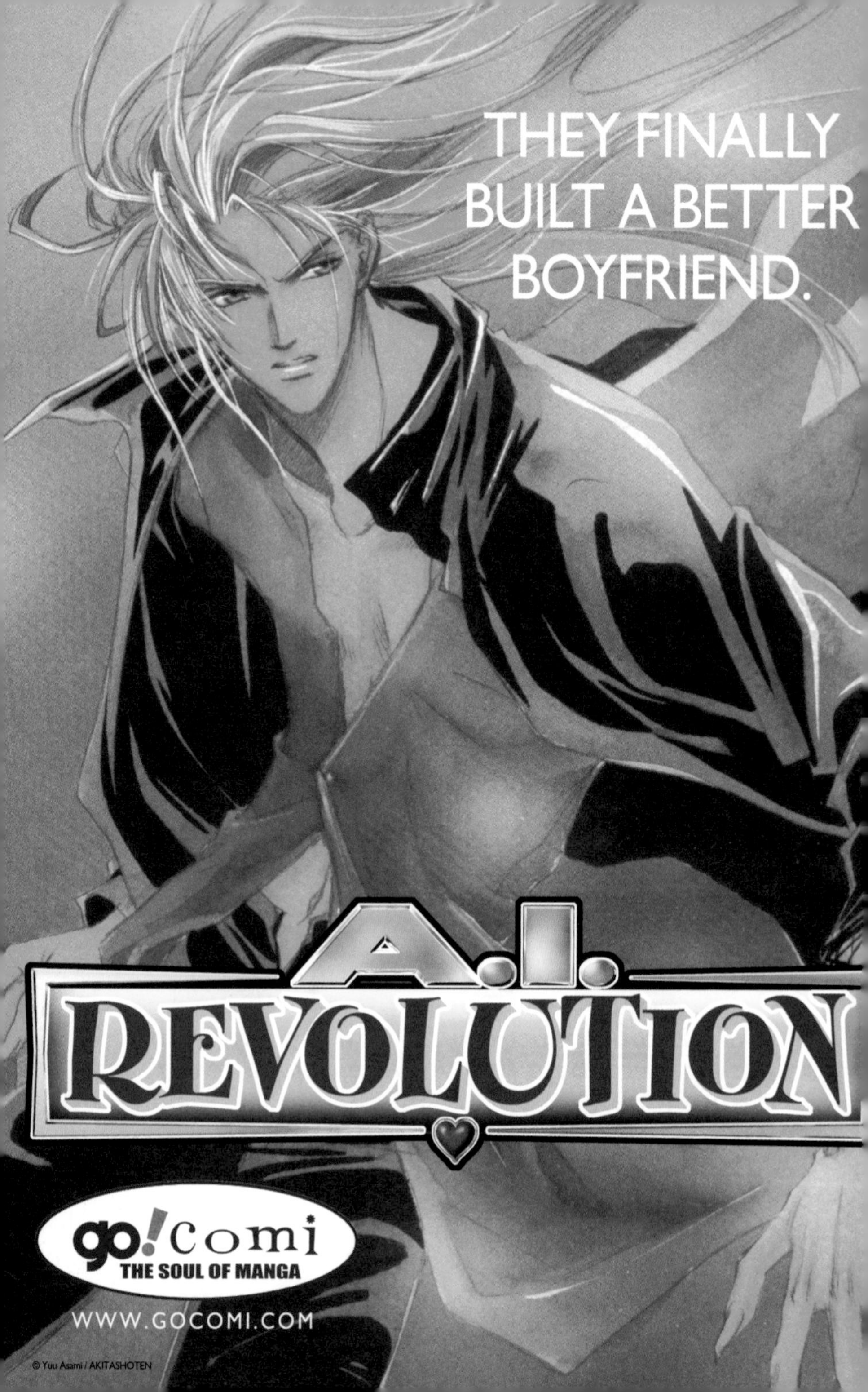
THEY FINALLY
BUILT A BETTER
BOYFRIEND.
A.I.
REVOLUTION
go!comi
THE SOUL OF MANGA
WWW.GOCOMI.COM
© Yuu Asami / AKITASHOTEN